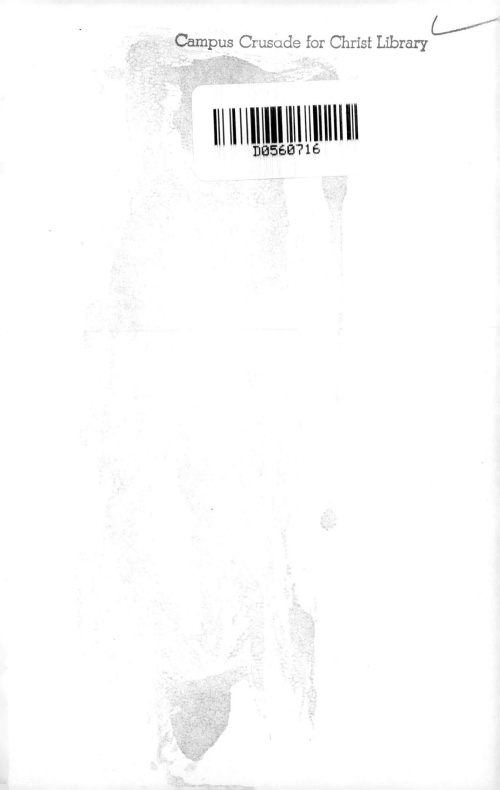

D0560716

UNHOLY SHADOWS

and

FREEDOM'S HOLY LIGHT

UNHOLY SHADOWS

and

FREEDOM'S HOLY LIGHT

By

J. H. Jackson

TOWNSEND PRESS - NASHVILLE, TENNESSEE

By J. H. Jackson:

"Stars In The Night"

"The Eternal Flame"

"Many But One"

"Unholy Shadows and Freedom's Holy Light"

DEDICATION

To the 6,300,000 members of the National Baptist Convention, U.S.A., Incorporated in whose tradition of freedom I was born and nurtured.

PREFACE

THIS BOOK IS designed as a realistic approach to the gains and remaining problems of the civil rights struggle. It acknowledges with appreciation all of the lofty achievements in the struggle for freedom, and without seeking to discredit any, it ascribes the basic advancements in the practical growth of freedom to the nature and dynamic power of the mental, moral, and spiritual principles in the American society. The author draws a clear distinction between goals and methods. All true Americans are for the goals of the civil rights struggle for they are the promises of the Federal Constitution and a part of the expectation of all people who believe in freedom. But there is a division of opinion regarding the methods by which the accepted goals can be reached. The point of view here is that the best method is through law and order according to the principles of the Federal Constitution and all of those ideals by which and through which a free society of free men can be built.

Non-violent civil disobedience is rejected as the best instrument for achieving civil rights in a nation like the United States of America. Historically, civil disobedience, however non-violent, has never been used as a means of correcting the errors of a social order but rather for the purpose of overthrowing the established order. The supreme law of this land, the Federal Constitution, prescribes the measures and the methods by which the errors in the American system may be corrected—whether said errors are found in unjust laws or in social customs and traditions. But civil disobedience is not one of the methods prescribed by the Federal Constitution. Civil disobedience is a form of lawlessness and, is in reality, not far removed from open crime. For it violates the citizens' pledge of loyalty to the American way of life including the way of correcting errors as well as the way of sustaining the democratic principles of the nation.

Those who have practiced segregation as their creed and as their way of life have lived a life of civil disobedience to some of the most lofty principles of the supreme law of this land. They have done this not to correct any errors of the nation but for the purpose of destroying the democratic claims and intentions of the nation by substituting for the defeated institution of slavery, racial segregation, and discrimination. Many people who practice racial discrimination believe that they are right and hence follow the guidance of their private conscience. Those who practice civil disobedience in their quest for first-class citizenship are adopting the same methods to defeat segregation that segregationists have used to support segregation.

The use of the term non-violence is a deceptive term when applied to acts that are unwholesome and illegal, when measured and evaluated by the principles of the Federal Constitution. The term does not preempt any act of its moral or immoral content. For a thing may be immoral, unjust, selfish, illegal, and even criminal, and not be violent. Confusion, disobedience, disrespect for law and order and for the rights of others in the name of patriotism and in the quest for first-class citizenship may create what the author calls *confusionism*, but cannot build a democratic society.

Public officials and all United States citizens must return to, and rededicate themselves to the principles of the Federal Constitution and the American philosophy of freedom. They must be dedicated without reservation to the American prescription of equality of opportunity for all. But they must no longer pamper those who break the law be they Negroes or white, for it is just as wrong for Negroes to break the law in the name of integration as it is for white people to break it in the name of segregation. Negro people must not any longer allow themselves to be used by leaders, Negro or white, for the purpose of increasing their own popularity and their purse. Negro people must do more than spend their talents and efforts in opening doors of opportunity, they must go in with dispatch and claim all that rightfully belongs to them, for they have the power even now, to take on the full responsibility of first class citizenship. They must go from protest to production, from complaints to creative endeavors.

The next forward step in racial development and progress will not be made by white friends for their Negro neighbors, but will be made by Negroes for themselves. And this step depends not on what Negroes can force other people to give and do for them, but on what Negroes in the light of their existing ability and in the light of available opportunities can and will do for themselves and for the social order in which they live.

The author acknowledges and expresses his debt of gratitude to all of those who have inspired his thinking in this field. He gives peculiar credit to his critics and opponents whose misinterpretation of his philosophy inspired him to give his own story and his own testimony before the bars of public opinion and to students of both races whose questions on the issues of civil rights have been informative and inspirational.

I am indebted to the loyal members of the Olivet Baptist Church, Chicago, where I have served for the past twenty-five years. They have been as a family and a shield from intimidations, a source of encouragement and comfort when opposition seemed most dangerous. They have given to me a free pulpit and have at no time counseled silence on the most vexing social problems of our times. To further encourage my ministry, this church by unanimous vote December 29, 1958, gave to me life tenure so that I could be freed from that type of insecurity that goes with the hazards of possible unemployment. Now I carry on the mission of true patriotism, and advocate respect for law and order, first class citizenship for all Americans, and the redemptive mission of Christ for all mankind.

Also, I owe a great debt of gratitude to the 6,300,000 members of the National Baptist Convention, U.S.A., Incorporated for the opportunity they have given me to serve my race, my nation, the peoples of the world, and the cause of the Kingdom of God. For the past fourteen years they have given me a national platform from which to speak and have permitted me to carry a message of freedom to all races and nationalities, to the poor as well as the rich of the earth, to the learned and the unlearned. As their servant I have stood before city councils, mayors of cities, governors of the several states, two vice presidents of the United States, two presidents of the United States, kings and lords of the earth, and the Pope of Rome. The National Baptist Convention had a large share in making me what I am. For these and many other reasons, this book is dedicated to every loyal member of the National Baptist Convention, U.S.A., Incorporated.

I am greatly indebted to Mrs. Maude T. Jackson, my wife, for the help and encouragement she has given both day and night as I have struggled with the composition of the manuscript. For helpful suggestions on structure and organization the author owes a debt to Dr. Kenny Williams, his daughter, who read the manuscript more than once. I am indebted to my private secretary, Mrs. Naomi Mason, who was responsible for taking much of the dictation and typing of the manuscript including the final form.

While the author acknowledges his indebtedness to all of those who in any wise influenced his thinking, he takes the responsibility for the ideas and conclusions of the book.

J. H. JACKSON,
Chicago, Illinois

May 15, 1967

CONTENTS

UNHOLY SHADOWS

and

FREEDOM'S HOLY LIGHT

1

THE NATURE OF OUR DEMOCRATIC SOCIETY

Introduction

WHAT IS AMERICA? It is 3,615,211 square miles of land including some barren areas, deserts, valleys, hills, mountains, fertile plains, and some of the richest soil in the world; but America is more than a geographical spot. Although we are proud of the physical and material wealth of this nation, her topography and all other physical characteristics do not exhaust the meaning of America. While we take keen delight in all of the comforts supported by the physical and material riches of this great country, we realize that America is not only a geographical spot for it is a community of almost 195,129,000 people comprising all races and nationalities. These people have been drawn together from practically every continent and country that the sun has smiled upon. They have come with many languages, beliefs, philosophies, and cultures. Furthermore, America is an opportunity. All chronicles of America make clear the many possibilities which pervaded the colonial experience. When I was a boy I studied a history book which made the following statement:

The voyage to America was like a journey to another planet. It made the people of Europe acquainted with the new race—the Indians—and with new animals, new plants, new features of nature, new fields of enterprise. Everybody felt that America meant opportunity. It filled the minds and hearts of men with new hope, new courage, and stimulated them to undertake what they would not have dared before.[1]

And so the myth of America has grown.

There are some unique elements that characterize our democratic society. Without a knowledge of these components the possible solution to the problems that confront our society can never be fully grasped. The primary element here, or the least common denominator, is the individual human being. There can be no democratic society if there are not individual human beings. But before we seek an answer to the question "what is the purpose and destiny of our society?" we must begin with the prior questions: "what is the nature of man?" "What are his needs, aspirations, and desires?" "And what are the best methods by which he can more nearly realize his goals or more completely fulfill himself?" Any social order is influenced by the doctrine of man that supports it. Sociology, social psychology, politics, or any form of social organization rests upon the answer to the questions: "What is man?" "What is the object of his striving?" "What is the outreach and the purpose of his being?" If man is the object and the tool of the state, the servant or the slave of an existing social order, then the state owes him no debt and the social order in which he lives has for him no responsibility beyond the use of his talents and the use of his being as means to whatever ends best serve the existing state. A totalitarian state takes unto itself all the responsible values and virtues, thus rendering man a puppet, a meaningless cog in the wheel of the socio-economic life of the state. As shoe leather is raw material of the finished product, so man is the raw material to be used to help construct the economic and political structure of the state. His place and value are determined by the state. The respect for man in a totalitarian state grows out of the fact, primarily, that he is a producer of commodities, a potential soldier to defend the state, a servant of the ideals and principles of those who are the organizers and

[1] D. H. Montgomery, *The Leading Facts of American History* (Boston, 1910), p. 39.

the leaders of the existing social order. A totalitarian state then cannot change its nature or pursue more lofty goals until the doctrine of man has been changed.

The difference between our American pattern of democracy and the totalitarian state is not due wholly to the difference in a philosophy of economics. Our method of free enterprise and our competitive approach to the distribution of materials do not define the basic differences between the structure of the American system of democracy and the philosophy of the totalitarian states. Rather, the basic difference is due to a difference in the concept and the doctrine of man. In our democratic society man is the end; he is the reason and the object for the existence of every type of legislative and social organization. The state is made for man and not man for the state. Man possesses certain mental and moral faculties that render him a sacred being worthy of all respect. He comes forth endowed with certain inalienable rights that no one can justly take from him. Even the state itself must respect these rights. These inalienable rights are not affected by place of birth, economic and political circumstances, or by the social rank in which his early life was cradled and nurtured. These rights are not derived through the findings of committees, nor do they rest upon majority vote of members in the halls of parliaments or in the sacred chambers of any national congress. For normal human beings these rights spring from within. They are not in any way externally determined. No toga of honor can produce them and no garment of praise can create them. They cannot wholly and completely be snatched from human beings by institutions of slavery, nor can they be wholly bound by chains of servitude and cursed fetters of oppression. A human being is a human being defiantly. He defies the negative forces thrown about him. He carries upon his being the weights that a cruel society may impose upon him, he may be hindered and handicapped by the oppressive limits set upon his spirit and upon his being; but at no time can his rights be completely snatched from him without his will, commitment, or consent. Man comes forth potentially endowed and blessed with certain inalienable rights. In the Declaration of Independence adopted by the Continental Congress July 4, 1776, the founding fathers discovered certain truths about the nature of man that they said were "self-evident; that all men are created equally; that they are endowed by their Creator with certain inalienable rights; that among these are life, liberty, and the pursuit of happiness."

Life is a sacred trust which is too important and too lofty to be desecrated or marred by the evil purposes of any oppressive system and any despotic tyrant. The right to live, and to live meaningfully, belongs equally to every creature who passes through the gates of birth into the broader field of human existence. In spite of all the accumulated evils of our society, and notwithstanding the corruption and the errors that have crept into our body politic, the organized life of our society seems keenly conscious of the sacredness of human life. Under normal circumstances society goes to great extremes to protect, to rescue, and to save one individual human life. In their frenzy, animosity, anger, and bitterness, men may take the lives of others but never with the total consent of their better judgment or by the dictates and approval of their consciences. And if through passion or wrong directions a human life is taken, human beings are so controlled and influenced by a CONSISTENCY URGE that they can never deny that the victim did have the unquestioned and unimpeachable right to live.

The philosophy of the golden rule rests largely on the assumption of and the existence of this CONSISTENCY URGE: "Do unto others as you would have them do unto you" implies and suggests that there is within the mind and spirit of normal human beings an awareness that they should not take from others what they did not desire others to take from them. They should not destroy what they themselves can never create or bring back into existence.

A second right as set forth in the Declaration of Independence is a right to liberty; that is the right to be free, the right to follow the constructive outreaches of one's being and to labor by the light of the oughtness of his conscience to fulfill all of the existing potentials of his life. Men may not know the particular things to which they are entitled. They may not know the rules or the laws under which and by which they are to pursue their goals in any existing society. But it seems to be a part of their inner nature and the voice whispers to them in foul weather as well as fair, in darkness as well as in the light, "you ought to be free." Freedom in the truest sense of the word, then, is the right of all men. Men cannot be satisfied to be hemmed in by barriers that set limits not only on the aspirations of their spirits but also on the visions and dreams of their inner being. Furthermore, it is the right of man in a democratic society to pursue those things that will bring happiness, inner satisfaction, peace of mind, and harmony in his entire being. Man has a right not only to escape the things that penalize and afflict his being, he has a right to pursue that course of life that will bring to him the greatest possible joy and satisfaction. The food-getting habits of man are a part of the total pattern of satisfaction. His quest for shelter and his search for comforts are milestones in the total pursuit of happiness.

Enlightened educational psychology is aware of this aspect of life even in a growing child. The best teachers are those who are more concerned about discovering the natural-bent, taste, and aptitudes of the child than those who are more concerned about achieving complete submission to the imposed routine of an existing system. If he can pursue the things that give him the greatest degree of satisfaction, the child may be led into fields of creative endeavors. This, of course, does not grant license to those who think they find their greatest satisfaction in making others miserable or in destroying the rights of others. The truth is man is so constructed that he can not find happiness through destruction, neither can he arrive at peace through confusion and war.

The right to be happy is not the right to be gay at all times.

The right to be happy does not assume the right to avoid burdens and heavy responsibilities. A happy person is a person who finds harmony within his being and satisfaction in his mind as he goes forth doing those things that he is conscious that he ought to do in his attempt to fulfill his purposes and to arrive at the complete destiny of his life. There are other rights that are important in the life of man. One of these is the right to worship God according to the dictates of his conscience. He has the right to follow the invincible surmise of his spirit and the lofty directives of his faith. But these things do not fall within the confines of a democratic state as we know it. The existence of governments is for the purpose of securing the rights to life, liberty, and the pursuit of happiness. Our form of government does not exclude the right to worship but is not committed to leading individuals into that field. The field of religion is not the field of the political state as we know it.

What man possesses is not only what has been achieved by him; he is endowed by his Creator with certain inalienable rights. This comes very close to the expression of the Christian concept of man. Here man has a creator and this creator has endowed him. It stands to reason that if we accept the fact that man is endowed by his creator, we must also assume that in the process man received some of the nature of the Creator himself. The outreaching for a quality of life higher than that which is defined by economics is an indication of a higher kinship. In our form of government the citizen's whole life is not regulated or determined by government. He has the right to privacy: the privacy of his home, the privacy to choose his own friends, the freedom to pursue his own calling, to follow the guidance of his genius and his aptitude. In this category also comes the freedom of religion. While the government makes no attempt to define, determine, or explain the existence of the nature of the Creator in the human creature, the United States government does not sit in judgment on any form of religion, neither does it concern itself about making laws regulating or even regarding an establishment of religion. But when it accepts the idea of a Creator who has the power and who has endowed man, then the government comes close to admitting the Christian concept of man.

When the eighth century prophets described man as being worthy of justice, righteousness and truth, they spoke of him as a creature of Jehovah in whom the image of God was placed. In man and to man the good had been revealed. Said the prophet Micah: "He hath shewed thee oh man what is good." [2] The ancient theocracy of the Hebrews emphasized man as a creature endowed by his Creator. In the message of Jesus of Nazareth this concept of man was not weakened or watered down. According to Jesus man had been endowed with a hunger for righteousness, with a thirst for ever living water, and with a soul that was immeasurable in value and far more precious than embellished stones. But man did not attain these values by his own efforts, they were a part of the endowment of his Creator.

The American government has not and does not engage in a theology of man beyond the statement that he has been endowed by his Creator with certain inalienable rights. Having committed itself to this, the government has left all human beings free to pursue the ends of religion without being molested and free to worship God according to the dictates of their consciences. Freedom to worship assumes that men do possess inner values to guide them and inner compulsions to control them. This country in its infancy experienced what could happen when the religious beliefs of men were tampered with and their religious faith regulated by the laws of state. The Massachusetts theocracy had stained its hands with human blood, and innocent people had been consumed in the fires of religious prejudice and hatred. When it came into being, this

[2] Micah 6:8.

nation reflected a maturity that put witch-hunting in the past and banished religious persecution as one of the ancient relics of colonial days. The founding fathers of this nation believed that the worship of God had constructive effects upon the lives of men and that the principles of Jesus of Nazareth were undisputed assets in building human character and human personality. Therefore they refused to interfere with the exercise of religion and made no attempt to foster it by force. It may be that when historians shall analyze the constructive life of this nation and when the most gifted minds shall seek the reasons for the lofty values reflected in American life, they may put high on the list the nation's doctrine of the freedom of religion. This is the foundation for the dignity of man set forth in the Declaration of Independence and espoused in the Federal Constitution.

There have been those who have sought to deny this lofty concept of man as a part of our Federal Constitution. They have said the Constitution in this respect did not include slaves and hence originally it did not include Negroes in its doctrine of man. The Constitution was adopted in 1787 when slavery was still a part of the accepted pattern of American life. But when the great minds had assembled to write this historic document, they faced many serious questions. Three of them occasioned much debate that finally resulted in three judicious compromises. The first dealt with the relation of the small states to the large ones in regard to representation in Congress. This question was finally settled with the decision that Congress should consist of two houses: The House of Representatives chosen by the people of the different states and representing them; the Senate, or upper house consisting of two members from each state irrespective of size.

The other two compromises were concerned with the slaves. One of these dealt with the matter of apportionment. In arriving at the number of representatives in Congress the North insisted that slaves should not be counted, the South insisted that all of the slaves should be counted. They finally reached the compromise expressed in Article I, Section 2. Three-fifths of all the slaves were to be counted. But here the lawmakers were not concerned about the doctrine of man they were concerned about economics and plain politics. It is strange and rather ironical that the South, where most of the slaves were held, argued in the defense of the slaves saying they should be counted equally as persons while the North said they should not. The North was competing with the South, for the North did not hold slaves in large numbers. The South was in contest against the North, but in its attempt to protect its rights—economically and politically —the South became a strong defender of the rights of every slave for the South insisted that each slave should be counted as one person. The South in this particular was both right and wrong. It was wrong in its desire to continue the institution of slavery but it was right in its assertation that each slave was a person. While the third compromise dealt with the right of slave-holders to transport slaves from one section of the country to another, the most vital of these compromises for our purpose is the second. This debate regarding the person of slaves revealed how deep-seated was the problem that the lawmakers confronted in their attempt to write a great document of freedom and justice and to hold—at the same time—a part of the population as slaves.

For seventy-eight years this compromise regarding the person of slaves found a place in the Federal Constitution, but the Thirteenth Amendment (ratified in 1865) banished this compromise from the supreme law of the land and said at least in theory that an institution like slavery or involuntary servitude shall no longer exist in the United States or any place subject to the jurisdiction of the United States. In the light of the Thirteenth Amendment it is clear that the supreme law of the land proclaims the dignity of every human person. With such dignity this nation is committed to guaranteeing the rights and the equality of opportunity of all of her citizens.

The Place And Function Of Law
In A Democratic Society

Freedom does not mean the absence of law. There must be a governing principle of a democratic society to avoid individuals converting liberty into license. A great republic like the United States of America required a supreme law. This law had to be comprehensive enough to gather the concern and interests of the several states while addressing itself to the problems of state and local governments. This law in turn demanded the respect and the obedience not only of the states but also of all the citizens of the nation. The Federal Constitution, the supreme law of the United States, prescribes the privileges and the rights of all groups and all citizens individually and collectively. If any state denies these rights or withholds these privileges from any citizen or group of citizens, there is the recourse to this supreme law, and one may appeal to the same through the agencies of the courts. Individual citizens are not to fight their battles alone in such a situation. When they are aware of the enemies that confront them, citizens do not assume the responsibility of punishing and correcting them. Such functions belong to the federal government if and when the states fail. It is to be remembered that all those functions that are not entrusted to the federal government are thereby left to the respective states. No group of citizens is obligated to determine what methods should be employed to correct the errors of the opponents of justice and freedom nor to regulate the actions of those who stand between citizens and their rights. The supreme law of the land is very specific and is very clear on the rights of citizens and how they should be achieved. Citizens then must have faith in the legal machinery of the nation and in the justice for which the nation stands. This supreme law binds all citizens together in a great fraternity and welds them into one family under a common flag. When any group of citizens charts another course of action and draws up another strategy of action and design to gain the desired rights, confusion is bound to result in the long run. All citizens must obey and follow the methods prescribed by and through the supreme law of the land in their attempts to settle their problems or to achieve their rights. If citizens are convinced that the supreme law of the land is not adequate to solve the problems that they face and if they are convinced that there is little or no hope in the established system and principles of said law, they should make it clearly known and be honest enough to confess their inability to be loyal to that in which they do not believe. It is not the duty of each citizen to fight his battle in this republic. It is the responsibility of the nation by the promise and the directives of the supreme law of the land. The purpose of the Federal Constitution is to guarantee and to provide a social order that is so united that each part can work for the establishment of justice in order to insure domestic tranquillity, to promote the general welfare of all citizens, and to secure the blessings of liberty to generations present and future.

The supreme law of the United States is the basis and the foundation for the rights of every citizen. The equality of opportunity for all is also a far-reaching promise of this sacred charter of liberty. Equality of opportunity is impossible unless there be a common standard by which all values that are offered to citizens may be determined. In the supreme law of our land there is no place for caste, class, or special-privileged groups. Obedience to these principles is essential for maintaining a democratic system.

But there is another aspect of citizenship aside from the privilege and the security of the individual by the nation. It is the obligation and the responsibility of the citizens to the government and to his nation. There is, in reality, a contract between the citizen and his nation. Each party to the contract has a specific responsibility. The forfeit of either one of these will greatly damage and endanger the other. The nation pledges, as has been indicated above, to protect each citizen and to guarantee to each the security and well-being with all of the resources, vitality, and power that the nation possesses. In accepting these pledges of the nation and in calling upon the nation to fulfill its side of the bargain, the citizens are obligated to keep their pledges of loyalty to the nation, for they swear to defend their country against all enemies foreign and domestic with all the resources and power of their being even to the giving of their lives. The pledge includes then not only the citizen's possessions, but also his life as well.

There is very little latitude left for the citizens to select or pick out the areas of his preference in which he wills to be loyal. His pledge is to the country as a whole including its weakness, its pleasures and its pains. It is most difficult for individual citizens or groups of citizens to free themselves completely from their obligation to the country's call of duty. Even the idealism of an individual citizen does not exempt him from his duty to his nation unless said idealism exempts the nation from its responsibility to secure, to defend, and protect the citizens. If for conscience's sake, one refuses to bear arms in the defense of one's country, one must still be involved in other auxiliary duties that contribute to the defense and the security of the nation. While the pacifist may not pull the trigger that fires the gun that kills the enemy, he is involved in helping to create the conditions that make the work of the fighting soldiers easier. In a democratic society such as America, every citizen is involved in the total life of the nation, and it cannot be otherwise. We are part of the nation's strength and ideals. We are also a part of the nation's errors and sins. We cannot in the name of conscience refuse to be partly involved in the failures of the nation any more than we can be exempt from participation in the nation's success.

No citizen is an island unto himself. He is a part of this vast republic. If as citizens we share in the benefits that the nation gives, be it police protection, security through military might, or any other economic and cultural blessings, we must also be counted as partly responsible for the means and measures by which the nation's protection and security come. We cannot escape the fact that the citizens and the nation are bound together by an agreement which is designed to protect and preserve both of the parties involved.

But in our system of government the nation is not wholly external and set apart from the people. The people themselves participate in making the government. Here the government that is *for* the people is *of* the people and *by* the people. Out of the thoughts and collective desires of the people the government arises as the administrator and the servant of the people's needs. In the citizen's pledge of loyalty he waives the right of option. He does not take it unto himself to select the laws that he will obey and to abide by the principles that he himself chooses and admires. The nation prescribes the duties, obligations, and responsibilities that citizens owe to the government, and also the nation defines the obligations that the individual citizens may expect from their government. Ours then is a fellowship by consent and not by compulsion, a government designed to protect the rights of all citizens both from the domination of the state and from the encroachment of fellow-citizens.

Every American citizen is so involved in the nation's life and struggle that he cannot extricate himself at will. He who enjoys the benefits of the country's pleasures and securities obligates himself to share in the nation's pain and responsibility. Young men who burn their draft cards and make a public demonstration of it are not acting in the defense of their consciences. Rather, they are acting in the defiance of their country and must be recognized in that context. It is not expected that an imperfect state comprising imperfect people and existing in a world of imperfect nations can arrive at perfection in any area of its life by a single thrust. Citizens must not only pledge themselves to work for the defense of their country, they must also pledge themselves to work for the moral enrichment of the same so that the corporate desires of the nation might always be just and good. The United States of America makes no attempt to regulate the private lives of its citizens completely. It demands of them loyalty to country and respect for the rights of others.

The nation cannot take the full credit for the growth in all areas of life. Much of this is done through private enterprise and through the initiative of individual citizens and groups. Because of this there are some things in the United States of America for which the individual citizen must blame himself. In our present system of free enterprise the government has some responsibilities for the existence of poverty and ignorance and other weaknesses and failures in our democratic society. But the government is not wholly to blame. It is the government's responsibility to set up the guidelines, create conditions for justice in employment and every other phase of life. The government has made public education compulsory up to a point, but those young people who drop out and fail to take advantage of these opportunities must take their share of the blame. In this country there are no special classes selected to receive an education. It is made available to all. In a free country much of the responsibility for what a citizen might become is determined by the citizen himself. For this reason there must always be self-examination along with government censure for the evils that face us. The efforts of citizens must be marshalled against all private problems as well as public ones. We must not always spend the time blaming others and blasting the forces that oppose us. As the wise farmer, we must fertilize the land, till the soil, cast in the seed, and trust the power of growth to push back the clods and allow the plants to reach forth in their vitality and accept the blessings of the sun and the rain.

The system of democracy in the United States recognizes the

divisions of areas of responsibility and trust. And for each of these areas there are accepted leaders who specialize in their respective fields. The political leaders or the leaders in government are, for the most part, elected by the people and the people entrust to them the responsibility of leading and guiding the state in its function of protecting and securing the freedom of all citizens and supervising the affairs of the nation. As leaders in government these public servants are called upon and are expected to keep their pledges to defend this nation against all enemies foreign and domestic. Many of these leaders are called upon to give full time as specialists in their areas and to give their best in service, loyalty, and devotion to the welfare of this republic.

The managers and the captains of industry represent another group of leaders who have the responsibility for developing the economic life of the nation. This group is granted the freedom by the government to develop the highest and the best economic system as long as the system does not impinge upon the rights of other groups and individuals, and with the further provision that all rules and guidelines established by the government in the best interests of the citizens and the nation are observed. With the freedom granted to pursue and to develop the best possible economic order, this free enterprise system becomes productive not only of better machinery and better products, but also it develops or allows to be developed some of the finest talents and most creative and productive brains. Every progressive business and industrial firm is equipped with a department of research in which experts seek daily for better methods of production.

For the past fifty years there seems to have been an economic lag in those countries where the leaders of government have also been the leaders and the directors in industry and business. It seems that farmers who own their own farms and work for themselves in the interest of developing the best possible crops make better crops and are greater assets to the total economy of the nation. It also seems that the business and industrial achievements of nations of free enterprise are greater than those in totalitarian states. Although the government of our form of democracy concerns itself with the task of quality education and is committed to equality of opportunity for all, it does not assume the responsibility of dictating to educational specialists what and how they should teach. The educational leaders are granted the freedom of investigation, the freedom of discovery, and the freedom to use their experiences to produce the best in learning and culture.

We must not overlook the constructive roles that organized labor has played and still plays in the task of economic growth and production. Labor is not a tool of government, neither is it any longer the helpless victim of the captains of industry and the managers of business. Labor leaders are not only concerned about the most efficient and most skillful productions of each laborer and each group of laborers, but also they are concerned about the welfare, the well-being, and the security of the laborers themselves. While they enjoy the freedom of bargaining with management in the interest of the health of the worker and the best possible working conditions, they are also interested in the laborer's participating in a fair share of the profits from the business in the form of living wages and fringe benefits. The history of the labor movement in the United States is another story of the growth of freedom and the realization of some of the lofty goals for human betterment that could not have been possible without this historic movement.

The freedom of religion in the United States has been a means of further enrichment of the nation's life. The chapels, churches, temples, synagogs, shrines, and cathedrals are concrete illustrations of the concern and of the sacrifices that American citizens have made to the nation's life through the belief in the support and the devotion to the faiths of their choice. Here believers have drawn on sources of the universe that have led them to face the most difficult problems with hope and to brave some of the most tragic hours in life without yielding to despair. The government has allowed these groups of believers to develop their own cults, their own organizations, and their own leaders. They have been left free to use their own methods to inspire the highest type of thought and to help steel the souls of the individuals with the greatest armours of courage and to lead citizens to make the greatest possible sacrifices for the purification and enrichment of society and the salvation of all mankind. Those who have specialized in the task of the refinement, re-making, and the re-demption of men and women have had a share in lifting the cultural, moral, aesthetic, and spiritual standards of the nation's life. Because of these and other constructive forces, along with the scientific growth and the economic expansion of this nation, there has been developed improved thinking and planning for the well-being of all citizens. The spirit and the influence of religion have been felt in the growth of concern for local communities, towns, cities, counties, and the nation itself. There is not only con-cern for making money in this country, but there is also a concern for the health, well-being, and happiness of all citizens. This na-tion is so organized that the common people enjoy the blessings of many of our scientific discoveries as well as the rich, for by the blessings of our economic and cultural growth, the standard of living has been so lifted that the humble people of this country live better than many of the so-called wealthy in other countries. For example, with radio and television available to so many humble people today, it is difficult to withhold information or to keep a people ignorant of the march of events and of the unfold-ing of contemporary history.

Islands of Freedom

In our social order there are small freedom units that make their own laws and form their own programs of action and patterns of behavior. These smaller in-groups, which frequently defy definition, experience a natural and significant kinship and share certain responsibilities jointly, but they are subject to the supreme law of the land. These groups are not organized by the national government, they are not pressured, interfered with, or directly supervised by the central government. So long as these in-groups do not in any way violate the letter and spirit of the supreme law of the land they are free in their choices, in their modes of living, and in determining their own destinies. These little cells of freedom might be termed schools of experience in which persons and citizens may learn more about life and how to bear the responsibility as members of a democratic society; for within these groups the members think of themselves as belonging each to the other. Some are dependents, relying on their seniors and on their trusted leaders who feel a sense of responsibility to those who are dependent upon them.

The most natural and the most significant of these units is the family. The child is born into this small community, is nurtured by it, shielded by it, and receives from it not only its first initiation into life as a person but also receives his first directives regarding the primary task of living. The close proximity of this fellowship is indeed a unique and significant theater of life in which the members learn or refuse to learn what the individual's place is in a social order. What happens to the plastic self of every child in this first social community affects his attitudes, emotions, and outlook throughout the rest of his natural life. The burden of the child falls upon the home, and the home is guided by the parents who make it. The laws of association, a sense of sharing in a larger democratic society, are in a sense implanted in the growing members of the family circle.

There are many other in-groups in our American system that have been given the right of existence as a part of the life of a free nation. One of the largest (and most diversified), in-groups within the fellowship of the United States of America is the sovereign state. These fifty political and governmental units are granted certain rights and certain responsibilities, some of which are related directly to the welfare of the individual state. The state has many rights regarding its local citizens as the federal government has over the citizens of the nation. The states are free to act and to conduct their affairs as long as they recognize and are subjected to the principles and guidelines of the Federal Constitution, which is reality binds the fifty units into a working composite and democratic whole. These larger islands of free people have a chance to experience freedom in its many phases and can come to a knowledge of its responsibilities in a most unique way. There are many significant advantages in having this type of social organization in the United States of America. It guards against the danger of over-centralization and is a safeguard against a speedy dictatorship. While the federal government tends to balance all of the local units and merge them into one strong united nation, the individual states have the power to check the federal government in any attempt at over-centralization in favor of an unwholesome dictatorship.

The many separate and distinct in-groups in America show how dependent is the nation on freedom at its best. These respective groups are not related to one another and to the central government in the light of their competitive force and power. If force were exerted as the determining principle of the relationship of these groups to the whole life of the nation we would soon find ourselves caught in the fires of conflict without any hope of survival. The vitality and the freedom of the several in-groups assure and guarantee the vitality, the stability, and the freedom of the nation.

What then are some of the essential principles that must undergird and support this kind of nation? It cannot be blind competition. It cannot be exploits in pressure or any force that assumes the power of fear to generate the principles of faithfulness. If such a nation is to survive, there must be the principles of faith and loyalty in and to the American system, a mutual trust for one another and for one another's respective groups, and a spirit of cooperation and goodwill. Without these principles suspicions will develop; fears, ill-will, tensions, mistrust, and doubt will destroy all the wholesome principles that are designed to bind the states and peoples of this nation together as one great family.

But this is not the whole story of this nation of ours. It would take far more than a chapter to tell so vast a story of so great a country.

But we must take another moment to point out that when one has dealt with the positive achievements of the nation and has pointed out the greatness of the country as one dedicated to the proposition that all men are created equal, one must not overlook the presence among us of those who have not accepted the nation's principles as a way of life and have not resolved to apply themselves to the ideals of this great republic. Those among us who would abuse their freedom, interfere with the rights of others, and try to become what Lillian Smith called "killers of the American dream" are saboteurs of the rights of others, enemies of the sacred cause of an all-inclusive freedom. Because our nation is not complete, because all of her ideals have not been realized, and because there are still among us men with hearts of traitors and minds filled with evil designs of treason and destruction, we must work unreservedly to remove the diseases that affect this body politic and adopt every means and method to make the nation healthy, happy, and strong. Hence there are some virtues that we must still affirm, and there are some vices that we must protest, seek to remove, and to destroy. Every citizen is a soldier of democracy, and every American should be a committed servant of freedom and a keeper of his pledge to live, and—if needs be—to die for the eternal values of this great country. Because America is a free republic, because men are not regimented or controlled by government, and because there are no concentration camps and no standing firing squads, the citizens must be provided with some means in harmony with the American tradition and American way of life by which the spotlight can be turned on the enemies of freedom; and citizens can express their disapproval and dissatisfaction with peoples and policies of government when they seem contrary to the laws of justice and injurious to the bodies and spirits of other citizens. Hence there has been provided what is known as *protest* as one of the ways by which citizens seek to help build public opinion in harmony with the nation's theories and promises, and according to the prescriptions of the Federal Constitution.

2

THE REASON AND THE
RIGHT OF PROTEST

IN OUR DEMOCRATIC society there are various forms of expressing objections, disapprovals, or dissents in opposition to something that a person may be powerless to avoid or to change. Protest is a means by which the blame for a certain act or deed is fixed and the liability assessed with the reasons for the same clearly expressed, loudly proclaimed, and forcibly demonstrated. Protest has been a vital part of the life and growth of the United States of America. It is seen in the history of the labor movement, the cause of women's suffrage, and the cause of civil rights.

There is a reason for this aspect of life in America and it must be sought both in the fabric of the very being of the nation and in the minds and souls of the people who protest or utter their cry of dissatisfaction and their thirst for the refreshing waters of liberty. Let us first turn to the historic events of the past to study the origin, the genesis, and the continuity of this problem.

Historically this nation was born in the throes and aspirations of those who longed for and who sought earnestly for the gift of freedom. The early settlers who braved the dangers of a strange and surging sea, and who came to these shores were inspired, motivated, and sustained by a desire for freedom. The pilgrim fathers came to the new land committed to the task of building a great free community on this side of the Atlantic, and the work of the great leaders who helped to shape the destiny of America laid well the foundation of this republic on the eternal rock of justice and built its super-structure out of the raw materials of liberty and in the spirit of freedom. In sacred documents, in the laws of the land, in social organizations, and in all declarations and pronouncements, freedom has been at the very heart and at the very core of this nation's life. In this new nation the spirit of freedom filled the air. It touched inspired lips with fitting songs and even the works of art carried the same message and the same spirit. When the Statue of Liberty was erected in the port of New York, this jeweled-headed woman held a scroll of promise in her left hand and uplifted torch high in her right hand thus symbolizing the spirit of freedom in the United States. But in order to assure that no visitor would miss the meaning of the symbol these meaningful words were inscribed on its base:

> Give me your poor, your huddled masses
>   yearning to be free,
> The wretched refuse of your teeming shore,
> Send these, the hopeless tempest-tossed to me.
> I lift my lamp beside the golden door.

In spite of the vision of freedom and the idealism that spread throughout the broad domain of this vast new land, the cruel institution of slavery found a place and negated many of the noble thoughts of the founding fathers by casting a long and dreadful shadow across America's "golden door" for more than three hundred grim and purgatorial years. Then when the soul of the nation was purged by the fires of four cruel blood-stained years of a civil war, destiny rung from the hands of the nation's chief executive that immortal document, *The Emancipation Proclamation,* which broke—in part—the spell of chattel slavery and offered the blessings of freedom to some of the weary slaves. The promise was theory but created great hope and expectation. But the ideals of freedom for all were caught in the web of political expediency; carpetbaggers and other practical political leaders thought a compromise would be sufficient and the unity of a divided nation could be purchased by selling the freedmen back into a new form of slavery in the form of racial segregation and discrimination. So the old scars of servitude became the open cancers of discrimination. There was then developed a new concept of American citizenship; one for white, and another for people of color. The freedmen had heard of the story of the land of promise rich with unlimited opportunities, gracious with the balm of justice, and beautiful with the brotherhood that transcended creed, nationality, and previous conditions of servitude. The chains of oppression had been snapped, but the scars of the past still cursed the souls of a helpless people; their natural and God-given robes they wore became badges of infamy and subordination.

The ex-slaves were caught in a straight betwixt two; the old order of slavery now lingered on in the form of racial segregation, and the promise of freedom now seemed a vanished star in a hopeless night of despair. The children of former masters were trying to hold the children of ex-slaves in a new type of bondage. The children of ex-slaves were struggling to keep the doors of hope open, and they sought desperately to reconcile the theory with the practice and the high promise of the nation with the awful deeds of those who sought a polarization between subjected Negroes and oppressing whites. Some Negroes saw the task too great for any hope of deliverance and they relied on the shadows of fate; they followed the footsteps of many of the American Indians and refused the pains of tolerance and the burden of effort and retreated from the struggle. But there were others who kept looking towards the skies of promise with a desire to follow the faint but real star of hope. What could they do? They could not deny the theory of freedom because it appealed to them. They could not wage war against the opponents of their freedom because they had no army commensurate to the task. The only thing they could do was to protest, refusing to accept as final the curse of discrimination that had fallen upon them. For them protest was effort, it was warfare, it was struggle. It was the act of bound men denying the actuality of their chains. Protest dramatized faith in America, faith in many of the leaders of government. Those who protested believed that the citizens of the majority group possessed an ear for freedom that would hear their appeal.

Historically there has been an undying faith in the sincerity and the reality of the promises of freedom made by the nation; because of this the depressed and the victims of segregation have continued to inquire and to seek the full blessings of this promised value. There is another reason why protest has continued; it is found in the very nature of man himself. Man need not be taught to desire freedom, it is a part of his primordial nature. It is stamped in his very being. The voice within that cries out for deliverance is as a prodigal son crying for that portion of goods that he feels rightly belongs to him. This promise of freedom has been written more deeply into the very nature, soul, and life of man than it has been in parchment or in books of law. It is as natural as the search for water by the thirsty and food for the hungry. Man cannot be himself and deny the inner urge for freedom. The psychological nature and the ethical character of man compel him to reach for the greatest possible fulfillment. Any state that denies this essence of man will never appeal to the best or satisfy the highest in him.

In addition to these, there is the right of protest which has been bequeathed to every United States citizen; that is, the right to sit in judgment on the leaders of state, to analyze and evaluate the actions of their government, and to register complaints against any individuals or groups when their actions seem to be out of harmony with the ideals and principles of the nation. The first amendment to the Federal Constitution gives and guarantees the right of protest. This embraces the freedom of speech, the freedom of expression, the freedom of assembly, and the freedom to petition the government to redress any grievances. This law grants the right of expression and the right to testify in the defense of those things in which one believes. Whatever the view, or how deeply the hurt, the right of expression remains; if this speech or this act cuts to the very heart of any political plan or program, it must be allowed and the speaker must enjoy the right to speak. The government of the United States and the several states thereof cannot assure itself a continuing life by shielding itself from criticism or from the investigation of its citizens. The freedom to express and to convey the notion that one possesses is the right that every American citizen is permitted to enjoy.

Protest is not only the right of individual citizens, it is also the right of groups. People do have the right to assemble peaceably. They may seek through public forums and assemblies to correct the evils of their society and to help shape public opinion in favor of a type of life that is in harmony with their ideals of justice and fair play. People may go further than general discussions regarding any of the evils and errors of their government. They can petition the government directly for redress of grievances. Here they can do more than make known their grievances, they can petition the government that a remedy be found and that relief be granted. They may request not only relief from their injuries but also that the wrongs be set right, the damages be repaired, and the offensive cause be removed. At this point protest does not grant to any citizen or group of citizens the right to redress their own grievances or to take the law into their own hands by intimidating, punishing, or humiliating the offenders. It does not grant the offended or the aggrieved one the right to try to pronounce the guilt and the punishment of the offender. This is the work and the responsibility of their government, and no other group or organization can perform it.

While it is the democratic right of citizens in this country to protest, the right of protest ends when one has expressed his grievances and then petitioned the government for redress. When protest moves into the act of accusing and finding one guilty without due process and then proceeding to measure and mete out punishment, those who are protesting have moved into a new area and have assumed new rights that have not been prescribed by the law in question. It must be remembered that the just laws of this country are of the people and by the people as well as for them. They originate within the desires and wishes and aspirations of the people, but they are hammered out by the minds of lawmakers who are guided and in some cases motivated by public opinion or the corporate mind of the people. The people then can never retreat from this scene of responsibility or abandon the political arena of constructive action. They must remain forever vigilant, the watchdogs of the law, and the courageous champions of those reforms and principles of renewal that will guarantee the continuous growth and evolution of all of the laws and principles of our government itself.

Laws need more than public officials and political servants to insure their enforcement and their effectiveness. They also need the assistance of aroused and alerted citizens. This is in part the meaning and the significance of the ballot or the right to vote. It places a part of the responsibility for good government where it ought to belong; that is, on the shoulders of the citizens themselves. The citizens must be responsible for the type of officials that head their government and the kind of laws that are written on their statute books, and how they are enforced. In the final analysis the ballot is the most concrete and final weapon of protest in our American system. We cannot have the type of government we have in the United States without the citizens having the right to use the ballot to determine the quality of leadership which they elect to follow. In the long run, no government is good for the people that is designed for the people but is not of and by the people.

There is another set of rules that supports and guarantees the right of protest and that is moral law. As we indicated above man's knowledge of the good and his ability to desire, to love, and to seek the good puts on him the responsibility to work for the achievements of the good. A person then must stand against and oppose what he believes to be wrong. Not only must he oppose it, he must do all within his power to remove it. The wrong ought to be avoided, discouraged, and destroyed, but this is the negative aspect of protest. The positive aspect is guided by the dictum: "the right ought to be done." The right of protest then is a vital part of the enlightened conscience of men. At times it has required some genius, some gifted apostle of truth, who is influenced and controlled more by the light of his own inner being than by the rewards and punishments of the political state. By insights, wisdom, and the power of thought this gifted sage sees a higher and a better way. He is obsessed by the dreams and desires which lead to things richer, higher, and more powerful than the whole order of injustice and corruption. By faith he sees the land of promise and leads others to seek it as the goal and object of life. Such great spirits have not been lawbreakers. They have transcended the lower order of rebellion that falls beneath the law to fulfill the laws of the land and have found the right of action from moral and spiritual resources that organized society cannot give or wholly take away. Some of these leaders have been more than statesmen, scholars, and philosophers. They have been men inspired of God, prophets who live on the vision splendid. Hence they protest the old way not by opposing it on the level of its existence but by embracing and demonstrating a creative power higher than themselves. Such men are the founders of institutions and charters of new courses in history, the saviors of a decadent and dying social order. The age in which they live may hate them, abuse them, and maybe crucify them, but they will leave a loaf of bread to sustain life at its best and a torch to light the path of the weary feet of men in this and in another generation. Righteousness here does not begin in acts that lead to lawbreaking, rather it begins on the level of personal, moral, and spiritual refinement. The prophet's life is a judgment on and against the sordid things of his present, a challenge to those who know him best. He puts into his social order new moral and spiritual content.

The supreme law of the land, the Federal Constitution, makes no provision for any citizens to disobey said law even in the interest of conscience. This law does not in any way invade the sacred domain of personal conscience. It has the power to sit in judgment on any laws of town, city, county, or state. As we have stated above, it is the citizen's right through the courts to appeal to the principles of said law in quest of redress. The morality of the Federal Constitution is higher than that of the individual citizen. That is to say, the ideals and principles for which the Federal Constitution stands are far more lofty than those practiced by many individuals. This is what George W. Allport meant when he said:

> Actually, in the United States, state-ways—at least as expressed in the Constitution—are in advance of folkways. The Constitution is clear in its intentions that total democracy shall prevail. Thus the official morality of this country is high, although private morality is in many respects low.[1]

The Federal Constitution does not purport to invade the consciences of men or to violate any of the laws of their inner being. This is one reason for the freedom of religion. If by research and investigation it is found that the supreme law of the land at any point violates man's right to think, to believe, to obey the oughtness of conscience, then such rule is subject to change at this point by amendments. At only one point in American history has the Constitution been so amended in order to regulate the private lives of some of the citizens of the nation. When the attempt was made through the Volstead Act to legislate the consciences and the private lives of Americans in the matter of strong drink, this amendment failed and by the pressure of public opinion it was removed from the Constitution. Not that the people of the nation condoned or sanctioned the immoral conduct of drunkenness, but because the nation does not assume the power to regulate such private choices of people, this amendment was changed.

The oughtness of conscience may put before the mind, the life,

---

[1] The Nature of Prejudice (Boston, 1954), p. 471.

and the spirit of men some obligations that the law does not impose, (and they may do or not do these things). Here is the freedom to strive for sainthood, to sacrifice many of the pleasures of life, to work to become more efficient in the work of art and in the insights of mind and spirit. Religion includes the freedom to worship God as one understands and desires it. Here one leaves behind other patterns of thought aside from and above the legal call of the supreme law of the land. One is concerned about those values and those experiences of life that are not and cannot be defined by any law of state. They can here transcend the little evil hindrances that are placed in their way. One does not fear such things, one lives beyond the reach of them. He does what he does because he believes it is right to do it and because he feels he ought to obey the law of his being and of the universe rather than the laws of man however good they are. This level of moral and religious refinement is above and beyond the roadblocks of segregation and discrimination, and lives not by "the created goods" of government as Henry Nelson Wieman would say, but by the creative goods of human life and of the universe itself. For it is not economic, social, or political security that man seeks at this point in life, but moral refinement and religious enrichment. This is what the Old Testament prophet [2] meant when he said, "although the fig tree shall not blossom, neither shall fruit be in the vines; the labour of the olive shall fail, and the fields shall yield no meat; the flock shall be cut off from the fold, and there shall be no herd in the stalls: yet I will rejoice in the Lord, I will joy in the God of my salvation." On this level of experience a believer finds joy not through economic abundance, but he finds joy in a spiritual fellowship. Economic things are good and valuable, but according to this prophet they do not determine a man's attitude and spirit toward the highest things in life.

Jesus of Nazareth once made a similar statement to his disciples when they had returned from a certain town and brought

[2] Habbakkuk 3:17–18.

him food to eat. He said, "I have meat to eat that you know not of . . . my meat is to do the will of him that sent me and to finish his work.[3] Such faith and such religious insights and commitments are not required of any citizen of the United States of America in order to qualify as citizens of this great republic. But the supreme law of the land does not seek to curb or to control lives on this level of existence in any person. Men are permitted to believe and to act on this level, and when they so act, they are not under the responsibility and guidance of the Federal Constitution, for into this field the Constitution does not venture and on such delicate subjects and issues it does not speak. We can more clearly understand what Jesus meant when He gave His method of dealing with our adversaries and the kind of protest that He advocated.

There is a form of protest that does not aim at the physical or the legal change or the modification of any unjust law. In this form of protest one does not concern one's self with the removal of the law from the statute books; neither is one concerned about refusal to pay the price that an opponent places upon him so long as the act involved does not fall below the moral requirement of existing law and does not lead one to fight or to contend with the adversary on his level. If an adversary compels you to go with him one mile, you protest this unjust act by going with him two miles, thus taking from him the weapon with which he proposes to fight. The second mile is voluntary and reflects a new and high moral endowment of the one against whom the adversary seeks to carry on his campaign in asking him to go one mile. The one mile imposed is designed to vex, to insult, to humiliate the victim by the adversary. The willingness to go the second mile completely disarms the adversary who had relied wholly on the first mile to subdue and conquer his would-be victim. But when he voluntarily goes that extra mile the would-be victim displays a quality of life that the enemy does not understand and cannot conquer. This quality of life transcends the

* St. John 4:32–34.

life of the adversary, and he has no answer for it. Jesus said, if he takes your coat let him have your cloak also. Now the giving up of the coat does not compromise the moral quality of one's life, for one's life does not consist in the abundance of things that one possesses, but in the high values that one embraces that will not fade with old and worn-out clothing, or canker and perish with silver. The law of love that Jesus of Nazareth proclaims is far more rich and more divine than the love that depends upon and feeds upon the rewards and kind deeds of friends and well-wishers. Jesus took the position that this kind of love was never on the defensive and never put too much value on what imperfect men could give or take away in the name of love or hate.

The prophetic souls of history who have transformed society have not been those who have spent all of their time trying to reap the benefits of the material order. They have been men who have found a set of values for which they could live, values that were more inclusive and more comprehensive than all the material things that man could give. Jeremiah, the weeping prophet of the ancient Hebrews, was not put into a dungeon because he refused to take the humiliation of the king but rather because he brought to the kingdom a mission and a message that was more inclusive than the political order of his day and more powerful than all the soldiers in the armies of Judah. He was not jailed for disobeying the laws of state but because he would not allow the laws of state to come between him and his commitment to his God. In the United States of America the supreme law of the land makes no attempt at insulting a person's private conscience but defends the right of freedom on this level of experience. Hence there is no need for any citizen to defend his private conscience as competitor to the Federal Constitution. As a citizen of this country each person owes his allegiance to this nation without modification, reservation, or compromise. The growth of the conscience of any citizen up to the point proclaimed by Jesus will never lead him to fight with his own hands the enemies that face him. He does not take it upon himself to redress the grievances for which the government is responsible. He never turns to the task of blocking traffic, picketing private homes, or picketing churches, for such acts are not in harmony with the higher laws of conscience as we have discovered here. Jesus at no time threw himself against the petty laws of the Roman empire. He said, "render to Caesar the things that are Caesar's, and to God the things that are God's." [4] The ethics of the Federal Constitution are concerned only with the relationship of citizens to citizen, citizens to their government, and the government to their citizens. It has nothing to do with the relation between a citizen and his God or a citizen and his religious faith; consequently, as Americans, we have no grounds for disobeying the supreme law of the nation based on private conscience. There would be grounds for disobedience if the nation insisted that we refuse to walk by the light of the faith that inspires us to trust the Determiner of Destiny for the higher values in human life.

Forms Of Protest

Protest for civil rights is not new. Traces of it can be found in varying portions and aspects throughout the long history of the Negro's life in America. It was present among the slaves themselves long before the dawn of the day of Emancipation. These chattel slaves were strangers in a strange land. To them it was no particular blessing to be torn away from their native clime bereft of all the privileges of their native land. Their spirits, their minds, and their bodies were not as easily subdued as some have led us to think. They longed to escape the fetters and the pangs of slavery. Some of these slaves could not endure the perils of the sea and the solitude of the little vessel on which they were bound. When the opportunity came, some leaped overboard in a furious but futile attempt to swim back to the shores of their native land. An outstanding historian says:

[4] Mark 12:17.

Group protests against captive conditions had been made ever since African Negroes were first forced to go on the middle passage to the Americas. Hardly arrived in the Western Hemisphere, Negroes revolted in Haiti as early as the Sixteenth Century. Murderous insurrections in Venezuela and attempted escapes to the Indians from servitude in what is now South Carolina were well-known . . . Negro insurrections occurred in North America periodically from 1526 through the legal duration of slavery.[5]

During the Revolutionary War protest took the form of joining with the British forces when the patriots and the military leaders of the thirteen original colonies rejected the services both of the free Negro and of the slave. The conclusion was that Negro soldiers had not won the right to fight for the independence of the United States. General George Washington supported this idea, and the Negro was included along with deserters, strollers, vagabonds, and persons who were suspected as enemies to the liberty of America as being a part of an objectionable class. On July 9, 1775, an order was sent to all recruiting officers not to enlist Negroes as soldiers.

On September 26, 1775 Edward Rutledge of South Carolina moved in the Continental Congress to discharge all Negroes in the army. Although he was strongly supported by many of the southern delegates he lost his point. On October 8th however, a council of war composed of Washington, Major Generals Ward, Lee, Putnam; Brigadeer Generals Thomas Spencer, Heath, Sullivan, Green and Gates met and considered the use of Negroes. It was agreed unanimously to reject all slaves, and by a large majority to reject Negroes altogether.

Ten days later a group of civilians, among whom were Benjamin Franklin, Thomas Lynch, met with Washington and deputy governors of Rhode Island and Connecticut to discuss plans for recruiting a new army. It was again agreed to reject Negroes altogether. On

[5] Miles Mark Fisher, *Negro Slave Songs In The United States* (New York, 1953), p. 28.

November 12, 1775 General Washington issued an order instructing recruiters not to enlist Negroes.[6]

The slaves had no alternative but to express their protest against their rejection on the part of the leaders of the colonies by responding in the affirmative to the call of Lord Dunmore, the governor of Virginia, when in his proclamation he opened the doors for Negroes whether free or slave, to enter the royal army of the king of England. This they did in huge numbers, and so impressive was this move on the part of Negroes that the warlords and military leaders of the colonies reversed their position and extended to the Negroes an opportunity to join the army and fight on the side of the colonial patriots.

Some Negroes expressed their resentment to servitude by saving their money and then purchasing their own freedom. Others, through attempts at insurrection and other destructive means, tried to put an end to the awful shadow of servitude that haunted them. Among some of these were men like Gabriel Prosser in 1800 and Denmark Vessey, who tried a similar venture twenty-two years later. Then came a courageous leader from Southampton County, Virginia, who felt he had been called to deliver his people from bondage. In 1831 Nat Turner led his insurrection and frightened many slave masters, some of whom never again found absolute repose in the institution of slavery. Some Negroes expressed their resentment by joining that secret company of fleeing slaves historically called the underground railroad. Dr. Miles Mark Fisher sees in the Negro spirituals a sign language and one of the secret methods of communicating one to the other and making plans for the meeting of their secret society in which their resentment and opposition to slavery were freely expressed. Their songs were the expressions of their immediate desires and dealt with historic situations that in some cases helped them in their resentment against the conditions that

[6] John Hope Franklin, *From Slavery To Freedom* (New York, 1947), p. 132.

confronted them. Dr. Fisher holds that "Steal Away" was a song used by Nat Turner to assemble his companies for his insurrection.

Secret meetings were convened by songs. Negroes stole away from numerous plantations to African cult meetings just as Nat Turner of insurrectionary notoriety convened his companions by their ironic singing of 'Steal Away.' The external evidence of Turner's revolt against slavery coincides with the internal evidence of this song. He knew that should he be caught meeting with other Negroes the oft repeated burden of the song would be true: 'I hain't got long to stay here.' Yet, he was in a quandary how else to act when his personal Lord was calling him like a patrol officer with a trumpet, 'by the thunder,' 'by the lightening,' 'by green trees bending at will, and by signs of the judgment . . .' The saddened melody of the song bespoke that its author was melancholy about beginning his slave revolt in the house of his kind master. The circumstances all point to Nat Turner of Southampton County, Virginia as the author of 'Steal Away,' about 1825, the time of his call to be a prophet.[7]

Dr. Fisher through careful research has set forth a thrilling story of how the Negro slave songs were used to express the attitude of the slaves toward all the problems of life that he confronted. His songs were vehicles and tools by which he expressed the deep sentiments, attitudes, and feelings of his whole being.

Dean William Pickens, who for a number of years was a field secretary for the National Association For The Advancement of Colored People, frequently advanced an aspect of the doctrine referred to above. He was a scholar, a profound thinker, and yet carried a popular message to Negroes and white peoples North and South. His protest was not in bitterness, his sarcasm was cutting but not insulting. His wit was keen and penetrating. His contribution to the cause of civil rights in this country must never be forgotten. Those who knew Mr. Pickens personally and who often heard him speak realize his greatness. America has not as

[7] Fisher, *op. cit.*, (New York, 1953), pp. 66–67.

yet taken the time to honor sufficiently his genius and his leadership. There is no slab, crude or polished, that stands as a silent
reminder of his final resting place. This was rendered impossible
by a strange turn of providence. In failing health Mr. Pickens
took a cruise on the Caribbean Sea. On his ship he staggered to
rest and was buried in the arms of that far-off sea. In a jovial
mood Mr. Pickens frequently said Negroes had learned a technique of cursing their masters before their faces without insulting
them or calling down the wrath of the masters upon their head.
Said he:

They wrapped their curse words in songs, and when they would
see some of the masters visiting their worship services they would
frequently sing this song: 'You may be a white man as white as the
drifts of snow, but if you ain't got the love of Jesus in your soul to
hell you'll surely go.'

According to William Pickens the rest of the song was an intro-
duction for the sake of the last few words, namely; "to hell you'll
surely go."

Dr. W. H. R. Powell, the pastor of the Shiloh Baptist Church
in Philadelphia, Pennsylvania, and one of America's great preachers, used to thrill his audience with a story that reveals a unique
method of protest that slaves sometimes used in the worship
services of their masters. Whether this story be fable or fact, on
the lips of Dr. W. H. R. Powell it conveyed the message that he
had in mind. He recounted that in a particular church slaves
were not allowed to sit in the audience, at least on the main
floor; the balcony was reserved for them. One Sunday morning
the white minister had given a dynamic description of the
heavenly land, he had told his white parishioners about the
beauties of the eternal clime with the tree of life and the leaves
for the healing of the nation. He then described the beauties of
the streets paved with gold and told how the saints would walk
the golden streets with feet shod in slippers of gold. Their robes
were the finest, and they were to sit around the throne of His

Majesty and sing praises unto the lamb and crown Him Lord of
all. Wishing to include the whole of his audience in his message,
he then gazed upward toward the balcony and observed the
anxious looks and tense faces of the dusky sons and daughters of
Africa. He then said to them that they too would be in glory but
their lot would be different from their masters. They would be in
Negro heaven. They would have no wings, no robes, and no
golden slippers. Their streets would be heavenly but not paved;
they would stand and not sit. The eloquent sermon was over,
the congregation was almost ready for the benediction. One old
slave struggled to his feet and raised his hand. In getting the
pastor's attention he said, "I would like to offer prayer before the
meeting adjourns." A little surprised and stunned for a moment,
the pastor had no words. Finally one of the deacons said to him,
"let him pray." The old man stood with deep and mellow voice,
and reviewed the sermon as best he could, and said to God: "We
thank you for allowing us to get to heaven, but we have heard
strange things of Thee. The preacher has told us that we will
have a special section with no paved streets, no robes, no wings,
and no golden slippers, and we will be restricted and even
denied a place to sit. But O God, all we ask of you is to let us get
there, and we'll sit any damn place we please." This indirect
method of expressing one's feeling seems to have been a part of
some of the African customs. According to Dr. Fisher there was
the *Bo Akutia* custom among the Ashanti.

In it an aggrieved native took a friend to the house of his adversary. The offended person then villified his friend in the presence
of the adversary for whom the abuse was really intended.[8]

In the light of such a custom the method of protest as expressed by William Pickens and Dr. W. H. R. Powell falls within
the category of possibility. But suffice it to say, there is strong
testimony that much of the history, plans, and purposes of the

[8] *Ibid.*, p. 9.

slaves seem to have found expression in their songs. "Deep
River"⁹ is said to have originated in Gilford County, North
Carolina, and the "camp ground" the slaves longed for was their
native Africa the home of camp meetings. The deep river is the
vast ocean separating the slaves from the shores of their native
land. But our concern here is with the element of protest that
recurs again and again in the slave songs of the African people.

Dr. Fisher has made a strong argument and has presented
documentary evidence that is most convincing, and it is difficult
to deny the facts presented in support of his thesis. But there is
something else to be said about these slave songs that will extend
beyond the contemporary events of life and beyond the battle
for things physical, and hence beyond the elements of protest.
This other aspect of the Negro slave songs will claim our attention in our Chapter *From Protest To Production.* From our observations in this Chapter the facts are certain and clear that the
Negro in America did not as a whole ever accept segregation in
the church or in any other place as a matter of logic and life.
Protest against religious discrimination not only was a vital part
of the mind and disposition of both slaves and freedmen, but it
was also one of the reasons that gave birth to the Negro church.
History records many significant forms of protest in addition to
those that came from the church.

From the days of the abolitionists until the present Negroes
have not stood alone in their protest for equality of opportunity.
There have been dedicated white Americans who have joined
Negroes in this struggle. There were strong abolitionists who
lifted their voices against the cursed institution of slavery and
they gave their time and their talent to defeat the plans and
purposes of this cursed institution. It is not strange then, that the
first and the most powerful civil rights organization in the United
States of America came into being in 1910 as a joint venture
between Negroes and whites. This organization had as its primary and only purpose carrying on a work of protest in the

⁹ *Ibid.,* p. 41.

interest of the rights of Negro Americans. In that historic meeting in May, 1910, the following white Americans joined with Negro leaders in organizing the National Association For The Advancement of Colored People: Mary White Overton, William English Whaling, and Henry Moskowitz. From 1910 to 1954 this organization carried on the most constructive, the most realistic, and the most successful campaign of protest of any organization of its kind in the United States of America. At no time were they anti-white in their plans and purposes, for theirs was a cooperative venture between loyal American Negroes and loyal American whites. They took their stand on the side of, and in the light of, and by the power of the supreme law of the land. Time would fail us to tell in detail the contributions that outstanding Negro and white leaders made to this organization which is still the most powerful of the civil rights movement today.

Dr. W. E. B. Dubois, a scholar and a philosopher, was one of the early champions involved in the work of the National Association For The Advancement of Colored People. Earlier he had attempted to organize the Niagara Movement which was more hostile and antagonistic to the white community than was the above-mentioned organization. But with his pen, and with his deep thought; he made, in his own way, his voice heard in the defense of justice and freedom. James Weldon Johnson, a sociologist, a college professor, and a poet, brought to the National Association For The Advancement of Colored People his insights, his genius, and his devotion. And it was he who left on record that immortal song, "Lift Every Voice and Sing." His note of protest was seasoned with artistic splendor and with deep religious fervor. One can never mention the great pioneers and sacrificial spirits in this organization without referring to Mr. Walter White. Many people did not understand him, and many members of the Negro community have not fully recognized the great contribution and the sacrificial service that he rendered to the cause of justice in his method of protest. It was difficult to distinguish Mr. Walter White from any white American because his features and his color led many to mistake him as a member of the Caucasian group. He took advantage of these natural gifts and harnessed all of his talents and more than once took his life in his own hands by going south, forcing himself into angry mobs, and gathering the facts and even pictures of some of the horrible lynchings that took place. Through his ventures the United States of America learned increasingly more about how lynchings were carried on and the identities of some of the guilty persons. The present Executive Secretary of the National Association For The Advancement of Colored People, Mr. Roy Wilkins, was brought up in the tradition of these outstanding leaders and has caught much of their spirit, their courage, and their faith in victory through law and order and through the courts of the land. In spite of cross-currents and some opposition Mr. Wilkins and those who worked with him have maintained the higher patriotic approach to the problem of protest that has been a vital part of this great association. This national organization has not at any time as a whole, become anti-white, anti-America, or anti-law and order. Some of the most far-reaching and historic victories in the field of civil rights have been led, sponsored, and financed by the National Association For The Advancement of Colored People. It was this organization through its leadership and dedicated and committed legal talents that helped to win the victory of May 17, 1954. After the historic legal victory of May 17, 1954, new opportunities came forth, new victories were achieved, and in the light of these new opportunities many new and younger civil rights organizations came into existence and joined the army of protest. Some among these were the revitalized Congress of Racial Equality which had been organized in 1942 but which had not been actively engaged in the work of protest as we know it until after 1954. Some new organizations were the Student Non-Violent Coordinating Council, Southern Christian Leadership Conference, and scores and scores of other organizations, many of which came to pass as a result of individual and group response to particular problems and particular situations. Many of the younger civil rights organizations find their reasons for existence primarily to meet specific problems in specific communities, but basically most of them have in common the emphasis on civil disobedience. The announced objectives are the same; the securing of civil rights and first class opportunities for Negro Americans. These younger organizations must be evaluated more as spontaneous movements sustained by a passion for quick victories and the overthrow of all the obstacles that would hinder or impede their progress. They must be evaluated not only in the light of their enthusiasm but in the light of long-range goals, practical achievements, and their constructive relationship to the Federal Constitution and the American way of life.

We must not overlook the work of the United Defense League which organized the first bus boycott in the South June 1953, in Baton Rouge, Louisiana.[10] The issue involved with the Baton Rouge Bus Company concerned itself with the matter of seating. Prior to the boycott Negroes were not allowed to move beyond the center of the bus. Through the bus boycott they received all of the seats they sought but one, and then filed a suit for that and finally were successful in their effort. They used what they called "Operation Free Lift," by which Negro people were given free rides. This continued for a week. It required more courage to conduct such a boycott in June 1953, for this was eleven months before the historic decision outlawing segregation in education and virtually breaking the back of that historic evil in the United States. The president of the United Defense League was the Rev. T. J. Jemison, now secretary of the National Baptist Convention, U.S.A., Inc. At the time of the boycott his father, Dr. D. V. Jemison, was president. Fourteen thousand Negroes benefited by the free car lift and at that time they constituted

[10] For the authentic story of this first bus boycott read the following newspapers from Baton Rouge: Daily papers: *The Morning Advocate*, June 20, 21, 22, 26, 30, 1953; *State Times*, June 25–26, 1953; Weeklies: *News Reader*, June 27, July 4, 1953.

seventy per cent of the riding public on the buses. They had a fleet of one hundred twenty-five privately owned cars ranging from 1953 Fleetwood Cadillacs to T-Model Fords.

When the Montgomery Bus Boycott was started in Montgomery, Alabama in 1956 the leaders patterned their operation after the first bus boycott that had been led successfully in Baton Rouge, Louisiana three years earlier.

3

PREFERENCE AND PREJUDICE

THERE IS A VAST difference between preference and prejudice. This fact must be explored, known, and fully appreciated if the people of this country are to come to grips with the problem of race without misunderstanding. Negroes as well as whites must know and evaluate this difference. If not, the struggle for civil rights will more and more move too far from the main track, lose its perspective, and miss its true goal. We must know against what we contend and for what we struggle in the pursuit of justice and equality of opportunity. Do we struggle to break the spell and the pull of preference in all of its phases in American life and to deny to a person the right as well as the privilege of private choice and the right to private friends in this struggle for civil rights? Are we ready to conclude that our system would be richer and human relations more constructive if somehow the state or the federal government could control the preferences of men? Is it possible to develop any form of social organization or any kind of political state in which men and women do not have preferences in the realm of friends, associates, and in the choice of a multitude of other values? If one destroys the right of preference, one destroys the right of choice; and if one destroys the right of choice, one undercuts the very foundation on which freedom stands. The right of privacy as espoused and defended by the supreme law of the land is in reality a strong support of the right of preference. In some countries the right of preference in marriage is taken from the parties involved, and the match is made by parents or by other rules of procedure.

This was true in the days of the ancient Hebrews. Some times the bride did not see the groom until the plans of marriage had been developed and concluded. Leah was given to Jacob as a wife after he had served her father for seven years. She was not his preference, but the tradition and law of the family dictated that he accept the family choice. Jacob made it known, however, that he preferred Rachel who was a sister to Leah, but the seven years service that he had rendered for Leah could not and would not be honored for Rachel. Jacob had to work seven years more for Rachel. He enjoyed some degree of preference when the labors were completed that had been required by her father, but in this case Rachel the bride had little or no choice, and hence enjoyed no option but to take the man her father had chosen and bargained with. Rachel might have preferred cutting the time of the marriage by six years, but she had no preference in the matter. What her father said was final.

In certain countries in Africa similar customs are followed today. But we need not visit ancient countries or study people whose patterns of civilization and culture are more divergent from those peculiar to Western Civilization. In some of the most advanced nations of the western world we find some traces of the denial of preference in the matter of choosing a wife. In 1936 the British Empire was shaken from center to circumference when the King of the British Empire, the former Prince of Wales, was called upon to sacrifice his preference and to allow the upholders of the country's tradition of royal marriages to determine who should be his wife. The king of this great commonwealth was called upon to make a speedy decision. Should he embrace the crown for life, or forsake the crown and marry the woman whom he loved? He flung himself against the testimony of history, the advice of some of the best statesmen in the modern world, and even turned back the tender entreaties and tears of his mother and petitions from other members of his family.

In the United States of America it is our belief that the right to preference is a sacred right that each individual must enjoy and that no powers of government must usurp or destroy it. In preference one is allowed to set his estimation on what or whom he shall embrace. One determines what values he prefers, what friends he shall accept, and what fellowship he shall choose and cultivate. In preference one sets one's affections and determines the worthiness of the object of one's desire. In the United States of America public education to a point is compulsory, but a student is allowed the right of preference as to careers and professions. The basic rudiments of education are required and determined by the state or the nation in which the citizens live. But a democratic state does not take from one the right of preference in following the bent of his talents and the leadership of his own mind.

In another context our American republic determines and sets up the standards, goals, and requirements for citizenship. On these there can be no compromise. Each citizen must possess enough character to render him a loyal supporter and a trustworthy citizen of his country. But whether he shall be a member of a particular church or denomination, or whether he shall be a member of any church for that matter, is left wholly to the citizen's preference; for in this type of preference no injury is done to the rights of other citizens, no threat to the government, and no hindrance to the logical and legal flow of the democratic process. In private fraternities, lodges, and secret orders, the members are allowed the freedom to establish their rules, their codes, their principles of behavior. They are allowed to build their own fellowship as long as this fellowship does not threaten the life and security of the members or take from non-members their basic rights as American citizens. They can exercise their own preferences regarding membership and not be in violation of the laws of the land or at variance with the Federal Constitution.

This aspect of privacy is one of the vital parts of American democracy. In America there is no royal family. There are no rulers in the several states and in the nation itself who hold offices or positions of honor on the basis of the right of birth, blood, inheritance, or any other factors over and above the choice of the people. Racial preference of itself is no sin. The preference of one nationality for its own people is no evil. The truth is, up to a point, it is a virtue and is an aspect of racial pride, togetherness, and respect. It is not known by many how deep-seated is this same spirit of preference among Negroes themselves. Thousands of Negroes respect their heritage, love and honor their foreparents, and are thankful to God for the blessings of their past and their present. But because of the kind of battle Negroes have had to wage against segregation and discrimination many outside observers have arrived at the conclusion that Negroes do not prefer one another. Such may be the case with a few Negroes but not with the great masses. The great masses of Negroes in honor and dignity prefer one another.

There are some Negroes, however, who do not love or respect their own race. They use the cause of the unfortunate among them to promote and to make themselves great as supposed leaders of the unfortunate Negro people. Some Negroes who oppose racial segregation and discrimination wage their fight not to liberate their unfortunate brothers but for the purpose of winning a place for themselves in the white community that they prefer more than fellowship with their own people. The personal ambition of this group is to be respected and promoted by the white community. They discuss the Negro cause; it is the theme in which they are considered experts by the white community. Many of these so-called race leaders do not identify themselves with the Negro community as such or with the organizations owned and operated by Negroes. These pseudo-Negro leaders will not identify themselves with any cause in the Negro communities aside from the battle against the white community for the abolition of segregation in order to win a place for themselves in the white power structure of the community. They will not help Negroes to develop better churches, better communities, and better homes, yet they are leading a crusade against white people to liberate Negro people.

There are other so-called Negro leaders who use the Negro cause as a means of earning as much money as they can from the sympathetic white people of goodwill. Such Negro leaders are worse than parasites. They stand on the backs of the Negro masses and ascribe to them vices which they do not possess collectively. In the process of raising money for themselves and their little causes, they inflame the white community with fear, embitter many public officials. This in reality is a form of deception that does not serve well the cause of freedom and is a liability to both races. It is unpatriotic, unfair, and un-Christian to so use and victimize the minds and spirits of innocent people. It is difficult to analyze and weigh with care the sincerity and dedication of leaders when the freedom and the rights of individuals are involved. People who have long suffered oppression are put to a decided disadvantage to evaluate or to criticize any person who comes to them in the name of freedom and in the interest of their rights as first-class citizens. Many and confusing are the methods employed. The same parasitic leaders would return to the Negro community with their fiery speeches aimed at stirring bitterness, frustration, and despair. Sometimes they hold nightly meetings and group sessions in small isolated places. They say the purpose is to organize the poor and the disadvantaged, but they never organize these people to harness their own values within their community, to pool their little resources and join with other constructive Negro leaders to help build for themselves. There is no message from these apostles of mal-content to heal the hurt of their people, but they use the hurt of the people to convert it into hate and finally bitterness. Many of these leaders do not prefer the Negro race in any other context aside from the context referred to above. Many Negroes who prefer their race are afraid to make known their preference lest they be called supporters of segregation and discrimination and slaves of the power structure and "uncle toms"

who have not the courage of their convictions; hence they keep
quiet when deep within themselves they love and respect their
own race. Racial togetherness can be taught to a people without
bitterness and without strife against other people. Any racial
togetherness that is based on opposition to the white community
alone, and hatred, revenge and animosity against people of
another color is not true racial preference. It is tainted with a
selfishness and a corruption that can never bless any community,
any state, or any nation.

There are many white people in America whose present
bitterness and hatred against Negroes spring from the false
notion that Negroes hate themselves, love and revere white
people more, and are desirous of falling heir without effort to
those things that the white community has amassed. When it is
clearly known that Negroes do have a constructive racial preference, some of the bitterness in the white community will
subside; and when more leaders of the Negro race make a constructive appeal to the existence and the powerful resources of
such a preference, tensions between the races will be greatly
reduced and the Negro masses will be encouraged to teach and
preach racial togetherness as they continue the war against every
un-American policy that blocks their upward march towards the
high and sunny tableland of first class American citizenship.
People who recognize and cherish and appreciate the natural
tendency of togetherness will be less inclined to hate and to
antagonize other peoples who maintain such preferences on a
just, moral, and creative basis.

The practice of and the deep feeling of racial preference
among Negroes does for them what it does in any other group.
First, it strengthens and develops wholesome racial pride and
respect. It deepens the love of a people for themselves. They
realize that there are some virtues and values that belong to
them which are worthy of praise and adoration. When people
know and appreciate what they are, what they do, and what
they possess, they will develop the courage to admit and to con-

fess what they are not and what they do not have. Self-criticism is a sign of a greater degree of maturity and is one of the ways to correction and to growth. Secondly, the people can blame themselves for some of the things that they do not have and are not doing when they realize that they are in possession of a creative vitality that has not been and is not being fully harnessed and most wisely used. Self-development is as great a task as campaigning to condemn and to correct those who have wronged the race or group. The race here admits the presence of potential strength and finds in its development one of the means of improving not only the race itself, but also the larger community as a whole. At this point a new significance is attached to the actions, deeds, and events that take place within the race itself. This new significance will lead to the recording of these deeds and in the long run a greater appreciation of racial history. Furthermore, the Negro race must learn to think more of its worth and ability than to retreat into day-dreaming about the evils that are being done and have been done. Too often the race is painted in the colors that have been imparted by those who hate and discriminate.

In their fight against segregation some Negroes have developed a phobia that leads them to feel that what is black is bad, and what is owned and controlled by Negro people is inferior or wrong. In 1963 the National Association For The Advancement of Colored People met in Chicago, Illinois. According to reports some of the young delegates allegedly complained and protested because at the entrance to the dining room of the old Morrison Hotel there stood a small carved figure of a boy with a black face. This little statue had stood there for a number of years. But the young Negro boys and girls attending this convention protested to the management and demanded that this statue be removed. The manager did not remove the statue, but he was gracious enough to the complaining delegates to cover the little statue with a piece of white cloth; after this the young people were perfectly satisfied. There is a dignity in the Negro race that is worthy of respect and appreciation, and it can and must stand on its own supporting feet. It does not need a white veneer or a white covering to enhance or to enrich it. Young Negro Americans who have this anti-black phobia would do well to visit some of the countries in Africa and learn how deeply the people revere and respect themselves and honor that which is black. If the Negro race is ever to receive its rightful place in society it will come through and by Negroes themselves respecting themselves, preferring themselves, and harnessing their resources and raising their own standards and stock. Negroes have the ability to do far more than they are doing on every level of life. To be sure, there are handicaps and forces to hinder and to defeat, but the material that Negroes possess is strong enough and rich enough to match and to overcome the negative forces that are thrown against them.

The greatest sin that any people or group can commit against themselves is to underrate their own talents and to refuse fully to harness their latent abilities. Negroes in certain cities have bought and developed some of the finest homes and have built beautiful communities. They can do more of this even now in more towns and cities of the nation. There is nothing wrong with Negroes undertaking to make any community where they live as great as any other community. They can take on the responsibility of helping to save our young people from the ranks of school drop-outs and early delinquency, helping to reduce crime, and making our streets safe by night as well as by day. This can be done without any kind of war against other groups and peoples. Is it too much for Negroes to undertake to build such beautiful and attractive communities that other peoples will desire and seek to be a part of it because it is most desirable? The responsibility for such undertakings does not deny to Negroes the right to choose a home and to buy in any part of any city that their money and ability will permit, but we are here emphasizing the Negro's ability and his power of achievement through his ability. This type of action is not designed to become a separatist movement that would degenerate into an anti-white or an anti any other group. Such would be wrong and self-defeating both for the race and for the cause of democracy itself.

It is clear that preference does not in any way mean self-discrimination. There are certain conditions that now exist that require Negroes to make some efforts to save themselves from falling into the slough of despondency and disrespect. Historically our togetherness has been an enforced togetherness. We were once held together by the institution of slavery. Since then we as a race have been held together by the cruel hands of segregation and have had before us no other choice. Now that the walls of segregation are crumbling, what is left to hold the Negro people together? Or do we wish to be together? Such a togetherness does not suggest or imply racial segregation any more than the togetherness of other groups and nationalities would deny their part and place in the American fellowship. As long as this togetherness and preference do not degenerate into prejudice against others and a denial on our part of higher and bigger opportunities and responsibilities, we would sustain a great loss if we did not maintain a degree of togetherness in the interest of racial pride and appreciation.

It is true that the drive against segregation has been a hard and weary one and has at times given the impression to some that the Negro was against himself. One white American once asked in a forum discussion: "why do Negroes want to be with white people? Do they not have any respect for themselves and any appreciation for their race?" My reply was: "we must never confuse the quest for the equality of opportunity and a full share in the cultural and creative things of American life with a desire simply to be with white people." Negroes do not hate themselves and for the most part, maintain a preference that has enriched their lives and stabilized their thinking, and guided them as a people. It may be that the sincere white American referred to above missed the facts and objectives of the constructive civil rights struggle. There are some Negroes who in

pointing out the evils of segregation have at times over-empha-
sized the failures to be found in a segregated situation. These
Negroes have made segregation most powerful and the determining factor for life and character, and they have preached
directly or indirectly a gospel of self-surrender and self-discrimination in the face of segregation. There are some innocent
Negro children who have gotten the impression that whatever
is led or possessed by Negroes is inferior. Some of them have
been heard to say that if it is a Negro school it is inferior. But,
our reply is, it need not be inferior. If equipment and supplies
and the same rigid educational standards are set up as are set
up for any other schools, Negro teachers can qualify, and have
qualified, to meet these standards of efficiency. And Negroes
must not allow such negative thinking to deceive them to the
point of self-discrimination. A people can live a life that is self-
defeating and self-degrading, and this is worse than any form
of discrimination. The victory against racial segregation in the
courts, the classrooms, in business, sports, and all of the other
areas of American life cannot of itself save a prideless people.

It is clear to most Americans that racial discrimination as well
as all other forms based on pre-judgments are, in the light of the
Federal Constitution illegal, immoral, and unjust. But there are
many people who oppose racial discrimination when it is practiced by white people against Negroes but seem willing to accept
it when it is practiced by some Negroes against Negroes themselves. Unfortunately there are some Negroes who give lip service to the fight against discrimination but who practice the same
against their own people and even against themselves. Discrimination is the act of separating or dividing people by some
superficial standard and ascribing to them a status below merit
and below every standard of justice, and then treating them as
if they were not worthy of or did not have a right to equal
treatment with other deserving citizens. In such an act the
character of the victim is discredited and his resident ability
dishonored and disrespected. Such people are dealt with as if

they were not able to respond to or to achieve the highest possible goals of human life. To assign a passenger a second-rate seat in a second-class car when he has the money and the desire for first-class accommodations is discrimination. This is true because the accommodation is below the purchasing power and below the mental and moral dignity of the persons involved. The same principle is true when some Negro leaders call Negroes to a pattern of life that is below their capacities as men and women, a pattern of life which does not challenge the highest and the best in them. This has been one of the tragedies of some of the direct action programs in our civil rights struggle during the past ten years. Negroes have been repeatedly called upon to march and to use their feet not only to demonstrate against injustice, but to influence change and to force the leaders of the power structure to adopt new and better methods of dealing with minority groups who have been so long denied their rights. We do not sit in judgment on those leaders who are sincere in their beliefs that this is the best and the surest way to win first class citizenship on every level of American life. We do not deny any real good that has been achieved by these methods. But what we hasten to point out is that this type of protest does not summon or challenge the highest and the best in any people. Some civil rights leaders have frequently said that, "there is nothing as powerful as the tramp, tramp of marching feet." This statement and the philosophy on which it rests is too weak to become an accepted way of life in the struggle for civil rights or in any other struggle. It has several defects. First, it assumes that men in responsible positions will react more constructively and respond more positively only when their lower emotions are appealed to such as fear of intimidation, and fear of the loss of prestige and community standing because of these embarrassing experiences. The higher emotions of patriotism, respect for the dignity of other human beings, and the moral commitment to the ideals of justice and freedom are not appealed to in such demonstrations. Pacts and agreements made under duress and under the pressure of insults, threats, and intimidations may serve as expedient for the moment but will tend to crumble when the pressure is withdrawn or a new courage born of resentment is developed. If we are to build a democratic society according to the patterns prescribed by the Federal Constitution it must be done by an appeal to the highest in people which will call forth the best in them.

Furthermore, "the tramp, tramp of marching feet" underrates other gifts and talents and capacities that Negroes possess now. There is something in the minority group far more powerful than the sound of marching feet. It is a potential of a developed mind that can think, evaluate, and form constructive conclusions and make lofty decisions in the time of crisis. There is also the gift of moral stamina out of which flows a strong oughtness of conscience and the ability to labor with one's hands to win one's daily bread as one accepts the responsibility of building his share of economic and cultural structure of this great republic. "The tramp, tramp of marching feet" must always be matched with the "thought, thought" of active minds and with the "work, work" of willing hands. To develop a mass philosophy that leaves the burden of thought to a few while the many individuals are reduced to the level of a blind animal existence is a discrimination against the high powers. Such a philosophy and such a pattern of action sins against the higher concept of man as a moral creature whose significance lies in the fact that he is a child of freedom and a son of God. A method of protest that tends to ignore or rob human beings of their higher powers is the worse form of discrimination.

To call young inexperienced children out of classrooms to demonstrate against the existing evils of a segregated society is unfair to the child because at this point his time is not being spent most wisely. The child is being taken from important hours of training that every growing child so badly needs. It teaches him a degree of disrespect for teachers whom he must learn to respect if he is to get the best possible results from efforts in his behalf. This draws the child's attention away from his immediate task of studying and commits him to a job that adults have not been able to master: that is, the correction of educational systems manned by adults when the child is less equipped for such a task. The best guarantee to correct a weak educational system is to train young minds in the basic principles of thought and freedom inspired by a love of truth and justice. Let them get the best possible education that is available to them, and let them always be reminded that there are still more things to be gained, to be learned, and to be achieved. A child who is skilled in the act of protest but weak and untrained in the art of study and thought and the task of creating values and producing higher forms of life is a present and potential liability to himself and to his society of the future. To lead a child away from loyalty to those who are elected to instruct him is an act of discrimination that might in the long run put his feet in the wrong path or damn his life to the hell of anti-social and anti-human relations forever.

It is not enough to adopt a program of integration that assumes that the relation between the majority and the minority shall always be that between sellers and buyers; owners and renters, employers and employees. While there is nothing wrong with the above-mentioned relationships, an effort to improve and render them more just and more equitable should be put forth; for employees, buyers, and renters, have rights that employers, sellers, and owners must always respect and vice versa. But any programs that are based on the assumption that the traditional relations between Negroes and whites will and should always be the same, underrate the Negro potential and sin against his already existing ability. Too many Negro leaders consciously or unconsciously are discriminating against their own race by preaching the doctrine that whatever is all-Negro is all wrong whether it be school, business, profession or church. Playing down the Negro's ability and performing acts that demonstrate the lack of faith in his creative and productive abilities are acts of self-depreciation.

Of course there is much more that our country must do to help make this nation a more perfect democracy, and for these things Negroes as well as other dedicated Americans must always contend. We must insist that we stand as tall as our height and our reach combined will permit us and that we shall reach even now for the highest values that summon from us our greatest strength. Negroes who have won the right to vote must no longer refuse to vote, neither must they sell their ballot to the highest bidder. They must make the wisest and the fullest use of it. They must help to put in office the best possible persons irrespective of color or creeds. The ballot is not a weapon of revenge against those who are the children of segregationists or against those who once believed in segregation. If children of former slaves use their ballots to punish children of former masters, the children of segregationists will have the same right. To refuse to rise above a slave morality in our dealing with our fellow-Americans is a violation of our highest insights and our highest gifts and powers. Civil rights leaders and other Negro leaders who lead their people away from their higher responsibility and from a dedicated service to the improvement of their own people are not leading in the right direction. A life of protest does not exhaust all the resources of any man's being. A campaign of hate carries not to the heights for which normal people are equipped. Bitterness does not help men to be better or to build the best possible character. Acts of vengeance do not and cannot release in any people their higher virtues of manhood and womanhood, and wickedness does not make a people wise. No Negro is out of place who turns his face toward his people and sees in them powers that have not as yet been released and observe latent talents not yet harnessed. The cry must be uttered to Negroes: sons of men, and daughters of women, stand on thy feet. Contend for the highest mastery and let no man take thy crown. Bury not your talents in an untimely grave of complaints and compromises; be not ashamed to invest what you possess and leave the ultimate results to time and history.

> For when the one great scorer comes,
> To write against your name,
> He writes not whether you lost or won;
> But how you played the game.

Preference of race is no evil then as long as it does not lead a people from the wider cultural and economic values of the nation and the world to which all are entitled and as long as it is not a sin against any other group. When preference for one's own group leads to an act of prohibiting the membership of others in a larger group, preference here degenerates into prejudice. Prejudice as we know it, is a prejudgment that seeks to justify unkind thoughts, evil intentions, and destructive deeds against others. When one takes one's preference and tries to make it the preference of all others, a form of prejudice results. A group of American citizens may prefer a certain group as members of their clubs, fraternities, and private associations, but if in this act the same citizens seek to deny to others their rightful place and their rightful share in the life of the whole community and nation, this is an act of prejudice. The laws of justice in the United States of America do not deal with private prejudices so long as they do not extend beyond their jurisdiction and become a means of hindering the normal and rightful growth of others. Prejudice is an enemy to freedom and democracy when it comes out of its private domain and seeks to regulate the policies and practices of a whole nation. When Adolph Hitler developed a strong pro-German point of view and committed himself to the task of rendering the greatest service possible in restoring the dignity of his home and in lifting the German people to their rightful place in the family of nations, his preference was wholesome, just, and good. But when he goes a step further and deifies the Aryan race as a master race, then he moves into a category that is both dangerous and destructive. The horrors of the German concentration camps, the murders of more than six million Jews by Hitler and his group, have left on the pages of history some of the most sordid and most diabolical crimes of prejudice against mankind that have ever soiled the pages of human history. The German's right to living space did not necessitate the destruction of other races, nations, and countries. But Hitler's defeat and the fall of the Third Reich is a concrete and sad reminder of how self-destructive is hatred and prejudice when given free reign. A program of destruction dictated by the prejudice and hatred of one people against another carries with it and in it the same seeds of destruction for those who administered and perpetrated it against others.

What are some of the steps of preference which can lead to racial prejudice? They may be summarized as follows: the feeling that it requires the hand of segregation to guarantee the preservation of the white race in its biological purity; the use of the doctrine of white supremacy as a dogma and a duty to establish and to prove the inferiority of another group and to deal with them and to punish them accordingly; the belief that the blessings of one racial group can be best preserved through penalizing another; and the fear that the granting of full freedom to others will jeopardize the position and the values that the preferred ones have acquired. But prejudice is not essential to growth. If a group believes that it is superior, it need not turn to negative actions against others. It has nothing to do but to go on with its growth and development. Why fear the weak if you know you are strong? Why seek to build and to develop or to cause to be developed a weak and segregated people in a nation that you love and hope to lift to the highest level of democratic fellowship? Why plan for your health as a people of culture and then by design create slums in which diseases and ignorance and crime may breed and spread to all the community and attack all races and all peoples?

The supreme law of the land gives any group the right, the latitude, and the freedom to have and to develop its own preferences so long as these preferences do not in any way grow into prejudices that hinder and tend to destroy the lives of other people. For this breaks the fellowship of the nation and tends to destroy the very grounds of democracy. The battle against segregation and discrimination must not be, and is not a battle against legitimate, wholesome preferences, but against prejudice that is self-defeating and self-destroying. Any civil rights groups that insist on leading drives against people and private institutions because they would destroy or break legitimate and private preferences are leading the wrong campaign and cannot be supported by the Federal Constitution or the American philosophy of freedom. But prejudice must be opposed because it will destroy this democracy of the United States and destroy both the segregated and the segregator.

One constructive way to overcome prejudice is to expand the circle and limits of preference. By this act more individuals are included in the circle of vital kinship. The expanding of the circle here is dependent upon and an indication of growth and maturity biologically, psychologically, and morally. The child for a time prefers the members of his immediate family. He is dependent upon them for food, for comfort, for love, and security. But this circle expands to include playmates, school-mates, and other persons and groups. People who prefer their race and their race only are less mature than those who have been able to include in their accepted circle higher reasons than race. People who allow themselves to develop and to grow in depth of appreciation for the values in mankind can without a great strain finally include in their circles persons who are joined to them not by blood and birth, but by common interest, ideals, and some creative and all compelling causes. The greater the growth in these circles of preference, the more is the area and circle of prejudice reduced. Prejudice, then, exists where men have allowed hindering theories and philosophies to dwarf their minds and to fetter their spirits and distort their whole personalities. There comes a time when one can recognize membership and fellowship not by color, but by character; not by prejudice, but by principles; not through fear, but by faith. Negroes who insist in fighting all white people have not become mature enough to accept in all seriousness into their membership people who transcend the limits of their own race. When we become Americans in our thinking we will be as sensitive about the preservation of the nation's way of life as we are about the preservation of our own families and our own race. The solution to the race problem and racial conflicts in the United States of America cannot and will not come in a conflict between preferential groups in which one circle seeks to break the preferences of another and win for themselves a victory for their preferences. There must be an initiation into wider circles of responsibility, that will engage the minds and emotions of people of different races, as they seek to pursue a cause that is meaningful to both races and both groups. When we dedicate ourselves to the principles of the Federal Constitution and labor to build an American society purer in freedom, richer in goodwill and mutual understanding, all races and nationalities within the confines of this great republic can become workers and co-laborers together in a national circle of friendship in whose preference the bitterness of prejudice will be diluted if not wholly subdued.

Here we become brothers not by birth or blood but by a common relationship prescribed by the supreme law of the land and sustained by the American philosophy of freedom. When He would convey to those about Him the all-pervasive kinship through a common dedication to the ideals of the kingdom that He proclaimed, Jesus of Nazareth gave an astounding answer re-

garding His kinship when He was asked who were His mother
and brothers and sisters. He replied:

> For whosoever shall do the will of my Father which is in heaven,
> the same is my brother, and sister, and mother.[1]

Jesus at this point was expressing no disrespect for the members
of his family. He was not trying to discredit family ties and
family relations, but rather He was pointing out to those who
stood about the importance and the power of another and more
inclusive kinship. He will not allow even His family relationship
to disturb and to call Him from the work of the kingdom. His
was a great cause, and a lofty and inclusive purpose. His mother
and His brother could and were included in the wider kingdom.
But He could not fit His twelve disciples and other believers
into the narrow circle of the direct descendants of Mary His
mother.

Prejudice, a very serious malady both of the mind and emotions, is most difficult to cure. It has enough anchorage in the
rational faculties of the person to justify, at least on the surface,
the bitterness that it engenders and is so clearly allied with self-
interest and self-security that it sets itself up as an urgent and
essential principle and way of life. Prejudice can both be caught
and taught. It may be caught by the flare of tradition, devotion
to customs, or the esteemed mores of the community. It may be
the fashionable thing to do in order to gain and hold one's
status in the community. Also, it may be taught to the child by
its parents, its playmates, and its associates. Once planted, it
grows like a cancer until its roots are entwined about every
nerve of the body and every cell of the brain, and it tends to
color, affect, and influence every decision and every action of
one's life. It not only becomes a pattern of thinking and acting,
it becomes also a barrier to certain types of thinking and acting.

[1] Matthew 12:50.

It sets limits on the range and the height of one's outlook and holds the feeling tone of one's being in strict captivity and on the lower level of human existence. There are matters and issues on which a prejudiced one dare not think for fear that the canons of reason might invade the area of the mind that has been leased or sold to a particular prejudice. Further, such a one fears to disturb the feeling tone of life that has become the willing subject and helpless slave of prejudgments and blind imaginations. Such persons will not make a full and fair use of their faculties; instead they live cloistered in the foul and stagnant atmosphere of halls of experience that have seldom if ever been blessed by the fresh air and the pure light of truth.

Persons in this category are not only the victims of their prejudices, but they are the victim of those who know their prejudices and appeal to them in order to control their thinking and their acting. And they will think and act in such a way that they will defeat themselves and accept and make use of only a part of their ability and strength. Those who take the advantage of the prejudices of such people will never honor or respect their right and their ability to face the propositions of life squarely and think them through clearly, and then deal with the issues dispassionately. Hence, prejudiced people go through life the victims and the prisoners of the little, the ugly, the reduced, and the poverty-stricken world, when they are entitled to a broad, bright, clean, and beautiful world of the human mind and the human spirit. They will themselves into chains and submit to being led and controlled by them. This is what Lillian Smith meant when she talks about two men "Mr. Rich White" and "Mr. Poor White" and a bargain. "Mr. Rich White" was the boss of money; "Mr. Poor White," the boss of Negroes, was to run the schools and churches in any way he desired, make the customs, set the manners, and write the laws as long as he did not touch "Mr. Rich White's" business. "Mr. Poor White" and "Mr. Rich White" were in a car together. "Mr. Rich White" was driving, and "Mr. Poor White" sat on the front seat. A Negro was in the back of the car. Finally, "Mr. Poor White" thought:

'Mighty fine to sit in the front seat by Mr. Rich White, mighty fine to turn around now and then and see the Negro right there on the back seat where you shoved him. But still, you ain't driving. Mr. Rich White's driving and you get restless for it looks like he is driving down a road that goes nowhere, when you need to stop at the store to do some bying. Need to get flour and meat and milk for your younguns, and shoes for the family, a new roof over your head and medicine for the baby, and a job that won't wear out tomorrow, and a few games to play with.'

But Mr. Rich White says: 'Can't stop now, better keep watching that Negro!—Is he still on the back seat still there where you shoved him?' 'Yeh,' you say, 'he's still there.' 'Well, what's the matter, don't you like sitting up here on the front seat with me . . . You want me to let that stinking Negro come up here and sit with you. You want that . . .' 'No,' said Mr. Poor White, 'reckon that ain't what I want. I couldn't stand that.' [2]

Lillian Smith illustrates how one may be controlled by his own prejudice and sacrifice many values of life for which he is worthy and to which he is entitled. It is clear that a person who is dominated by prejudice is as much of, and maybe more, a victim than the person against whom the prejudice is vented. If a person who is hated by another will maintain a mind free from hate and an attitude that is guided by a spirit of love, he will remain more free and more powerful morally and spiritually though his body may be in chains. The question comes now, how to set free the man who is dominated by his prejudice, for he needs emancipation as much as his servants or his would-be slaves.

It is true that laws are needed to help to legalize the right and to set a standard of behavior in which the oppressed may be

[2] Lillian Smith, *Killers of the Dream* (New York, 1949), pp. 186–187.

delivered and the slaves may be set free. Laws are guidelines for private and public conduct in the interest of helpless individuals and in the interest of developing community. But laws alone will not rescue people from their personal prejudices. If we are to build a social order for free men and a free society the concern must be both for master and slave. There must be a program and a plan not only to rescue the would-be slave from physical handicaps, from inequality of opportunity, and all of the other evils of discrimination; there must be a plan and program to rescue the master or the segregator from the invisible chains of prejudice, bitterness, and hatred. How can this be? We can only make suggestions, the solution to this problem is a difficult and complicated one. But these are some suggestions. People who are prejudiced should be permitted to express their feelings, to talk about their impressions, and to empty themselves of all bitterness and animosity. They should be granted an opportunity to study objectively the persons whom they hate, to observe if they possess any positive virtues and values that had been overlooked in the blindness of prejudice. They should seek a cause bigger, greater, and higher than the cause provided them by their little prejudices and having found such a cause, they should live in it and live for it. American citizens who are afflicted with racial prejudice could be greatly helped and benefited by realizing that they are members of one great national family in which and by which the life and security of all are more definitely assured if the life of the nation is secured and the morality of the Federal Constitution is observed. A victim of prejudice needs an association with persons of principle, be they in life or literature, whose examples can shock the prejudiced mind, and whose light of inspiration can dispel the shadows of ignorance and hatred, and can lead an individual to examine himself and compare what he is with what a higher life has to offer. Prejudice is a difficult disease but it can be cured.

I have heard white people of the deep south tell of their conversion from a commitment to racial segregation to the wider responsibility of Christian fellowship and joy.

Some years ago I visited southern white missionaries working in Nigeria, West Africa. Some had come from Mississippi, Tennessee, Kentucky, and Texas. I visited their homes, spent days with them as their special guest. I saw the expression of their devotions at their morning and evening prayers, and heard their conversations around the breakfast and dinner table. Many of them had been completely emancipated from the old way of thinking and living. They were new men and women aflamed with a courageous truth, devoted to a world expanding kingdom, and apparently had invested their lives in a kingdom of values that had freed their spirits from prejudice and had committed their lives to the eternal principles of the gospel of Jesus Christ.

Negroes themselves can become prejudiced against white people. They may remember some past event, some bitter experience, some defeat and some handicaps that they can trace directly to the evils of segregation and discrimination. People who form their philosophy of life based on such experiences are operating from the point of prejudice and not from the lofty heights of constructive principles. I have heard some militant civil rights leaders explain their reason for their militancy. They go back to a peculiar event, to some unkind deed done against them, and justify their bitterness and their hatred against all peoples whose skins are not colored. Leaders of this type are not fighting a battle against prejudice, they are fighting a battle of revenge. They are not trying to correct the disease, they are seeking to inflict punishment on all of those who are related to the diseased patient as well as the patient himself. Campaigns of bitterness might create an image of Negroes that would tend to give comfort and ease and a kind of justification to white people of prejudice. Negroes who themselves are committed to racial prejudice in reverse are not the best apostles of freedom or the most effective messengers of human deliverance and truth. Negroes who are the victims of racial prejudice are in two categories; the physical category of discrimination, (which is passing away in the light of growing understanding and better appreciation for the American way of life and for her commitment to freedom.) The second category is that of inner prejudice, resentments, and hatreds against the white community for the sins of the past. From this captivity there can be no legal deliverance unless the individual commits himself to the constructive and creative forces which can save all men from the sins of oppression. If people knew the richness of a life emancipated from prejudice and racial hatred, they would be glad to embrace it and would take keen delight in proclaiming it.

As a boy I was reared in the state of Mississippi in Coahoma County where bitterness between the races was deep and dangerous. I have seen my father, a rural district Baptist preacher, close a crop year with nothing but debt. I have seen him lead his last mule from the farm up to the "big house" as a part payment on a debt of several years. I knew how vicious and how devastating was the economic system that left some penniless and others rich. Questions came into my mind to which I could find no constructive answers. Our only country school houses were the little frame churches built and furnished by the meager income from Negroes themselves. I had seen my father's horse and buggy stopped; the road completely blocked by lynching mobs with guns and torches and axes, and lanterns and blood hounds in quest of some colored suspect. I have stood beneath the tree where a part of the rope remained after the victim had been cut loose and buried nearby in a crude and untimely grave. As a boy preacher in Clayton, Mississippi, I saw an innocent Negro man mistaken and shot dead, and looked at the smoking gun and smelled the burned powder, and saw the victim die without a physician or a friend. These and similar events cast a shadow over my youthful mind and inflamed my inner spirit with a prejudice and hatred that almost blinded my

soul with racial bitterness. I do not recall making any definite
attempt to throw off the curse and the inner shackles of this
bitter experience and foul attitude towards other people. But
I began in earnest a pursuit of understanding and the true
meaning of life. I read incessantly the Sermon On The Mount,
and my spirit was mastered by the picture of the Preacher
standing quietly but defiantly proclaiming the earth-shaking
truths of divine love. I tried, but in vain, to keep my prejudice
and hatred against other people in the same mental and moral
compartment that I had reserved for the Preacher of Galilee, but
it did not work. He kept demanding more and more space, and
one day I discovered that my days of racial bitterness against
others had gone and I had found a new constructive and creative freedom. I saw and knew that all men were sinners, all
peoples related in the fact of imperfections and in the reality
of individual and social sins, but they were also potentially related in the broader fields of love and respect. These experiences gave to me a new bright world of understanding that
lifted former weights from my own spirit and burdened my
whole being with a part of the responsibility of helping all
mankind to see and to know the reality of universal brotherhood. In constructive thinking, creative endeavors, and in redemptive fullness the mind is more free, the feeling tone of life
richer. The vision of human reality and deliverance are things
that cannot come when a person is enslaved by hatred against
other people. It is my conviction that a man is more devoted to
his own race and more sympathetic to their problems and a
greater champion of freedom when he has the inner freedom
and the spiritual insights that take out of his inner being offensive stones of hatred and prejudice, and place therein the
tender flesh of love and universal respect for all mankind.

Some years ago as a student at Colgate-Rochester Divinity
School I met a young white minister. We had some classes together, I had occasions to visit his church and preach for him. I
knew from his spirit and attitude that he was deeply weighted

with racial prejudice. I never discussed it with him. I never showed to him any resentment because I thought he was trying to keep it hidden. I was in sympathy with him. Both of us finished the divinity school and went our respective ways. He was finally called to the First Baptist Church in Flint, Michigan. After some trying experiences it seems he got a new slant on life. He called and asked for a conference. We spent a day together talking, thinking, and praying. He finally said to me: "I want to tell you something. When I was in divinity school I was greatly afflicted with racial prejudice and for that reason I had a faint resentment and hatred towards you. But," said he, "that is gone and I feel much better. For the last few days I have not been too well and I am not certain how much longer the span of life may be, but I have come to ask that we would join together as an evangelistic team to go across this nation preaching the gospel of Christ." I finally consented. We began making our plans. In the meantime I went to Florida on an urgent mission. When I returned there was a letter on my desk from Flint, Michigan, announcing that Orval C. Hendrickson had dropped dead. We planned as a team; he died as a member of the team before our campaign was launched, but I have kept ever before me his dedication, commitment, and have never forgotten the serious look on his face and the sparkle of joy in his eyes when I shook hands with him and said, "I'll join you." I did join him, and he has been as it were a silent partner in every venture I have made in all parts of the world to preach the gospel of love and brotherhood among all people. What he cannot say I must say, and what we did not have a chance to do together I am impelled to try to do with the spirit and power of Christ who loved and died for us all. I desire and work for the full freedom of my own race, but I am moved by a sense of responsibility to work for the enlightenment, full emancipation, and redemption of all peoples who are slaves of prejudice, victims of bitterness, hatred, and strife. Our task is not done when we have been helped or rescued from the chains of doubt and fear; we must seek to lead others into a new way of life that can enrich the human spirit. Prejudice of race and religion can be conquered. In addition to getting what rightfully belongs to us in the present world, as committed believers, we must seek also to win the victory of truth and freedom that rightfully belong to all men.

4

THE NATIONAL BAPTIST CONVENTION UNITED STATES OF AMERICA, INCORPORATED, AND THE CIVIL RIGHTS STRUGGLE

IT HAS OFTEN been asked, "What has the National Baptist Convention United States of America done in the struggle for civil rights during the past twelve years, between 1954 and 1966?" This Convention, which has a history of eighty-seven years as a religious fellowship in the United States of America, has produced many outstanding leaders who have helped in the struggle for human freedom. These leaders have not restricted their concern to one particular period or one particular phase for freedom. They have worked throughout their entire history, but the period referred to above marks a new phase of the civil rights struggle made possible by the Supreme Court Act of May 17, 1954, outlawing segregation in education and, in reality, in American life.

The National Baptist Convention, U.S.A., Inc. is an organization of 6,300,000 Americans who are believers in Christ, dedicated to first class citizenship and to the freedom of all mankind. Out of this fellowship has come many leaders, many strong leaders, of the current civil rights movement. This would suggest that the atmosphere of the fellowship has been conducive to freedom. It has engendered a manner of life and thought which has taught and inspired others to seek the ways of freedom. This climate did not begin in 1954. It has been a part of the long history of this convention. Our founding fathers left this legacy, and it has been a means of inspiring thousands to love, respect, and honor the cause of freedom. Free people dedicated to complete freedom, not only for their own brothers but for their fellowmen everywhere, left to us a legacy that has put us in debt to our country and to all mankind. Many of us still remember the work of Dr. E. C. Morris of Helena, Arkansas, who was one of the strong leaders in the South. He served as President of the National Baptist Convention for more than twenty-seven years. It was his influence, his counsel, and his guidance that helped to settle the race riot in Elaine, Arkansas, many years ago. He was a statesman who loved his fellowmen and who was respected by all Americans, North or South. Following this staunch leader came Dr. L. K. Williams of Texas, later of Chicago, who led the National Baptist Convention as its President for more than nineteen years. He, too, was a champion of brotherhood and better race relations North and South. His counsel was sought, his influence was much needed, and he made a distinct contribution to the Negro race and to the United States of America. The late Dr. D. V. Jemison of Selma, Alabama, who was President of the National Baptist Convention from 1940 to 1953, was another great champion for freedom. He led more than 400,000 Baptists in his state before he became President of the National Baptist Convention. In his own way, he encouraged among Negroes a spirit of independence and advocated the finest possible relations between the races. His integrity, strong and persuasive character made a great imprint on the peoples of this state of both races.

Not only were the official leaders of this organization committed to first class citizenship, but also thousands of their followers had caught their spirit and walked in the paths laid out by them. The structure and government of the individual church grants independence, freedom of expression, autonomy to each local congregation, as well as to each member, so that all the member churches of this Convention, separately and collectively, were freedom-conscious and freedom-directed. Any member of this historic body would soon catch the spirit and heed the cry for freedom, for it was a part of the very life, structure, and nature of this organization. Therefore, any man called to the leadership of the National Baptist Convention is called to a great heritage and enters into a great legacy for freedom that not only influences him but compels him. It was to be expected that the leadership of the National Baptist Convention in 1954 would catch the spirit of the times and would reflect concern of the unanimous decision of the nine judges of the Supreme Court of the United States of America. When we combine the inspiration of the pioneers and great Baptist leaders with the compulsion of this high Court and the aspiration of all freedom-loving Americans, we have a situation that not only the Baptist leaders but the members themselves could not and would not resist. Their recommendations, the cooperation with other freedom loving groups and all of the attending events indicate that the leadership of this organization for the past twelve years has given undisputed and unqualified leadership for the cause of freedom, justice, and the advancement of this great nation. Many of the young leaders in the cause of freedom have been brought up and nurtured in the tradition and spirit of the National Baptist Convention.

The leader of the first bus boycott in the South was the Rev. T. J. Jemison, the son of the past President of the National Baptist Convention and pastor of the Mt. Zion Baptist Church of Baton Rouge, Louisiana. He is also the Secretary of National Baptist Convention and has been since 1953. He was moved, inspired, dominated by the cause of freedom, but he was a direct descendant and heir of the work that had been done by pioneers in this great Convention. Many of the members of the Montgomery Improvement Association, with headquarters in Montgomery, Alabama, were staunch supporters of the National Baptist Convention and pastors of some of the strongest churches in that city. We do not, in this statement seek to ignore or underestimate the fine leadership that had been given to the drive for freedom by others, especially by a layman of the A. M. E. Church, Mr. E. B. Nixon, a pullman porter who was highly respected not only by his national union but by the citizens of Montgomery and Alabama. Dr. Martin Luther King, Jr., President of the Montgomery Improvement Association, was also a member of the National Baptist Convention as was his father and as his grandfather had been. The President of the National Baptist Convention encouraged the work of the Montgomery Improvement Association and sought to give all the help possible without seeking spotlight or trying to take any of the credit for what the leaders in Montgomery were doing. Because of his interest in this noble cause for freedom and because these men were members of the National Baptist Convention, he kept in constant contact with them and sought their advice as what we could best do to help in the cause they had espoused. He suggested that our Convention would buy a bus to help with transportation. After meeting with Dr. King and Dr. E. D. Billoups, President of the Baptist State Convention of Louisiana, and Vice President at large of the National Baptist Convention, and the late Dr. H. H. Humes, the leader of the Baptist Convention in Mississippi, it was suggested by Dr. King and agreed upon that it might be better to give money instead of a bus. After this, as President of the National Baptist Convention, I sent letters and communications to all of the leaders of state conventions, urging them to send gifts directly to the headquarters of the Montgomery Improvement Association. From the Olivet Baptist Church in Chicago, we sent $1,000.00 and then another check for the same amount was sent directly from the Treasury of the National Baptist Convention. This represented a small part of thousands of dollars that were sent or carried from Baptist friends and Baptist churches and organizations. In response to an invitation from Dr. King and his cabinet, I went to Montgomery and delivered one of the anniversary messages for the Association. I was received with enthusiasm and enjoyed the fellowship of the ministers and lay people of Montgomery, Alabama. In 1956, we featured the bus boycott on the program of the National Baptist Convention, U.S.A., Inc., and most all of the young leaders were presented. Many of them made speeches and addresses. This reflected the Convention's concern and interest.

Later on, the Southern Christian Leadership Conference was organized. The pioneers and organizers represented leaders of the National Baptist Convention, U. S. A., Inc. It is true, the Southern Christian Leadership Conference was not a National Baptist organization, but the leaders, at least most of them, were dedicated servants of the National Baptist Convention. Many of these men were and still are outstanding leaders in their own right. They have worked in civil rights across the years and they still work in this particular field. The Southern Christian Leadership Conference was organized in the Mt. Zion Baptist Church in New Orleans, Louisiana. This church was and still is pastored by the Rev. Dr. A. L. Davis, who is an outstanding member of the cabinet of the National Baptist Convention. Also, he is one of the strongest civil rights leaders in the state of Louisiana. Joining him, were men such as the Rev. W. T. Crutcher of Knoxville, Rev. R. E. James of the same city, the Rev. T. J. Jemison of Baton Rouge, Louisiana, and many others— all of whom were National Baptist men. One of the purposes for organizing this association was to bring together the separate and scattered units of civil rights organizations in order to make a strong, firm, and well organized civil rights movement of the South. Many of us felt that in this particular move we, of the National Baptist Convention, would have within our reach a group dedicated not only to civil rights but to America and to the Christian point of view. We believed that now the Convention by nurture and inspiration has brought into existence a group of young men who understood the visions of the founders of their convention and who were now willing to make the sacrifice and to put forth every effort to make the Christian ideals of brotherhood a practical reality in the United States of America. It was not our purpose nor our dream to join with any group, or groups, to become hostile to and work in opposition to the

National Association for the Advancement of Colored People. These acts of helping to organize and support civil rights groups has been a part of the work of the National Baptist Convention, U.S.A., Inc.

But, with the development of new attitudes and new emphases, the leadership of the National Baptist Convention became convinced that they must speak and give expression to their point of view as religious leaders without doing any violence to others who are committed to their way of thinking and understanding. We continued our support for the National Association for the Advancement of Colored People, some of us becoming life members of this organization; but we still felt that, as religious leaders, there were some things we could do to help in this great undertaking. In 1954, in St. Louis, Missouri, as President of the National Baptist Convention, it was my recommendation that we further the cause of freedom by emphasizing the historic significance of the 17th day of May.[1] It was the recommendation that we would observe the 17th day of May, 1956, as a day of mourning, thanksgiving, fasting, and prayer. We would give thanks because at long last a great victory had been achieved for freedom through the Supreme Court of the land, and this represented the evolutionary growth of the American ideal of freedom. We suggested we would spend a season of prayer while we fasted because there remained so much yet to be accomplished and to be done. The goal of first class citizenship had not been fully attained. There were still roadblocks to the cause of freedom and hindrances to the free and constructive operation of America's machinery of justice. This recommendation was the first of its kind in the United States. This venture was most successful. It represented the first attempt to put prayer in the struggle for civil rights. All over the nation, this day was observed in churches, chapels, and cathedrals. Roman Catholics, Protestants, Jews, people of all races and nationalities took part in this historic celebration. It was recommended by the President of the National Baptist Convention, sponsored by said organization, but it claimed attention of members of other groups whose faith was different from ours. A step further was taken when we, through Rep. Adam Clayton Powell of New York, petitioned Congress to make the 17th day of May a legal holiday because of what it represented as the second great emancipation proclamation. This Bill H.R. 3016, died in the Judiciary Committee, but it represented the first attempt on the part of a religious body to insert into our history a historic legal holiday. This was an attempt to emphasize the virtues of America, the strength and progress of our nation, and to inspire those who had not supported the cause of freedom to join with others in a constructive effort to build a stronger and greater democratic society. We did not cease our efforts.

In 1957, when it was concluded that President Eisenhower's Civil Rights Bill was dead and there was little or no hope for its passage, we believed that the bill had enough value and virtue to be supported and to be passed. As President of the National Baptist Convention, I organized what became historically known as the "Urge Congress Movement." We met at the Olivet Baptist Church in Chicago. Thousands of citizens gathered. We resolved to send telegrams and letters to all of our Congressmen and Senators, urging them to reconsider this bill and pass it. So many telegrams were sent that the Western Union headquarters in Chicago set up an emergency station at the Olivet Baptist Church. After this historic night, the message was taken all over the nation to great cities, small towns, and rural areas, urging people to send letters and telegrams to their congressmen. One historian stated that without the "Urge Congress Movement" the 1957 Civil Rights Acts never would have passed Congress. This was the first piece of civil rights legislation to pass Congress in eighty-three years. We were a part of a dramatic turn of history. This was done without bitterness, without threats or intimidation, but with a direct appeal to the spirit of patriotism and to the American way of life, based on the validity and the strength and the promise of the Federal Constitution. This successful act laid well the foundation and paved the way for what transpired in 1960, 1963, and then in 1964. In 1964 the National Baptist Convention took an active part in working for the passage of the civil rights bill of that year. Leaders of the convention in several states were asked to contact their congressmen and senators and make an urgent plea for their support in the passage of a strong civil rights bill. In addition to this type of work requested in the several states the Board of Directors of the National Baptist Convention itself on January 22, 1964, sent an urgent plea to Congress for a strong civil rights bill. The full text of this plea was entered in the Congressional Record of February 7, 1964 by Senator Paul Douglas. Some brief quotes from the seven-point plea will reveal the forceful, comprehensive, and patriotic tones of this message.

To The Congress of The United States of America As a Whole, And To Every Member Individually:

Dear Honorable Sirs:

Thousands of us are aware of the tremendous responsibility that is yours, and know well the multiplicity of your duties and the complexities of your task. You must look well to the needs peculiar to your several districts that sent you to Washington, but also you are bound by oath of office to work for the well-being, security, preservation, and continuous growth of the nation's life and character. And by the events of history and the demands of the times, you now carry a major share of the responsibility for the peace of the world, the distribution and the administration of the economic well-being and social justice to the peoples around the world, and maybe on your shoulders and that of your nation rest the fate and future of Western Civilization and the whole of mankind.

With due regard for all the pressing issues before you both foreign and domestic, it is the earnest desire of millions of Americans that you in this session will pass a strong, meaningful, comprehensible, and creative civil rights bill for the following reasons:

The issues of civil rights are basically the unanswered questions and the unsolved problems of the full freedom of the individual in a democratic society and the practical application of the ideals of the Federal Constitution in matters regarding the rights of persons and groups in our body politic. Here, as you well know, we deal with the very nature of our country and you are called upon to help answer the question, can a nation of all the people, by all the people, and for all the people, really exist? Can this lofty theory be put into practice? The Congress of the United States of America has the power to help or hinder this Nation in answering these most important questions. There are social, economic, and political philosophers who have already given a negative answer to these all important American questions. This 88th Congress has both the authority and the power to refute all of these false philosophies by a very positive action in the defense of and in the support of first-class citizenship for all Americans now.

These things we petition you not in the name of group prejudice and group antagonism, but in the name of the Federal Constitution and in the name of the Nation as a whole, and in the spirit of justice, freedom, and goodwill. We have confidence in your integrity and we await with hope the verdict of your actions.

While many of the members of this great convention were also lending their support to some civil rights organizations they were also doing all within the framework of their church to influence the passage of a strong civil rights bill. The efforts were not in vain and the expectations were satisfied, for Congress did pass the strongest and most comprehensive civil rights bill in its history.

In the *Congressional Record* of March 7, 1960, Page A1932, and March 24, 1961, Page A2079 there are other statements from the National Baptist Convention in support of a just, free, and more democratic America. None of these statements indicate any elements of compromise but all reflect the convention's confidence in the nation's ability to fulfill its nature and to achieve its own destiny. It is clear then that while this great religious body sought to help the grass roots people to engage in the struggle on the level of law and order and petitioned the lawmakers to do their part in making the laws that would help to determine and build a great democratic republic, it has at no time ceased to encourage other groups and peoples to continue the struggle for these worthy goals. The National Baptist Convention is a part of the National Leadership Conference On Civil Rights and has given its influence to help the National Association For The Advancement of Colored People to dramatize the interest and the constructive desires of the people of this nation in the interest of freedom. We have not only appreciated the work of Mr. Clarence Mitchell in Washington among the political and congressional leaders in the nation's capitol, but we have lent our influence to strengthen his efforts and to support his constructive endeavors.

"What has the National Baptist Convention done?" It has been in the thick of the struggle. It has used its influence and its talents to urge people not only to support their government but to love and respect it. Our leadership in the cause of civil rights has not been restricted to getting advantages for our own people. We have also taken a part in helping to push the frontiers of freedom further and by helping to expand the borders of opportunity for all people. When the then Senator Kennedy became a candidate for the Presidency, there was much prejudice and animosity expressed against him because of his religion. Many said "It is not safe to elect a Roman Catholic as President." As the leader of a large segment of American Christians I felt urged to make a speech on this issue in St. Louis, Missouri, and became one of the first Protestant Ministers in America to make an open and clear statement in the defense of Senator Kennedy's right to run for the Presidency of the United States. My position was that there was only one document that determined and defined the fitness of a man for the Presidency of the United States of America and that document was the Federal Constitution. In this sacred document, there is no reference to religion. No man need be member of any church or of any denomination in order to qualify as President of this great country. I wrote two pamphlets in the defense of Mr. Kennedy's right to run. When Mr. R. Sargent Shriver heard of my position, he sought and finally reached me by telephone and invited me to come to Washington. It was some time before I could accept the invitation. In private conference, Mr. R. Sargent Shriver asked what was my attitude regarding Senator Kennedy. I gave to him the benefit of my thinking, my conviction, and my impression. Mr. Shriver remarked, "I wish Senator Kennedy could meet and talk with a man of your vision and insights." But, at the time, my schedule would not permit. Shortly thereafter, I received a letter from Senator Kennedy, inviting me to come to Washington for a conference. I finally went; but, before going, I prepared an agenda and presented the same to Mr. Kennedy at his office in Washington. I informed him in this document that he would be elected President of the United States if he could overcome the historic objection that had been held against him because of his religion. I said to him, "You cannot plead this cause alone. There needs to be some outstanding Protestant leader who, without prejudice, bias, or animosity, will tell the country how much the country needs to overcome this prejudice of religion." In the statement that I made to him in this document and that was finally put in pamphlet form, I advised him and the country that prejudice of religion was just as vicious as prejudice of race. That statement was repeated time after time across the nation. Finally, I was invited to head this department of religion in the campaign. I refused because I did not have the time and could not get away from the pressing problems of the work of my own local church and the National Baptist Convention. But, there was organized a Department of Religion and an outstanding theologian and religious leader from the National Council of Churches was assigned this task. My work in helping to elect the first Roman Catholic as President of the

United States of America was due to the fact that I believed the cause of civil rights cannot be served by working for one's own group alone, but by working to expand and deepen the ideals of freedom and America's concept of democracy at its best. I respected the late President John F. Kennedy because in the short span of time that he served as President of this great republic he justified the concern of all of us who expected him to rise above the limitations that any one denomination could set upon the spirit of a national leader, and he dealt with all men as members of this tremendous American fellowship under a common flag and a common constitution. I did not get a chance to talk much with the President of the United States after he had been elected to this high office, but I cooperated with him at a distance in working for the advancement of America's cause, not only at home but abroad.

What has the National Baptist Convention and its leadership done for civil rights? We have raised a clear voice in the defense of law and order. We have taken the position that America is the great ship and all individual citizens and groups are as secure and as safe as is the ship of state at sea. No group can work for its own emancipation without giving due regard for the security, the growth, and strength of the nation. We have taken the position that the Federal Constitution, the supreme law of the land, is a sufficient guide for building a democratic society. We have taken the position that the combined wisdom of the Congress of the United States of America is far more trustworthy than the conscience of any individual or the conviction of any group. The National Baptist Convention and its leadership have been keenly conscious of those gestures and movements which in many instances have become anti-America, anti-Federal Constitution, and anti-our philosophy of freedom and, in some cases, anti-Christian, and anti-God. It has been the work of the National Baptist Convention that has emphasized again and again the aspect of goodwill. In the address delivered before the National Baptist Convention in Memphis,

Dr. J. H. Jackson supports President Lyndon B. Johnson's efforts to bring the Vietnam issue to the conference table in White House Conference January 20, 1967.

John F. Kennedy and J. H. Jackson together in the cause of freedom.

Tennessee in 1955, the President pointed out that in addition to the legal aspects of the struggle for civil rights, there is also the aspect of goodwill.[2] Said he:

We need goodwill for it is by means of goodwill that communities are held together and that people learn to respect each other and they work for a common cause. Goodwill has never dropped a poisonous bomb of destruction on any city or community. Goodwill has never sunk a ship. Goodwill has never burned down a neighbor's house or taken the life of another. If the battle for freedom is won in the United States of America, it must be won in a spirit of goodwill.

In its approach to the problem of freedom within the context of the Federal Constitution, the National Baptist Convention in 1965 launched a drive for national unity. We drew up a 10 point program and emphasized that all groups, be they civil rights groups, religious groups, or political groups, must work together for a common cause. This message was taken to Governors of states, Mayors of cities, and to members of City Councils. In personal interviews with Mayors of cities and governors of our many states, we discovered a most encouraging response and many governors North and South endorsed wholeheartedly the National Baptist Convention's Call for National Unity. The editorial in the *Nashville Banner* in Nashville, Tennessee was strong and powerful in support of this drive. We are continuing that emphasis because we believe in division there is weakness and in weakness there is a threat to security and a danger that enemies might find the nation an easy target for defeat and destruction. We are continuing our efforts as American citizens to help win the struggle for peace, not by negating America, not through bitterness and intimidation, but through a militant patriotism, that is a patriotism that is willing to risk all values of American citizenship in the hands of the Federal Constitution and the just laws of the land. A militant patriotism is a patriotism that is not only willing to sacrifice, suffer, and live

[2] Annual Address, 1955, p. 15.

for the ideals of this great Republic, but even to die for the eternal truth for which it stands.

Our approach to civil rights has made a tremendous impact on peoples of all walks of life. Our message has been heard in the great metropolitan centers of the United States. It has been heard in small towns and villages. It has been carried to the countryside by dedicated preachers of the gospel, by laymen, Sunday School workers, and members of missionary societies. This great organization has not been quiet, silent, or still. It has gone on working for the advancement of the rights of all peoples and for the victory of freedom, not only in the United States of America but in the hearts of men.

The National Baptist Convention manifested the key interest in helping to solve the problem of Tent City at Somerville, Tennessee. Some farmers had been evicted from plantations because of their interest in voting. They found living space in the outskirts of Somerville and neighbors erected tents, and here families were thrown together contrary to all the laws of sanitation and expected human decency. Food and clothing and other essential commodities were solicited and sent from all sections of the United States of America. When the problem was presented to us, we also made gifts; but, in addition to these gifts, the President of the Convention went in person and visited the scene and spent some time in the tents, and, in fact, spent several nights in the home of the mother of one of the men who was carrying on the relief work in Tent City. It was the President's conviction that the people needed more than clothes and food. They needed better living quarters and a long-term program if they were interested in living in Fayette County as voting citizens. We recommended that we would not only protest the conditions, but we would buy and own a part of Fayette County where opportunity could be given to people to live and try their hands at an independent living for themselves and their families by working and tilling the soil without fear or intimidation. When this was known in the community, the price of the

Mayor Ivan Allen, of Atlanta, Georgia receives copy of The Call To National Unity from Dr. J. H. Jackson and endorses the same.

*Mayor Richard J. Daley of Chicago, Illinois receiving copy of The
Call to National Unity from Dr. J. H. Jackson and endorses the same.*

land went up—in some cases 50% and, in others, 200%. A doctor heard of our concern—Dr. M. L. Fuller, a professor of Dentistry at the University of Tennessee—called me by 'phone and said "I have 414 acres of land in Fayette County that I will sell to your organization for the purpose that you have in mind." A committee was sent to inspect the land and, when they made a favorable report, we entered into contract with Dr. Fuller to purchase the land in question. We were given eight years to pay for this farm, but accomplished our objective within eight months. The first tenant to move on the land from Tent City received from the sheriff of the county an eviction notice and was informed he had no right to occupy the premises. We went into court. The matter was presented to the judge. The case argued. And, at the end of a long, weary and bitter day, a solution was worked out by which we received full use of the land and the tenant remained in the house. That farm remains intact today, giving opportunity to unfortunate people who desire to live in the rural districts, to enjoy the freedom of labor, and the opportunity to exercise their rights as American citizens. In the year 1966, one of the men who work on the farm contracted to buy his own farm. This, we greatly encouraged. All of the modern equipment has been paid for. A herd of sixty-two cattle now graze on the pastures green. In 1967 the first hog was killed and the meat shared with the people on the farm. The families are also allowed to receive the milk and butter from the cattle without cost and their children can enjoy fresh milk as well as fresh air. The county sends to this farm each day buses to transport the children on the farm to their respective schools. They receive the same services as other people receive. This is an illustration of a doctrine that we have espoused over the years, that is, protest alone is not enough—we must also move to production. There has been a spirit of goodwill. We enjoy the fellowship of the businessmen and farmers in the county, and we work together to make the county a better place in which to live. We did not go to Fayette County to march—we went to market. We did not go to Fayette County to rent—we went to buy and own. We did not go to beg—we went to build. This has been the story in brief of the Convention's efforts to solve constructively the problem of Tent City.

In the summer of 1966, the National Baptist Convention set aside $10,000.00 for the purpose of sending a team of four college students with a director to work in the interest of national unity, to spread the pamphlets written on the subject, to visit churches and communities, and to discuss the ideals of American life and destiny. This project was carried on and was welcomed to the state of Mississippi. Mississippi Vocational College at Itta Bena, Mississippi, was the headquarters. The trustee board of the institution of higher learning made our team welcome and President J. H. White of the Institution gave to us every facility and all advice that he could. The campaign was led by Mrs. C. C. Coleman of Grenada, Mississippi, and at the end of the campaign they reported much good had been accomplished. The four students had earned their tuition for college for the next school year, and they had discovered the joy and the constructive reaction in attempting to become producers of a wider fellowship and messengers of goodwill in the state of Mississippi. The governor of the state had already written to the President of the National Baptist Convention a letter endorsing the Call to National Unity, and we were most encouraged because of the response received not only from Negro people but from many of the fine white citizens of that state. This, too, was in harmony with the National Baptist Convention position of going from protest to production. Our young people must be included in the program and in the efforts of our denominations to help press for the ideals of American citizenship, both by theory and by practice.

Another project in the field of civil rights sponsored by this Convention is what is called "Citizenship Education." A special conference was called in Chicago in 1966 when our Sunday School Publishing Board, along with our B. T. U. Department, brought manuscripts that were read for our approval in the field of voter education. It has been the request that this material be put at the disposal of Sunday Schools, Missionary Societies, and Baptist Training Unions so that our young people may learn and understand the significance of citizenship rights and the technique of voting and why. It is our hope that Pastors and all leaders in our denomination will take this practical interest in American citizenship. With more doors being opened, greater opportunities extended, these must be seized and harnessed by people who love the nation and who are interested in working out the problems within the confines of the nation's laws and ideals. It is the studied opinion of the leadership of this great organization that voting, political actions, and the participation in the matter of shaping policies for the present and the future must not be left wholly in the hands of those who would trust the way of bitterness and resentment and, in some cases, a counsel of despair as a way to victory and success. There must be a higher participation in the political field, not for selfish purposes alone, but for the strengthening of a wider fellowship between the peoples and groups of these United States of America.

5

NON-VIOLENT CIVIL DISOBEDIENCE IN THE QUEST FOR CIVIL RIGHTS

SINCE MAY, 1954, *civil disobedience* has been emphasized more and more as a significant instrument in the struggle for civil rights. For an understanding of this instrument we shall make some observations of some of the principles of it as advocated by Henry David Thoreau in his essay on the subject which was published in 1849.

Thoreau was a bachelor who never knew the responsibilities and the joys of family life. Neither was he a member of any organized church. On one occasion he objected strenuously to paying a tax that had been levied against him by the state for the church. This occurred eleven years before his essay under discussion was published. Thoreau lived when slavery was still a part of the life of the United States of America. The *Emancipation Proclamation* had not been issued or signed, breaking (at least in part) the power and the shackles of chattel slavery. The Thirteenth, Fourteenth, and Fifteenth Amendments had not been written into the Federal Constitution. It is to be stated further that he was a poet with keen mind and with gifted insights. As a transcendentalist he learned to emphasize those mystical gifts in the individual, and from this came, in part, his belief and his emphasis on the superb place that the conscience of man had in his life. Also Thoreau was somewhat of a recluse who loved nature and who believed that the best way to freedom was through living with nature without the handicap of rules and regulations in the form of organized government. What he has to say about government emanates from his interpretation

94

of human conscience, his love for nature, and his belief that a person could discover the finer values of life apart from the association with other human beings. Henry David Thoreau was not a specialist in political science nor had he made a thorough and scientific study of the function and the philosophy of government. He brought to his task nothing of the genius of George Washington, Benjamin Franklin, James Madison, Thomas Jefferson, or Alexander Hamilton in matters pertaining to the historic significance of political organization.

When we come to deal with his principles of civil disobedience, it is significant to know that we are not dealing with the expressions of a political scientist nor a student of government nor one who by study and experience had come to grips with the gregarious instinct peculiar to all normal human beings and hence with the knowledge of the force and the function of government in relation to the harnessing and the constructive control of human desires and emotions. One of the first pronouncements that Thoreau makes in his essay "Civil Disobedience" is as follows: "That government is best which governs not at all . . ."[1] In this one bold statement he dismisses completely the need for any function of government whatsoever. For him government is at best an expedient, "but most governments are usually, and all governments are sometimes, inexpedient."[2]

His criticism of the American government was just as trenchant. He saw in it less vitality and less power than can be found in any single man. He says:

This American government,—what is it but a tradition . . . ? It has not the vitality and force of a single living man; for a single man can bend it to his will . . . *It* does not keep the country free. *It* does not settle the West. *It* does not educate.[3]

[1] Henry David Thoreau, *Walden and Civil Disobedience*, Norton Critical Edition (New York, 1956), p. 224.
[2] *Ibid.*
[3] *Ibid.*

In spite of all that Thoreau says against the American government, he comes back to admit that it does have value.

Seen from a lower point of view, the Constitution, with all its faults, is very good; the law and the courts are very respectable; even this State (Massachusetts) and this American government are, in many respects, very admirable and rare things, to be thankful for, such as a great many have described them; but seen from a point of view a little higher, they are what I have described them; seen from a higher still, and the highest, who shall say what they are, or that they are worth looking at or thinking of at all? [4]

The United States government is not designed to deal with the highest realm which includes art, poetry, and finally, religion. As we have stated in a previous chapter the courts of America make no effort to regulate the highest outreach of conscience and has no word for or against religion. It is designed to function on the lower levels of human life such as the materials, the economic, and all those various aspects of life that define the security of the individual as well as the security of the nation itself. Although Thoreau draws the sharp distinction between the higher and lower aspects of the Constitution and the American government, he admits that on the lower level the Constitution is very good, laws of the Courts are very respectable, and the American government itself very admirable. Here, then, is no conflict between Thoreau's evaluation and the appreciation of government as expressed by some of our Founding Fathers and some of those who took part in the writing of the Federal Consitution. As has been stated the higher and the highest concepts are not considered fields in which the Federal Constitution operates. Here men are left free to make their own choices and decisions without any attempt at regulating man's behavioral patterns through the courts or by any laws. Thoreau believes that whatever the weakness some govern-

[4] *Ibid.*, p. 240.

ments may have, there is the possibility that conscientious men could form a corporation with a conscience.

Can there not be a government in which majorities do not virtually decide right and wrong, but conscience?—in which majorities decide only those questions to which the rule of expediency is applicable? Must the citizen ever for a moment, or in the least degree, resign his conscience, then? I think that we should be men first, and subjects afterward. It is not desirable to cultivate a respect for the law, so much as for the right. The only obligation which I have a right to assume, is to d) at any time what I think is right. It is truly enough said, that a corporation has no conscience; but a corporation of conscientious men is a corporation *with* a conscience.[5]

From what has been said above there is no conflict between the consciences of men and the Constitution. Since the Constitution appeals to the consciences of men for justice toward one another and the state and vice versa, we have every right to believe that it was written by conscientious men and hence there is a conscience of the Constitution. It is this conscience that is followed until we develop a conscience stronger and greater. Of course, the state is imperfect, but the state has an intention to be just. The sole purpose of the Constitution of the United States is not slavery, for by it slavery in its institutionalized form was outlawed. It is not in defense of injustice, for by it the justice of many has been protected and assured. The closing paragraphs of Thoreau's essay *Civil Disobedience* give a clear statement on the principles of our nation that we here support. He notes what all of us are aware of: imperfections and impurities in government. But in noting the evolution of government or the progressive steps from an almost absolute to a limited monarchy and from a limited monarchy to a democracy, he finds in each step the movement is toward a truer respect for the individual.

[5] *Ibid.*, p. 225.

The progress from an absolute to a limited monarchy, from a limited monarchy to a democracy, is a progress toward a true respect for the individual.[6]

In Chapter I we have noted that the individual person is the basis and primary unit in our democratic society.

I am not ready to say that our present form of government is the highest possible form of social organization, neither do I conclude that in it the constructive power of man for the building of a better social order has already been exhausted. There is still a future for mankind, for civilization, and for the American nation. But I do not believe that the best and surest road to success is the act of destroying what has been achieved and "starting from scratch" to build the so-called *better form of government*. The writing of the Federal Constitution and the building of this American Republic is work well done, and I agree with Thoreau when he says: "For it matters not how small the beginning may seem to be: what is once well done is done forever." [7]

The conscience of an enlightened democracy like ours should not be sinned against nor ignored. We should follow the oughtness of it until some enlightened genius or hero with new prophetic insights shall arise to inspire other lawmakers and leaders to lead the people forth on their chosen road to a more perfect democratic state. We need the insights of the past as fertile soil in which to plant and cultivate the social idealism of the present. So we may look forward to the growth and fuller realization of a greater democratic state in the future.

It is not then "civil disobedience" that we need, but civil obedience to the highest achieved ideals of the present and a pledged and a dedicated loyalty to the directives and the dictates of the oughtness of the enlightened conscience of the United States of America. The type of freedom the Federal

[6] *Ibid.*, p. 243.
[7] *Ibid.*, p. 233.

Constitution proclaims, grants to the individual conscience the latitude and the opportunity to survey the fields of new ethical standards and the possibilities for improved and richer qualities of human relations. Those who advocate civil disobedience as a means of improving the present government of the United States of America miss the total picture as set forth in Thoreau's essay on civil disobedience. It could be considered as a wholesome critique of the government of his day and could also be considered as an appropriate criticism of those forms of government that have come into existence within the last fifty years and which tend to negate the conscience of man and to treat human beings as if they were clods of clay or images of wood.

If there is a possibility of building a still better social order and a wiser government then the mission of man must be different from that which Thoreau ascribes to himself in the following lines: "I came into this world, not chiefly to make this a good place to live in, but to live in it, be it good or bad." [8] We must join with others in an attempt to help enrich the conscience of the nation so that the nation always has a sense of obligation to lead men to do justly, and to love mercy, and to teach others to do the same.

The nation and peoples of western civilization must accept one of two possible tasks. The first is they may help to plan the total destruction of all the cultural achievements of the past and maybe the total annihilation of all mankind. This is indeed most grim to contemplate. Or, on the other hand, they must assume the more pleasing task, though not less tedious, of building a society of peace and goodwill where men are not ashamed nor afraid to deal with one another and to live with one another as brothers.

Much of Thoreau's essay is protest; it is protest against slavery, against injustice before the law, against the oppression of the many by the few, and against corruption in government. This type of protest was much needed against the evils in

[8] *Ibid.*, p. 232.

the government of his day. Much of it as protest can, and should, be applied to the indifference, the apathy, the dishonesty, and the corruption in some governments of the present day. In this essay Thoreau did not intend to go beyond protest. Hence, he makes no attempt to set forth measures for building an orderly state or just democratic society. He who is in search of a technique and a method to improve our democratic society must not stop with Thoreau's treatise on *Civil Disobedience*. Thoreau gave his protest because he was moved by the evils he saw in the government of his day rather than being inspired by the achieved values and the potential growth of his social order. A concentration on what is wrong in society leads to negative reactions and a temptation to try to overthrow the imperfect order, and to destroy that which is full of evil and error. From a careful study of Thoreau's doctrine of civil disobedience, it is clear that he did not think of it as an agency for correcting the existing errors and evils in any government or as a means of strengthening the same by removing the evils therein.

Thoreau, then, is not a patron saint or a safe guide to be followed by enlightened Americans who seek to overcome the shortcomings of their nation and to build a more perfect social order.

James Russell Lowell said of him:

He seems to me to have been a man with so high a conceit of himself that he accepted without questioning, and insisted on our accepting, his defects and weaknesses of characters as virtues and powers peculiar to himself. Was he indolent, he finds none of the activities which attract or employ the rest of mankind worthy of him. Was he wanting in the qualities that make success, it is success that is contemptible and not himself that lacks persistency and purpose. Was he poor, money was an unmixed evil. Did his life seem a selfish one, he condemned doing good as one of the weakest of superstitions. To be of use, was with him, the most killing bait of the wiley, tempter uselessness. He had no faculty of generalization from outside himself, or at least no experience which would supply the material of search, and he makes his own whims the law, his own range the horizon of the universe.[9]

This sheds some light on the doctrines and philosophy advanced by Thoreau. A man with an almost anti-social attitude cannot be trusted as a safe guide in dealing with the problems of human relations and government.

Mahatma Gandhi was a great disciple of non-violent civil disobedience. He began his work in South Africa against tremendous odds but learned something of the effectiveness of this weapon because he faced a difficult situation where the organized life of the community was against him; but his greatest and most effective work came in his native country, India. He, doubtless, was the first leader who applied civil disobedience in seriousness and made it an effective weapon against the great British Empire. The purpose of civil disobedience on Gandhi's part was not to correct the evils of the British system nor to improve it, but to completely overthrow it. He was committed to this because he discovered the laws and the government of Great Britain were not just to India and were not designed to improve the lot of his people. Indians had no part in the formation of the policies and principles by which the British Government operated in India; hence Gandhi sought to overthrow this system in the defense of justice and freedom to the people of India.

There were certain situations that made this approach to the problem favorable. The British were in the minority. They did not control the labor unions, the labor leaders, the business men and the basic life of the Indian people. The British were foreigners attempting to control and master the life of the Indians. When he applied the weapon of civil disobedience to the po-

[9] James Russell Lowell, "Essay on Thoreau," *Walden and Civil Disobedience*, Norton Critical Edition (New York, 1966), p. 286.

litical situation, Gandhi was strengthened by the kind of support that he received from his people. If Indians had been in the minority, it is doubtful whether civil disobedience would have been such an effective weapon in the hands of Gandhi.

It is said by many that Gandhi was greatly inspired and influenced by the doctrine of civil disobedience as proclaimed by Henry David Thoreau. George Hendrick presents some interesting statements on the influence of Thoreau's civil disobedience on Gandhi's passive resistance.

Since *Indian Opinion*, the South African newspaper published by Gandhi from 1903 to 1914, is now available for study, much new material on Gandhi's knowledge of Thoreau has come to light. Before *Indian Opinion* could be studied, information about Gandhi's indebtedness to Thoreau was scattered and fragmentary . . . Gandhi, in his 1942 appeal to American friends wrote, 'You have given me a teacher in Thoreau who furnished me, through his essay on the Duty of Civil Disobedience; scientific confirmation of what I was doing in South Africa.' [10]

Louis Fischer takes a similar position regarding Thoreau's influence on Gandhi. He says, "Thoreau's civil disobedience essay did influence Gandhi; he called it a masterly treatise. 'It left a deep impression on me.' He [Gandhi] affirmed." [11]

There seems to be strong indication that Gandhi received ideas from Thoreau's civil disobedience and employed these ideas in his Indian campaign, but no one can deny that these ideals in the mind of Gandhi were put to original use, and he was the first to experiment with them in a political venture. As has been intimated, much success was achieved in India. But we must not overlook some unfortunate aspects of Gandhi's political leadership. On the eve of Indian independence Gandhi realized and discovered that his people had not been won to

[10] "The Influence of Thoreau's Civil Disobedience on Gandhi's Satyagrah," *Walden and Civil Disobedience*, Norton Critical Edition, p. 364.
[11] Louis Fischer, *Life of Mahatma Gandhi* (New York, 1950), p. 87–88.

his political way of thinking. When the time came to petition India and to set up Pakistan as a separate and independent country, Gandhi objected to this very much. Lord Louis Mountbatten advocated and urged a division of the country as the best way of solving the problems originating from the religious conflict between Hindus and Moslems. Gandhi opposed such a division to the last and insisted that the division of India was an absolute evil. But in spite of his opposition, India was divided and during his campaign of objection to the division, Gandhi discovered that the vast majority of the people in India had decided against his point of view. During this time of debate over this question of partition it is said that 95% of Gandhi's mail was abusive and hateful. The Hindus were against him because he seemed to be partial to the Moslems. The Moslems, who were to benefit by the creation of Pakistan, were angered with Gandhi because he seemed to obstruct the creation of the country that they desired and which would belong to them. In the midst of this, Gandhi admits his grief and disappointment. Says he:

Thirty-two years of work have come to an inglorious end. On August 15, 1947, India would become independent, but the victory was the cold political arrangement; Indians would sit where Englishmen had sat; a tri-color would wave in the place of the Union Jack. That was the hollow husk of freedom. It was victory with tragedy, victory that found the army defeating its own general. Gandhi announced, "I cannot participate in the celebration of August 15 . . . I deceived myself in the belief that people were wedded to non-violence." Indians had betrayed non-violence which was more important to him than Indian Independence.[12]

As powerful and as successful as Gandhi was, he was not the most successful political leader with the weapon of non-violent civil disobedience. On the very eve of India's Independence and months thereafter, there was much rioting, bitterness and

[12] *Ibid.*, p. 473.

bloodshed between Hindus and Moslems. It seems that Gandhi's greatness was reflected more in his sainthood than in his ability as a political leader.

Lord Mountbatten made this report of Gandhi:

> [He] was not compared with some great statesman, like Roosevelt or Churchill. They classified him simply in their minds with Mohammed and with Christ. Multitudes tried to kiss his feet or the dust of his footsteps. They payed him homage and rejected his teachings. They held his person holy, but desecrated his personality. They glorified the shell but trampled the essence. They believed in him, but not in his principles.[13]

All honor be to Gandhi as one of the truly great spirits of modern history. A tragic death brought to a close one of the most humble and saintly men to walk this earth since the days of Jesus of Nazareth. His love for his people was beyond question. His commitment to their sorrow and suffering no one could deny. His courageous determination to withstand the imperial power of Great Britain is well known both in the British Empire and throughout the world.

When we were in India in 1962, Mrs. Jackson and I had a chance to visit the homes of some of the fine people of India. We heard their personal testimonies on the greatness of their former leader. To them, Mahatma Gandhi was not only a statesman and a great political leader and father of free India, but he was a saint worthy to be praised and honored. Our visit in the homes of some of the members of Parliament and with the late Prime Minister, Nehru, himself, deepened our appreciation for the Indian people and for the leadership of that great country. Newspaper reporters, as well as the man on the street, were committed to the greatness of Mahatma Gandhi. We paid our respects to Gandhi's memory by leading a pilgrimage to the Rajghat where stands the great monument erected by the state in Gandhi's honor. With others, we took off our shoes and ap-

<hr>

[13] *Ibid.*, p. 473.

proached the spot with reverential and prayerful silence. We cast our floral pieces on this hallowed spot and joined with others in singing the Christian hymn that Gandhi so much admired and loved—"Lead Kindly Light." This was, indeed, a great religious experience as men from different sections of the world paid their tribute to a great but fallen leader. Bishops from many of our churches in the United States gave eloquent testimony. Representatives and leaders from other countries told of their admiration and appreciation for Gandhi's greatness. The hotel in which we stayed was not far from the home in which Gandhi stopped on his last and final visit to New Delhi. More than once we visited the little garden spot enclosed with small hedges where Gandhi had come for evening prayers for the last time. We stood with bowed heads on that little marked but tragic spot of earth on which his wounded body fell from the impact of the assassin's gun. One cannot stand in the presence of such hallowed scenes and behold people still pausing in silence, in prayer, and some in tears as if in communion with the spirit of a hero and a martyred saint without feeling the impact of Gandhi's genius and greatness. I have taken this time to state my personal admiration for Gandhi and his noble work so that no one will misunderstand when I interpret and evaluate the place that non-violent civil disobedience has in the struggle for civil rights in the United States of America.

I do not discuss the personality of any leader when I am concerned with the doctrine of non-violent civil disobedience. I am concerned about it not as a method for India but as an essential method for helping to solve the problem of civil rights as we know the problem in this great country. Here we come not to praise or to blame any persons of ancient or modern history, however great and deserving, but we come in a realistic approach to the quest and for a strategy and method of solving problems of civil rights. We must answer the following questions: Does this doctrine furnish us with a better tool in dealing with this problem than does the Federal Constitution of the United

States and the American philosophy of democracy? Can we gain more under the Federal Constitution by obedience than we can by disobedience? As we look at the problem of equality and opportunity for all Americans and compare the prescription with the prescriptions of non-violent civil disobedience, we are convinced that we have here in America the tools, the strategy, the energy, and the spirit by which we can solve not only the problem of civil rights but all the problems of human rights that face this great nation. And, if we have not solved the problem, it has not been due to the inefficiency of this supreme law, but it has been due to our failure to harness and follow the ideals of the supreme law as a guide line and as a standard by which to measure and by which to walk.

For almost ten years now, certain civil rights groups in the United States of America have advocated and tried the technique of non-violent civil disobedience in the struggle for civil rights; history is marked by these efforts and the highway of time is littered with the wreckage or the worth of these efforts and these attempts. We can now observe with objective analysis what has been achieved and what has not been achieved.

What is the non-violent disobedience technique as advocated and practiced in the United States of America in the present civil rights struggle? It is an act of creating tensions short of violence in order to force changes in the interest of civil rights where changes have not been forced or realized before. Civil disobedience is an act of disobeying certain rules and regulations that an individual or a group may decide are unjust and a stumbling block to the achievement of the goals of first class citizenship. This method relies on the emotion of fear and seeks through harassment, threats, and intimidations to force an official or an unwilling person to surrender to the demands made by the group upon him. At best, these protest methods can create opportunities, open doors for those who have been denied their rights but can go no further in arming people with ability and the determination to seize these rights. Protest through non-violent civil disobedience seeks to harness a people's hurt and move them to acts to embarrass and to punish those whom they consider to be responsible for the continuation of their oppression. Any means are justified that are short of violence. Some gains have been made and some opportunities created by these methods of protest because we still have among us some political leaders and some so-called Americans who are not inspired by the lofty principles of this great nation. When they are moved to act, they act out of political expediency and for fear of their own security. Such persons are enemies to the American way of life and are liabilities to her body politic. They have helped to create the belief that civil disobedience is better than civil obedience and civil responsibility. Some political leaders have often honored those who dishonor the law and have respected more the groups who disrespect them than they do those patriotic citizens who respect them because of what they represent.

We do not discredit those who believe in such methods nor deny any of the values and goods that have actually been achieved, but we must admit non-violent civil disobedience is not the best method to gain civil rights in a nation like the United States of America. It does not enhance our supreme law of the land. It does not deepen respect for the American way of life. It does not harness or appeal to the highest emotions and the most creative potential of those who engage in it. Neither does it appeal to the highest emotions and the highest in thought and in value judgment of those against whom it is employed. The emotions and attitudes involved and released at this level of experience are not of the quality to produce community, a sense of joint responsibility and the wholesome relationship that is essential for building a democratic state and the highest possible type of community. Non-violent civil disobedience was never intended or designed as a method of social, economic, cultural, and political correction in a country whose established order was one already committed to justice and freedom as is the United States of America through its Federal Constitution. Civil disobedience as practiced by Mahatma Gandhi in India was designed not to correct but to overthrow the imperial power of Great Britain. India belonged to the Indians. They comprised the vast majority of the people of the country, whether in labor, business, the professions, education and every other walk of life. Hence, when Gandhi used his technique, he had with him the weight of numbers, the wealth of the country, and organized labor. They labored with Gandhi not to correct any of the deficiencies of the British rule but to totally defeat it and to overthrow it.

When the thirteen original colonies in these United States rose up in serious protest against Great Britain, they employed civil disobedience not to correct but to overthrow a great colonial power that was not interested in justice, equality of opportunity, and freedom for the colonies. Britain, as the established order, was committed to oppression, over-taxation, and all the other vices that go with these things, and the colonies were in their rights in their method of approach for they had no other avenue for deliverance and no higher power to which to appeal. There cannot be successful coexistence of this type of social and political disorganization and an accepted established order supported by laws to which all loyal citizens subscribe and on which all depend for protection and guidance. Civil disobedience is designed to overthrow; for, in order to be effective, civil disobedience must disregard, disrespect, and work against the established order and will its ultimate defeat.

There is a very thin line between civil disobedience and lawlessness, law-breaking and, finally, acts of crime. Every loyal American pledges his allegiance to the ideals, principles, and laws of this republic. By that act, have committed themselves not only to obey the laws of the land but to follow the American method of correcting policies and practices, of changing unjust laws wherever they exist. This latter is done through due process —the courts of the land and through amendments and revisions, and even the writing of new laws to take the place of the old if such is needed. The Federal Constitution is the bedrock of our American democracy, the guarantor of the rights of each citizen, and the protector of the freedom of all Americans. It is so constructed that it lends itself to corrections and yields to cultural and political growth through evolutionary processes and not through revolution. Since the American legal system lends itself to correction through due process and through the courts, it has made no legal provision for corrections by means of civil disobedience and, since every loyal American has pledged himself not only to obey the laws of the land but to uphold and support the Federal Constitution; by any acts of civil disobedience, one becomes a lawbreaker and a violator of his own pledge and oath of loyalty to ones own country. People who advocate and practice civil disobedience in the United States against the laws of the United States not only dramatize their lack of faith in due process but employ some of the same methods and attitudes toward the orderly procedure in the United States as do the persons and groups that are avowed enemies of the United States and who have pledged themselves to the overthrow of the government of this great country.

The term non-violence sounds lofty and can be used to cover many undesirable acts and attitudes, but we must remember that the term "non-violence" does not preempt any act of all of its moral or immoral content. For an act may be non-violent and still wrong, immoral, vicious, destructive, and contrary to the rules of fellowship and a creative togetherness which are most essential in building a wholesome and stable democratic society of free men. Acts of non-violence may so victimize some of the people involved with hate, unexpressed resentment and bitterness that they will resolve to get revenge on those who are the objects of their protest and non-violent acts. Some of the racial bitterness that is abroad in America today is due not only to the oppression of the past but to tensions that have developed over racial hurts and racial afflictions. In spite of the growth and gains in this country, many of us are inflamed by the constant statements of the viciousness of the oppressors past and present. This repeated council of despair has made many of the minority group desperate and has created a climate that has produced disrespect for the nation and for many of its laws and public officials. Non-violent acts that become seeds that in due course would produce bitterness, violence, and riots must be construed as contributing factors to violence itself. There is a statement which says, "By their fruits ye shall know them." By the fruits of non-violence, civil disobedience, we shall know it for what it is. It has assumed that those to whom the message is proclaimed are on the verge of violence. It is a part of the modern *powder keg* philosophy; that is, the doctrine that some leaders proclaim as they go about the country saying to officials, "you must do what we suggest if you would keep the peace; we happen to know that unless you do what we suggest there is going to be an explosion, for this community is seated on a powder keg." But, many of these *powder keg* philosophers carry their own explosive and hatred and bitterness and their own match of malcontent by which they ignite the frustrations that they have created and set our communities in flames. We have seen more violence since 1954 than ever before in our history. We have had more concentrated doctrine of non-violence for the past twelve years than ever before and those who have put their confidence in non-violence to solve the problems of civil rights could well join in the pathetic words of the great Mahatma Gandhi when India was near the time of independence, August 15, 1947. Gandhi witnessed how deep was the hatred, antagonism and bitterness between Hindus and Moslems. When he observed the riots and bloodshed among his own people, he said, "Thirty-two years of work have come to an inglorious end . . . I deceived myself in the belief that people were wedded to non-violence."

Civil Disobedience

One of the outstanding weaknesses of this doctrine is that we must disobey certain laws of state because if we did not we would violate the law of our conscience. In the United States of America as we have stated, all laws are to be judged, regulated, and corrected according to the principles of the supreme law of the land, the Federal Constitution. If in the process of obeying this law one finds one's self in conflict with some unjust sectional law one has access to the courts that will defend and protect such a person according to this supreme law. The burden of proof is not on each individual citizen or each voluntary or involuntary group, but the courts.

The purposes of the Federal Constitution as set forth in the Preamble are worthy and lofty purposes and they do no violence to the visions, dreams, and outreaches of the individual conscience. These purposes are roughly stated as follows: . . . "To form a more perfect union, to establish justice, insure domestic tranquillity, provide for the common defense, promote the general welfare, and secure the blessings of liberty to ourselves and to our posterity." These goals are morally sound and are as lofty as any that the individual conscience of any person can commend for himself and his immediate group. If the social and moral goals of the Federal Constitution are realized the standards and qualities of life for all the citizens of the United States will indeed be as high as any that can be found on the most lofty peaks chartered and prescribed by the oughtness of conscience. It is difficult to imagine the conscience of any individual transcending or calling persons individually and collectively to higher social goals than those stated in the Preamble of the Federal Constitution. Obedience to such a law or the principles thereof is a virtue, but civil disobedience in a country blessed by such a law is a dangerous venture both for the individual citizens and for the peace and harmony of the nation itself.

Civil disobedience means far more than disobedience of segregating laws or any unjust laws that are in violation of the supreme law of the land. Civil disobedience means exactly what it says; that is, it is disobedience to the rules and laws of the civil order in which and under which one lives. It is non-cooperation with the policies and directives of the state or nation in which one has membership. Such non-cooperation is not restricted to segregating laws. It is applied also to any requirements, demands, or laws governing the lives of the citizens and it leads people to go beyond the provisions for protest as set forth in the Federal Constitution. In the name of civil disobedience young citizens may burn their draft cards and trample the American flag beneath their feet and march through the streets of cities in an attempt to control and amend the foreign policies of the nation. It has led some Americans to be bold enough to sit in judgment on the nation's policy in Vietnam in such a way as to give the impression that the nation can no longer trust the president, his cabinet, and the Congress of the United States of America to guide the nation and its people in an hour of crisis. When one says that the United States of America is on the wrong side of the revolt in Vietnam one says by implication that those who are in the opposite position are on the right side thus taking one's stand against the United States and with other nations and countries who are anti-American in their philosophy and attitude. This goes beyond the freedom of speech and becomes almost the frivolity of prejudgments without supporting investigation and facts. We can be against war as most Americans are, but that does not arm us with the facts or put us in a position to discredit the leadership of the nation. At this point the Federal Constitution prescribes how the nation behaves in a crisis and what steps to take when individually one becomes dissatisfied with policies and procedures of one's government.

Another weakness in civil disobedience is it puts too much stress on one's physical deliverance from those conditions that are below the level of merit. Men who are governed by such attitudes and outlooks are more concerned about quick self-deliverance and self-preservation than they are about social salvation, human redemption, and the purging and purifying of a set of circumstances that are both unjust, immoral, and impure. A conscience pure enough and sensitive enough to respond to the highest values in the universe can render the greatest service by risking itself on the battlefield for truth and righteousness. Even good men must be willing to live in conditions and environments that cannot and do not reward them for their vision, for their insights, and for the righteousness of their purpose. In his *Republic* Plato taught well this lesson. He set forth the fact that if the philosopher kings had attained the clear and the most profound insights into the needs of the state, and after they had been blessed with the visions of the heights, then they are called upon to go back into the shadows of the darkened cave to render unselfish service to those who are less fortunate than they are. Then some asked why would such a task be assigned to the philosopher kings? Is such not an act of injustice? The wise philosopher taught that because of their vision they could see better and hence render a better service to those in the cave.

"Then, I said, the business of us who are the fathers of the state will be to compel the best minds to attain that knowledge which we have already shown to be the greatest of all—they must continue to ascend until they arrive at the good; but when they have ascended and seen enough we must not allow them to do as they do now . . . I mean that they remain in the upper world: but this must not be allowed; they must be made to descend again among the prisoners in the den, and partake of their labours and honours whether they are worth having or not.

But is not this unjust? He said; ought we to give them a worse life, when they might have had a better? . . . There will be no injustice in compelling our philosophers to have a care and providence of others . . . we have brought you into the world to be rulers of the hives, kings of yourselves and of the other citizens, and have educated you far better and more perfectly than they have been educated and you are better able to share in the double duty. Wherefore each of you, when his turn comes, must go down to the general underground abode, and get the habit of seeing in the dark. When you have acquired the habit, you will see ten thousand times better than the inhabitants of the den, and you will know what the several images are, and what they represent, because you have seen the beautiful and just and good in their truth." [14]

In this episode the philosopher Plato reaches his highest peak as a thinker, and at this point Greek philosophy was at its best.

The Christian religion teaches that the highest duty of any believer was and is the act of bearing His Cross. This is the act of relating the best in one to the worse in men and situations for the purpose of purifying the situation and redeeming men from the low way of life and lifting them to the heights. The humble preacher of Galilee gave little or no time to the task of getting from the people of his day all that rightfully belonged to Him. He threw himself unreservedly into the struggle for the Kingdom of God. He endured the insults of men with dignity; suffered persecution without bitterness, and refused to make the merit system of the Roman Empire determine the measure of His character and the heighth and depth of His commitment to truth, to his task, and to His God. He endured the laws of the Roman Empire in order to release in Palestine and in the world the ideals of His kingdom and the spirit of truth and righteousness.

The Cross of Jesus Christ was the act of enduring the demerits of men in order to keep within reach of the eternal merits of His father. The Cross is the sign, the symbol, and the power of human redemption, and represents the highest and the deepest in the Christian religion.

When the Apostle Paul turned his face towards Rome with all of its pagan philosophies and its anti-Christian practices, he accepted the challenge of Rome as a personal debt. Said he,

[14] *The Republic,* Translated by Benjamin Jowett, (Cleveland, Ohio), 1946, pp. 255–256.

I am debtor both to the Greeks and to the Barbarians; both to the wise, and to the unwise.

So, as much as in me is, I am ready to preach the gospel to you that are at Rome also.[15]

In the act of calling men of sensitive souls and enlightened minds to endure the evils of a political state in order to help bring to pass a better quality of life among men we are at one with some of the highest thoughts of the ages. Here the best in Greek philosophy is joined to the highest and the deepest in Christian thought.

We must now do all within our power to change every unjust law and to put down every vestige of segregation and resolve that we will not tolerate any evils in our society that we can change. But in the process we must not refuse to think, to live, and to be our best in spite of the evils of our environment. While we work for fair housing we must live as well as possible in the houses that we now occupy. While we struggle to improve the quality of education for our children, we must encourage them to make full use of all available educational and cultural facilities.

[15] Romans 1:14–15.

6

NON-VIOLENT CIVIL DISOBEDIENCE BY NEGROES AGAINST NEGROES

FREEDOM IS UNIVERSAL both as a right and as a desire and human quest. A trustworthy method to gain freedom must be as valid in one situation as in another. It is impossible to have a free America if one section of the country is allowed to seek freedom and security through disrespect for the Federal Constitution and through the use of segregation and discrimination. Also, any method employed by Negroes to gain freedom against white segregationists must be as valid as an agency or as a means of securing freedom against any Negroes who would prove themselves enemies of the rights of others and members of a clan whose purpose is human oppression.

In our study of non-violent civil disobedience as a valid means of securing civil rights it has been most difficult to be objective when racial segregation is the obstacle that we seek to remove. So many observers confuse an objective study of the method with the goals to be achieved. If one does not believe in these methods employed against segregation then one must be in sympathy with racial segregation. Some extremists have taken the position that non-violent civil disobedience is the basic if not the only reason why certain changes have taken place in this country to advance the cause of human freedom. It is our position that non-violent civil disobedience is not the best method to correct the existing evils of our society and to build a better democratic fellowship. A study of this technique when applied by Negroes to correct any errors in organizations manned by Negroes gives a better opportunity to observe the method for what it is worthy. For this purpose we have elected two examples for observation. The National Baptist Convention, U.S.A., Incorporated, and the National Association For The Advancement of Colored People.

The National Baptist Convention
And Non-Violent Civil Disobedience

In the light of the authentic records as revealed in chapter 4 the National Baptist Convention has been committed without question to the struggle for civil rights. No other religious organization among Negroes has been any more vocal in this field than has the 6,300,000 member religious body under discussion. The leadership of this body has been courageous and an active participant in some of the stronger civil rights organizations, and yet the National Baptist Convention and its leadership have been targets and in some instances, victims of direct action led by some so-called militant civil rights workers. The questions have been raised, why would an organization of Negro Christians be subjected to such attacks? Why would some of the leaders be accused as supporters of segregation? What occasioned these attacks? It could not have been because the members were segregationists. As has been stated previously, many of the civil rights groups were organized by men who were members of the National Baptist Convention. This includes the United Defense League that was organized in June of 1953 in Baton Rouge, Louisiana, The Montgomery Improvement Association which was organized in 1955, and smaller groups in Birmingham, Alabama, Atlanta, Georgia, and Little Rock, Arkansas. But the National Baptist Convention gave more direct support to the Montgomery Improvement Association and to the Southern Christian Leadership Conference. Why did this close fellowship between the National Baptist Convention and the Montgomery Improvement Association and the Southern

Christian Leadership Conference diminish or discontinue? It was not due to conflict of personalities, it was due to a difference in emphasis. The Montgomery Improvement Association in its bus boycott effort adopted, or at least followed, the pattern that had been set two years earlier by the United Defense League in Baton Rouge, Louisiana, in its eight day bus boycott. There was not any attempt to interfere with the operation of the buses or to stop the movement of traffic, the people in Montgomery did what the people in Baton Rouge had done, they organized a car pool and people united their financial strength and co-operative efforts and produced a means of getting to and from work without supporting or encouraging a segregated pattern of transportation. The National Baptist Convention could whole-heartedly support this movement, morally and financially, for there was no attempt to break laws or to drive others to ill-convenience. The Negro community refused to support the segregated buses by producing other means of transportation. The leadership of the National Baptist Convention believed wholeheartedly in such constructive efforts.

When the Southern Christian Leadership Conference was first organized, as was stated, it sought to bring together new civil rights groups in the several towns and states of the South. It organized for unity and for the purpose of using its concerted efforts to aid in helping Negroes to register and develop their voting strength as American citizens. Some of the strongest workers in the Southern Christian Leadership Conference were strong supporters of the National Baptist Convention, U.S.A., Inc. When the Southern Christian Leadership Conference began to move towards a program of civil disobedience and began to throw its influence and strength against the functional responsibilities of the just laws of the land and the courts, then many leaders of the National Baptist Convention could not share its point of view. There was not at any time a vote on the part of the National Baptist Convention or any resolutions passed that the Southern Christian Leadership Conference would no longer be supported. Each minister and each participant made his own decision privately. The end-results were that practically all of the charter members of the Southern Christian Leadership Conference who were devout leaders in the National Baptist Convention discontinued their active support for the same reasons. They wanted to continue to work for civil rights but they wanted to work through the legitimate and prescribed channels of the United States of America. They believed that if in the process of obeying the Federal Constitution one violated state laws or laws supporting segregation, this was not civil disobedience, this was civil obedience and it was the job of the courts to decide who was in error; the victim who acted according to the Federal Constitution, or the institutions, and even state courts that believed in segregation. The leaders of the Baptist group said we must submit these matters step by step to the courts until we reach, if needs be, the Supreme Court of the United States of America. With the verdict of the Supreme Court outlawing segregation in public education in 1954, there was an assurance and almost a conclusion that any matter reaching the Supreme Court dealing with racial discrimination would be decided in favor of the full freedom not only of Negroes but all Americans. The National Baptist Convention continued to make annual pronouncements in support of first-class citizenship. It continued to participate in those constructive things that tended toward the full emancipation of all Americans but it did not sacrifice its responsibility as a religious organization. It refused to become an annual civil rights meeting with its program limited only to this important field. The National Baptist Convention insisted on preaching a gospel of redemption not only for Negro people but for all people. It was their concern and still is, that the gospel of Jesus Christ is not only for the segregated but for the segregators, and that men who are segregated have as much right to preach the gospel of universal salvation to those who believe in segregation as to those who do not believe in segregation. In each case the object is to save men from their sins and bring them to a loyalty to the principles and ideals of Jesus Christ. There were some pastors and some lay people who felt the convention should become a direct action organization specializing in civil disobedience. But the convention's interpretation of the social gospel related the church to business, to economics, to politics, to the struggle for civil rights, and to all the elements of human benefit, but this religious group did not so interpret the social gospel to mean that the church should give its wholehearted support to a program of civil disobedience. There were legitimate attempts on the part of some of the disciples of civil disobedience to win the convention to their point of view. This was their democratic right but fortunately they failed in this. The masses of the members of the convention remained loyal to the convention's tradition of a Christian ministry, a social concern, but primarily a gospel fellowship. After some years some of these civil rights leaders within the National Baptist Convention succeeded in influencing the public press to give to this great religious body an image of an organization that was indifferent to civil rights, indifferent to social and economic betterment. They also gave to some of the leaders that much hated epithet, "uncle tom." When all of these insinuations did not win the convention over to civil disobedience the campaign was finally launched in earnest and the program of non-violent civil disobedience was thrown in full force against the organized life of the National Baptist Convention. As it is the custom in a program of civil disobedience, they concentrated on the elected officials and had as their objective increased freedom for the members of the convention and the breaking of the alleged dictatorship of the established order. After months of campaigning and many weeks of propaganda the National Baptist Convention had a serious and direct confrontation with the strategy of non-violent civil disobedience. The campaign was led by some of the best known technicians and leaders in that field. The place of this confrontation was the Convention Hall in Philadelphia, Pennsylvania, September 1960.

We were soon to learn that this determined campaign against the National Baptist Convention was not restricted to Negro members of the National Baptist Convention, but there were white people who had no connection whatsoever with the convention who came in to help win the battle for civil disobedience over the National Baptist Convention. These strange white people knew little or nothing about the religious intentions, commitment, and background of this historic body. They came to see and to conquer. By some strange stroke of fate the delegates in 1960 had the most difficult time coming from the South, the West, and the Middle West to get into Philadelphia. A strike had tied up one of the largest railroad systems in this nation. But because of their devotion to the heritage of their fathers and to their religious commitments, the delegates flooded the city of Philadelphia; some coming by private cars, planes, and buses, but they came with a determination to withstand whatever negative force they might meet in the interest of the preservation of their right to remain free and to make their own decisions in the light of their Christian conviction.

The important hour had struck, the president of this great body sounded the gavel and announced that the 80th Session was now in order for business. The mayor of the city and the governor of the state made us welcome. Then the leaders of what was called the "Baptist sit-in" opened their campaign that continued from Wednesday morning until Sunday afternoon. After some hours of public demonstrations including speeches and any devisive methods at their command, some of the leaders were asked to come forward and tell the assembly exactly what they desired. They came forward but did not make a clear statement to which all persons involved could subscribe and agree.

It was impossible to ask for any protection from the law enforcement officers, for they did not know at what point to begin. It would have been very easy for them if it were a case of Negroes seeking their rights against white segregationists. The case would have been obvious and clear. The law enforcement officers were informed that these people who were demonstrating are not violating any law, they want freedom to control or direct their organization as they think right. The law enforcement officials were left to conclude that the demonstrators were right and the elected officials of this great convention were rebels; ungodly men and women, dishonest persons who had come to usurp the rights of people for their own selfish gains. All of these negative things were far from the truth, for some of these people who were following the pattern of direct action and civil disobedience as had been used against segregating institutions did not know themselves the real issues involved. They thought the whole issue centered around the elected officials, but the issue was deeper than that as subsequent history revealed. Officers were not allowed to make their reports. Fifteen thousand stunned delegates and visitors sat amazed and horrified when they saw preachers and pastors who had been transformed into apostles of civil disobedience and as demonstrators use every means at their disposal to keep the president of the National Baptist Convention from presenting to that vast crowd the annual address. Most of these were dedicated pastors from fine homes and communities, with fine college and seminary training; but they were now in the grips of the doctrine and the propaganda of non-violent civil disobedience. They thought it a virtue and a religion of a kind whose tenets they should follow rather than observe the principles of the Christian religion. Many of these persons who had organized the demonstration knew that their success depended on keeping the people from knowing the truth and hence noise was a far better weapon for them than silence, and disorder a more trusted ally than order, and disobedience of every code of ethics was for them more virtuous than obedience even to the rules and the prescriptions of the freedom of Christian worship. The gospel was not heard in that annual session. The National Baptist Convention as many of our other religious bodies in America has some of the greatest preachers in the United States of America; and yet, in the tension of civil disobedience men prefer the noise, the vicious behavior patterns of rabble rousers rather than listen to the inspiring words of some of America's greatest preachers.

Young people who had come from across the nation to engage in an Oratorical Contest for possible scholarships into their respective college for the next year were not allowed to appear on the platform. By arrangements of the Board of Directors these young people gave their address in the private office set up for the officials of the convention, and the Booker T. Washington Night address was delivered in this little crowded room because the space in the vast auditorium was held and blocked by the leaders of non-violent civil disobedience. Some urgent business that needed to be done was transacted only by informing the delegates through direct messengers what the issues would be that the secretary of the convention would read at a certain time and they would vote by standing when the documents were read.

There were some who thought that the coming of Sunday would soften the hearts of the demonstrators but they were just as determined that the gospel would not be preached on Sunday morning. Most of us who have attended religious bodies had never seen such a meeting as the one on Sunday morning; Christians surrounded by others who elected to block a worship service. The choir occupied its place, the officials took their stations but there was no singing from the choir, such was forbidden by noise. Fearing something dreadful might happen officers of the law crowded about the platform. What they saw were Christian leaders in their places making no effort to resist those who opposed them. But the greatest testimony to the Cross of Christ that morning were the silent tears shed by the people assembled who longed for the day to return when in their convention they could again preach the gospel of Christ with freedom and sing his praises without intimidation or interruption. The convention lost thousands of dollars because the session was an abortive one. It lost scores and scores of man-power hours because the delegates could only sit in silence while the opposers blocked the active work of the convention. It lost the available opportunities of a whole week to give testimony to the meaning and power of the Kingdom of God, and it will never be known how many people that week missed a chance to hear the gospel of Christ and be saved. It is not strange then that so many strong men and women wept bitterly in the closing moments of the convention. Some wept for sorrow at the plight and the emotional state of people whom they knew who were now victims of a strange mode and pattern of thought that had led them away from the idea of Christian fellowship to the way of conflict and confusion. Others wept because they knew that there were some people at that convention who were there for the last time and who were forced to leave with a picture of a broken fellowship, the parts of which they would never see put together again. Some wept because they were shocked by the strange foreign evil forces that had somehow been let loose on this great religious body with a design to wreck, ruin, and if possible, to utterly destroy.

But the leaders of the non-violent civil disobedience campaign resolved to continue their efforts whatever the cost. During a recess period on the second day of this session in the absence of all of the elected officials, this group conducted their own election and declared themselves the officers in charge of the whole organization. One distinguished civil rights leader stood in the presence of observers and some frustrated delegates and announced that by the power invested in him he was turning over all of the documents and giving full authority to these new leaders to carry on the work of the National Baptist Convention. The leaders of the "Baptist sit-in", by their own acts, became as they said, the leaders of the historic religious corporation against whom they had waged their battle. So determined were they that they brought legal actions against the official treasurer and secretary of the convention for the purpose of securing the convention's funds and assets. The civil courts ruled against them and this aspect of their campaign failed. But through news media bold announcements were made that these men were the representatives of the organization. And thus for twelve months it was proclaimed that there were two organizations each one claiming to be the National Baptist Convention, U.S.A., Incorporated. The Board of Directors of the convention held an early session thirty days after the Philadelphia meeting and organized their plans to go forward with the work of the denomination without in any wise saying or doing anything against those who claimed to have the right and the authority to act for the body in question. In this first meeting of the Board of Directors there was not a single state that was not represented. As usual, plans were made for the annual session in Kansas City, Missouri, for September, 1961. In the late summer of 1961 two of the well-known leaders of the non-violent civil disobedience campaign visited the office of the president of the National Baptist Convention in Chicago and suggested what they called a Christian solution to the problem. It was in reality a kind of compromise which would have given honor and dignity to the power and influence of the "Baptist sit-in" to which we have referred above. The committee was informed that their proposition was not a Christian solution, it was really a kind of doublecross and a sin against the orderly procedure of the convention. "This," said the president, "I cannot do; for it is not wise, it is not fair, and it is not right." Thirty days later the National Baptist Convention assembled in Kansas City, Missouri, according to plans. The "non-violent" Baptist group also assembled in the same city. They came as the convention with their officers and with their plans. They held their own board meeting, registered their own delegates. Then on the morning of the opening of our convention they came to the convention hall and interrupted the orderly procedure of our convention by staging a "march-in." They came down the aisle as football players charging and rushing against an opposing team. They had no regard for the fact that they were supposed to be separate and distinct from the incorporated body. They were not concerned about the danger and the hazard of such a march, they were rushing towards an already overcrowded platform. An innocent minister, a loyal supporter of the National Baptist Convention, made an effort to get out of the way of this charging crowd and fell backwards from the platform and suffered a broken neck from which he died that night. It required police officers to stop the hazardous so-called "non-violent march," but it had already occasioned violence and death.

The death of an innocent man who was seated on the platform in a convention hall that had been secured by the officials of the convention of which he was a part is a concrete demonstration of how violent the so-called non-violent campaign was and could be.

The leaders of the "march-in" having failed in their attempt to stampede the convention by their demonstration then hired lawyers and sought an injunction from the court to hinder the orderly procedure of the convention. This group with a pitiful minority was the group one year previously who had claimed to represent the vast majority. The National Baptist Convention Incorporated held the contract for the hall upon the payment of $7,500.00 rental two months previous to the time of the meeting. The "march-in" group had already declared themselves separate and distinct and yet having failed to take the hall by force they then sought to enjoin those who held the contract for the building. The informed members of the Board of Directors knew that no court of law had jurisdiction over the procedure and business of this religious corporation as long as said corporation conducted its affairs according to its own laws. As they had done previously the members of the Board of Directors decided to grant every courtesy to the brethren who now were in the "march-in" group. They had voiced the willingness to have a court appoint Dr. D. A. Holmes, pastor of the Paseo Baptist Church, Kansas City, Missouri, to preside over the convention at election time. The president of the incorporated convention recommended to the convention that it would elect Dr. D. A. Holmes to preside over the election. Knowing that the "march-in" group was holding their meeting at the church pastored by Dr. D. A. Holmes, some members of the cabinet objected to this procedure. When it was explained to them the purpose of this and when they were told that Dr. D. A. Holmes was a man of integrity, they accepted the suggestion. The president of the convention made a direct recommendation to the delegates assembled and Dr. D. A. Holmes was unanimously elected to hold said meeting. The president was then asked to inform Dr. Holmes of the vote of the convention. This he did. He further stated to Dr. Holmes that this was being done to give the opposing brethren a new opportunity to see if they could control the convention. Dr. Holmes was asked to go down town and allow the judge of the court to appoint him to hold the election. Dr. D. A. Holmes knew and so did the president of the convention that the judge had no power to appoint him or anyone else to preside over this body, but because the "march-in" brothers thought so, this procedure was tolerated by the regular convention leaders.

The next question that confronted the lawyers was what shall the judge put in the order that he was to send to the president, the Board of Directors, and the convention assembled. He did not know the rules and regulations of the convention, he did not know the issues involved. He knew, of course, that he had no authority or power to send any order to law-abiding citizens who knew the laws of their convention and who were conducting it accordingly. It became the duty of the man who had served the convention as president since 1953 to give to the lawyers, who in turn gave to the judge, the order to be sent to the persons involved. The terms were as follows:

1. All of the demonstrators who desired to vote in the convention election would be requested to do what all bonafide delegates do.

2. They would have to be orderly, not disturb the religious worship, nor in any way disrupt the meeting of the convention.

3. They must dissolve their organization which had been in operation for twelve months under the guise of being the National Baptist Convention, U.S.A., Incorporated and discontinue any further registration of delegates.

4. All the delegates that they had registered must now be registered with the incorporated convention, turning over both the names and the monies collected to the fiance committee of the incorporated convention.

5. They were to remove their badges and then receive receipts and badges from the convention in which they now sought membership.

6. They by the above acts were to recognize the staff of officers as the bonafide leaders of the organization.

7. The incorporated convention promised to give the same opportunities and rights enjoyed by those who had remained with the organized body. This was done without requesting an apology from the brethren for what they had done while under the influence of the philosophy of non-violent civil disobedience.

The convention after this moved forward in an orderly fashion and was not at any point disturbed further by the "march-in" group. For more than eight hours the delegates of the convention waited until the opposing group could fully qualify to vote according to the rules of the convention thus giving them the right to take over the convention not by noise and demonstrations, but through voting and the orderly procedure of the convention. They had full opportunity to make their speeches and say anything they desired to say, but more than this, the officers of the convention not only turned the gavel over to Dr. Holmes, but allowed two other men from the "march-in" group to assist with the election. The president and his cabinet left the platform and had nothing to do with the election procedure. This was done to show to the nation that the members of this body knew what they wanted and would do it if given the freedom to act. It was going the second mile with our brethren who had fallen victim temporarily to the non-violent civil disobedience technique. Also, it was for the purpose of demonstrating that the leaders of the convention were not dictators but the defenders of the people's right to hold their convention according to their own laws and accepted procedures. For none of the elected officials of this body gained their livelihood from said organization and would have no reason to contend for convention position because of economic necessity. Furthermore, there was a desire to remove every excuse and alibi that the apostles of non-violent civil disobedience groups could have.

With patience, determination, and courage the delegates in orderly fashion by standing vote, defeated the efforts of the so-called non-violent marchers. So tremendous and sweeping was the defeat that many of the principal parties were ashamed to remain for the closing of that session. The vote of the convention in 1961 not only vindicated the leaders of the convention of 1960, but repudiated the non-violent civil disobedience technique as a means of regulating and operating a religious organization.

As usual, the persons who had created the disturbances and had occasioned the death of one of the faithful members of the religious body at once placed all the blame for every tragic event against the convention and their leaders.

Why was the convention victorious in this matter? It was not due to any assistance given by any other religious groups. There was not uttered one word of protest through all America against this type of action against a religious organization. The victory came because there were, and still are, dedicated Negro Baptists throughout this nation who believe in themselves, who believe

in justice, freedom, and also in law and order. They believe they
possess the stamina and the ability to conduct the affairs of their
organizations and to maintain with honor the heritage of their
fathers that has come down to them through labor, sorrow, and
tears. Men of learning, labor leaders, dedicated civil rights leaders, college presidents, pastors of metropolitan centers, rural
district preachers, and laymen, stood as one in the defense of
the rights of Christian people to determine the policy of their
own organization.

The experiences that came to this religious body through the
technique of non-violent civil disobedience revealed some of the
following things:

1. That in the struggle for greater freedom and greater democracy in America the battle is not against white people alone,
Negroes themselves must help to defend the cause of freedom
against members of their own racial group. For the iniquitous
things that happened to the convention in question no white
people of America can be blamed. Negroes must blame themselves. Even the strange white people who participated in the
demonstrations in Philadelphia in 1960 were there only because
they had been invited and encouraged by some Negroes who
believed in the kind of demonstrations that were carried on.

2. It revealed that non-violent civil disobedience is not only a
special weapon to help Negroes gain their civil rights, it is a
weapon also that the minority uses in order to control the will
and wish of the majority. The tremendous vote in '61 in Kansas
City repudiated all of the charges of the past two years regarding the work of said convention. It was the minority that
sought by noise and confusion to control the thinking of the
majority.

3. The experiences revealed that non-violent civil disobedience as a philosophy and as a way of life does untold violence
to the better nature and better judgment of those who practice
it whether they be Negroes or members of other races and
nationalities. Many of the people who took part in the cam-

paigns referred to above were fine people, respected leaders, and we believe Christians who had fallen victim to the destructive dogma and ideology involved in civil disobedience.

4. The members of the National Baptist Convention saw at first hand how violent was the non-violent method and how destructive and dangerous; for it did not respect the laws of the institution, and had no regard for the rights of others.

There are people who are professed Christians but who feel that it is right to block a whole worship service if it is done through non-violence. Some feel that they can do anything and be justified as long as their acts are described as non-violent. There are people who are dishonest, deceitful, non-dependable, drunkards, and immoral in their habits, but who feel they are worthy, honored, and distinguished people because they believe in non-violence. Also, there are outstanding leaders in the United States who are distinguished in their fields; some as scholars, scientists, leaders in business, labor, and priests and preachers, but their worth is determined and measured according to some by non-violent direct actions. If they do not believe in this latter technique they are considered out of step with the times, useless, and unworthy. The Baptist "sit-in" in Philadelphia in 1960, and the Baptist "march-in" in Kansas City in 1961 are undisputed proof of how destructive the so-called non-violent method can be even against Negroes. They discovered that such actions could be used to intimidate them and destroy their self-respect, their families, their churches, and even the race itself.

The doctrine of non-violence as applied to the civil rights struggle has some merit and also some value. Its merit is in the valid doctrine that violence is not the means by which we can build an improved and better social order. Its peculiar value lies in the fact that a minority group cannot use the destructive weapons that are available to the majority and expect to win against the majority; and also violence is self-destructive and cannot be the means of building a stronger individual and a more integrated social order. In this context the survival of the fittest cannot mean the survival of the most vicious, the most ferocious, the most destructive, and the most violent. Fitness must include the elements of social, mental, moral, and spiritual integration which would lead to a fellowship of understanding among people of all walks and ranks of life.

But the doctrine of non-violence both in theory and practice has some outstanding weaknesses that we must not overlook. In the first place, it has become somewhat a monolithic standard in determining the ethics of the modern civil rights struggle. The assumption has been for the past twelve years that whatever is non-violent in the civil rights struggle is right. In our complex modern society it is difficult to use a negative term like non-violence as the definitive ethical standard for any pattern of behavior. It omits too many other essential qualities and overlooks too many essential moral principles in the building both of an integrated personality and of an integrated social order. Any movement or any philosophy dealing with the correct relationships between human beings must include many other virtues aside from that of non-violence.

The emphasis of non-violence does violence to the Negro race from at least two points of view. Indirectly it indicts the race as being not only potentially violent but being prone to violence with a strong tendency and urge to resort to the measures involved in violence. Historically this has never been true of the Negro race in the United States of America. The Negro race is not a perfect race; it has its defects as any other racial group. There are members of the Negro race who are violent, vicious, and criminal in thought and deed but the majority of the members of this race are not vicious or violent. A study of the Negro's experiences and his attitudes in the darkest days of slavery will reveal that for the most part they were a trustworthy people and were kind even to their enemies. Since the days of slavery until now the Negro race as a whole has never been a violent people. Notwithstanding the inflamatory campaigns during the past twelve years, at this present time the majority of American Negroes are still decent citizens who desire their full rights as all other Americans. But this desire is not accompanied with a racial tendency towards violence, and those who have constantly reminded Negroes not to be non-violent have through the psychological device of auto-suggestion planted the idea in the minds of some who had no previous thoughts of such. With the warning of non-violence goes also an implied, and in some cases, a direct indictment of an innocent people. In the second place this non-violent doctrine sins against the moral nature and the ethical achievement of Negroes. It has by implication as well as direct assertion ascribed a kind of slave morality to the Negro race by making non-violence the absolute standard for determining character in the civil rights struggle. Here the term non-violence means non-physical attack or the refusal to use bricks, knives, guns, or any other physical weapons against their opponents. Non-violence does not and cannot mean in this context the absence of mental torture, intimidation, community disruption or law-breaking and any form of social abuse. For in many cases non-violent acts in the name of civil rights have violated the code of self and social respect and have been most vicious in the attacks on the rights of others including the right of legitimate privacy. The rights of so many families to undisturbed repose have been violated by demonstrators who had a case against some one member of that family. Sometimes this particular member may be a public official, an educator, or even a religious leader. In public worship thousands of people have been deprived of the right to worship God according to the dictates of their conscience, to sing the songs of their choice, to listen to the gospel preached by their elected or appointed minister, because there were some people present in the congregation who were not in harmony with the purposes and programs of the leaders of the non-violent campaign. In the past twelve years advocates of non-violent acts in the civil rights struggle have participated in, and condoned the violation of practically every ethical standard that is designed to build community self-respect, the respect of others, and the good neighbor policy among all groups and classes. Therefore, the only standard for non-violence here is non-physical attack. This implies that Negroes along with others involved, are reduced to the level of brute instinct and brute action, leaving them at best with a slave morality or a morality that has little regard for the finer and more delicate virtues of life and society. This takes us back to the old concept of who and what a good Negro was. A good Negro slave was one who was not physically incorrigible. He did no physical violence against his master or anything that his master possessed. He was not included in the fellowship that demanded and required the higher virtues of goodwill, respect for the sacredness of other personalities, and concern about all of those virtues that made a community safe, constructive and creative of the highest types of fellowship. Under the ethics of segregation a good Negro was one that stayed in his place and his place was a servile one. He could disrespect his family, disregard the rights of other Negroes and be disloyal to those efforts and institutions through which and in which Negroes were engaged for self-improvement and for the betterment of their community. Under the most extreme system of segregation the only virtue required among Negroes was loyalty to their bosses and said loyalty was determined by child-like submission to their overlords which involved a refusal at any time to resort to physical violence. Negro Americans have developed great minds, a more ethical sense of responsibility for community building, and hence a respect for the virtues of human association that must be practiced if there is to be family and community growth and fellowship. Negroes already know that it is a sin against the highest moral standards to disrepect the personal rights and the property rights of others. They have already reached the cultural plane that makes them aware of other virtues and other laws aside from physi-

cal forces, brute strength, or any form of coercion. To reduce the Negro race to the level of a slave morality subjects
him to the notion that coercion is the highest possible form of
control in the building of a democratic society. Negroes as well
as many other minority groups know that mutual aid, cooperation, and love are the great forces by which a democratic society
can be built. They not only can appreciate, but they do accept
the principles stated by Arnold Toynbee when he says:

> On the cultural plane coercion is of no avail; for the only form of
> power that can here be employed with effect is the power of spiritual
> attraction through which one soul moves another by love and not by
> force.[1]

Further, the doctrine of non-violence has been for many a very
deceptive doctrine. It has been one of the elements in the civil
rights struggle that many people have called Christian, and they
have concluded that in following the doctrine of non-violence
they were following a Christian precept. But non-violence does
not reach the ethical standard as proclaimed by Jesus of Nazareth. It was not the overt act, it was not the use of instruments
of death, but it was the attitude of mind that Jesus evaluated
in his study of the moral content of an act. He said:

> Ye have heard that it was said by them of old time, Thou shalt not
> kill; and whosoever shall kill shall be in danger of the judgment:
> But I say unto you, That whosoever is angry with his brother
> without a cause shall be in danger of the judgment . . .[2]

Note here that whosoever is angry with his brother without a
cause brings upon him the same danger as those who kill. Both
shall be in danger of the judgment. It is not the act of violence
but it is the attitude of mind that determines the quality and
the moral content of the deed. The civil rights struggle needs
more than the morality of non-violence, it needs the morality

[1] *A Study of History*, Vol. VIII., 499.
[2] St. Matthew 5:31–22.

that would discipline every area of life both for those of us who seek our civil rights and those from whom we seek them. There is the need for sobriety, for temperance, honesty, self-respect, and respect for others; for it is impossible to win lofty moral battles in an immoral way. It is difficult if not impossible for men to be led to disrespect other people and at the same time win a battle against segregation which is a historic form of the evil of disrespect for the sacredness of human personality. When we have said a deed is non-violent we have not said enough. In a democratic society the deed must reflect loyalty to country, patriotic responsibility, respect for the rights of others, respect for personal ability, personal worth, and a respect for law and order. The civil rights struggle is important and must not at any time be neglected or taken for granted. But it is a part of the moral, social, and spiritual struggle of human life and the other facets of life must not be neglected as we work on the civil rights front. The methods we employ must be of such quality and such nature that they will not impede or penalize the growth of wholesome personalities and the development of a free and just society where the needs of all are met and rights of all are made secure.

Non-Violent Civil Disobedience
And The 53rd Annual
Convention Of The NAACP

As we have stated before the National Association for the Advancement of Colored People is the oldest and the strongest civil rights organization in the United States of America. When it assembles, whether in local units or in national conventions, it is expected that the finest traditions and the most lofty principles of freedom will be defended, espoused, proclaimed, and practiced. With this high expectation, thousands of people gathered in Grant Park in Chicago, Illinois, on July 4, 1963. The occasion was a gigantic freedom rally as a part of the annual conclave of this organization. The nation's flag was seen in the accustomed places floating in the summer's breeze reminding all observers of the 187th birthday of this republic. Thousands of American citizens in the tradition and spirit of patriotism had gathered at Grant Park on this historic occasion. They had come in the name of freedom though burdened with a consciousness that there were many problems still to be solved before all the lingering unholy shadows would give place fully to freedom's holy light. They had come as free men but seekers for greater freedom. They had come as citizens of a great democratic nation. They had come with the intention of listening to speeches by dedicated and committed leaders and citizens. Many of the delegates as well as visitors were anxious to know of the recent gains that had been made by the Association in the struggle for freedom. They came seeking new signs of hope and new grounds for trust, confidence, and sources of encouragement to make the essential sacrifices to carry even further the struggle for full deliverance and strength to bear the burdens essential to full emancipation. They had come as supporters of freedom of speech, freedom of religion, freedom of the press, freedom from fear, and freedom from want. The meeting was opened with appropriate patriotic hymns, including the National Anthem, and then the Mayor of the city was presented to bring his address. With courage and a forthright stand as a statesman, the Mayor faced the great audience and began a most courageous, effective, and patriotic speech. He was surveying the history of the Fourth of July, recounting the sacrifices of the great heroes of the American Revolution, pinpointing the magnificent achievements that this republic had made since its birth, and giving testimony to his faith in the future of this great republic, when there was a flurry, a noise, and banners raised. There were shouts of disapproval, and there were voices of protest lifted high with the assistance of their own walkie talkie loud speakers. Soon the noise became so intense and so difficult that the Mayor of the city paused and looked with disgust and surprise at the large crowd of people who had come to demonstrate against his presence. They were not all Negroes; many of them were white. Some had been seen in demonstrations in other parts of the city and country, but they stood defying the Mayor of the City of Chicago and calling in question his constitutional right to speak to a free people in a free country. As this continued, the Mayor folded his speech and walked in utter dejection from the podium and took his seat. In a brief moment, he departed from the platform, joined with his aides, and left Grant Park in his automobile. He had marched in the heat and had identified himself with those who were in quest of freedom; and yet, he had been howled from the platform although he was the chief executive of the city. He had been driven, through disrespect, from the platform to which he had been invited to bring greetings.

By any stretch of the imagination no one could classify Mayor Richard J. Daley with the enemies of freedom or link him with the avowed apostles of racial segregation. He had by his deeds proven himself to be a friend of civil rights and a devout supporter of the lofty principles for which the National Association For The Advancement of Colored People stood. The people who had interrupted the speech of the mayor and who had created the noise that drove him from the platform were either misinformed about the mayor's principles or had come to cast a shadow over the organization and the leaders who had come in the interest of a better America and the continuing growth of human freedom.

It was the democratic right of those who took part in the demonstration, but in so exercising their rights they had done wrong not only to the mayor of the city and the citizens of Chicago, they had cast a reflection on the sober, intelligent and dedicated leaders of the organization. Men like Bishop Gill Spottswood, the chairman of the Executive Board of the Association and one of the bishops of the A.M.E. Zion Church, represent some of the best leaders within the Negro race. But he was embarrassed and helpless as he stood before the demonstrators who gave him little or no respect as the presiding officer of the day.

Mr. Roy Wilkins the Executive Secretary of the Association with his staff of efficient helpers had prepared a most inspiring program and had sought to bring together representatives whom they believed were on the side of justice and freedom. This leader and those associated with him saw how impossible it is to operate a national convention of civil rights people when a few individuals decide to invade such a gathering with their program of non-violent civil disobedience. The demonstrators here contended they were acting in the defense of civil rights and the advancement of the Negro's cause, but by this act they cast a shadow over the acknowledged leaders of the organization and put under a cloud their intentions and their purposes. The demonstrators also took away, at least for awhile, the rights of all the delegates and visitors who had come to hear and listen to the program as presented.

After the departure of the mayor of the city, and after the restoration of order the presiding officer proceeded to complete the program as prepared. Two veteran American leaders were called to speak as programmed—Senator Paul Douglas of Illinois whose contribution to civil rights is known to all informed Americans, brought a most encouraging message. Bishop Joseph Gomez, the presiding Bishop of the Fourth Episcopal District of the A.M.E. Church, brought to the great crowd a logical, forceful, and powerful address. The delegates and citizens assembled would have been robbed of a great opportunity had they not heard the clear and searching words of a committed leader and religious statesman. As we listened to his address many of us thought how fortunate is the Negro race and how fortunate is America to have such able minds on the American platform today in these times of doubt, uncertainty, and confusion.

But just as Bishop Gomez was closing his eloquent address

there was indication that something else was in the making in the form of a second demonstration. People were moving about in the rear of the assembly exchanging banners and apparently re-grouping themselves for another attack. When Bishop Gomez had finished his address amidst applause and fitting expressions of appreciation the time had come to present the president of the National Baptist Convention not for an address, but to bring greetings from the National Baptist Convention, USA., Inc. Bishop Gill Spottswood turned to me and said, "Now Dr. Jackson, you have seen what has happened to Mayor Richard J. Daley. Do you care to speak?" My reply was, "If there is any opposition to my speaking I would rather not, but I would not wish to make the impression that I had disrespected the invitation to be present by choice. Ask Mr. Roy Wilkins the Executive Secretary what he thinks about it." When the Bishop returned, he said: "Roy thinks you should speak." Bishop Spottswood then said to me, "you will be next." He then attempted to introduce me to bring greetings to this great freedom rally, and when my name was called the non-violent civil disobedience demonstrators started anew their campaign of noise and demonstrations. I made no attempt to stand or to speak. One bearded white man in the audience who sat near one of the parishioners of our church was heard to say, "Where is the man, Dr. Jackson? Which one of the men on the platform and where is he seated?" Somebody then identified who Dr. Jackson was. Then he replied, "This is our chance—we can never get but so close to him at the National Baptist Convention. He is not as surrounded with friends as he is there—this is our time." The noise continued. Some of the same demonstrators that waved banners against the Mayor of the city moved toward the platform. Mrs. Sylvester White, the wife of one of the judges of our city and member of the local committee, came to me and said, "Will you please leave the platform? They will not discontinue the noise until you leave." My reply to her was, "I am waiting for the men who came with me. They know where the car is parked. I do not."

A few more minutes of delay and then the same person returned and said to me in a more tense and somewhat frustrated
tone, "Will you please leave this platform for your own personal
safety?" And then I got a slightly different slant of the climate
and the atmosphere. The press surrounded me for a statement
and, as I moved to the back of the rostrum to give a statement,
a crowd of policemen came to the door and said, "He must not
remain any longer—it is too dangerous here." Accompanied by
them, I walked out of the door of the back room in the pavilion
only to be greeted by a howling mob saying "kill him, kill
him", and then police officers linked their hands together and
put me in the circle and we marched towards the position
where I thought my car would be available. We paused for a
second and then Chief Kelly, one of the outstanding policemen
who, incidentally, was white, said to those officers standing
about, "We must not wait any longer. It is too dangerous. Have
Dr. Jackson to get in my car." And Robert Allen, one of the
members of my parish, got into the car with us. And when the
mob approached the car and began to rock it as if to turn it
over, Robert Allen raised the closed umbrella to strike the mob,
but I said, "No, Allen, put the umbrella down. Do not fight back
at these people." Slowly, the officer's car moved through the
great mass of humanity and headed towards the open street. In
driving south toward my residence, the officer said, half talking
to us and half soliloquizing to himself, "I never thought I'd live
to see the day when the Mayor of this city would be treated
like this on a Chicago platform." Driving further, he said, "And
you, Dr. Jackson, we consider you one of our outstanding citizens
of Chicago and one of our great religious leaders—not only in
Chicago but across the nation. And I never would have dreamed
that anybody would have given to you the treatment that you
received today." He took me to the door of my home and then
later he said, "I have been on the police force for a number of
years in Chicago and my closest brush with death came on the
Fourth of July, 1963, when I took Dr. J. H. Jackson in my car to

deliver him from a gathering mob in Grant Park." Said he, "They tried the springs of my car and I expected the car to turn over any minute, but I resolved that day that, if he died, we would die together." A brush with death revealed also the patriotic commitment and concern of the police officer whose face was not colored, but white; and yet he had such profound devotion to duty and such commitment to truth and honesty that he made the commitment "if he died, we would die together."

All of the people involved in this incident were not members or delegates to the Convention in question. Some had come from other groups and maybe some were not members of any civil rights organization. Their purpose was to discredit and, if possible, to silence the voices of people who espouse the cause of freedom and also the cause of the nation. Why should any American be intimidated on a public platform on the Fourth of July among people committed to Freedom? Why should public officials be disrespected and intimidated when they stand, not to censure or condemn or sit in judgment on any individual or groups, but for the purpose of saying "You are welcome to our city." And why would a Minister of Jesus Christ be denied the constitutional right to speak in a public meeting? Were there those who doubted the ability of the speaker? Did they fear that his utterances would not be in harmony with truth and freedom? Did they believe that the speaker would deal with the problems of freedom correctly? The only difference between the proposed speaker of that hour and some of the others who formed this mob crowd, he had simply insisted and still insists that he who seeks freedom can find the resources and techniques in the United States of America. What has happened in America and who is present in America that makes a public meeting in the interest of freedom on the birthday of the nation dangerous for American citizens? These persons who so act, if they be Americans, do not think as Americans, neither do they live in obedience to the nation's doctrine of freedom of speech.

I have said repeatedly: I do not prefer bootlegged freedom. I prefer that freedom that the United States of America has promised and the Federal Constitution has guaranteed and proclaimed. I do not desire to seek that deliverance that would compromise the ideals of the Supreme law of the land or threaten to destroy the gains that have already been made in the growth of understanding, justice, and goodwill in this country. Neither do I seek security that will put the nation under a cloud and force us to accept as allies people, be they colored or white, who have already pledged themselves to the destruction of the nation's way of life and have decreed the silencing of the voice of the church by rendering the right to preach the gospel of Christ hazardous and dangerous. We must be courageous and firm and committed to the ideals of freedom and truth. We must also withstand with all our might and courage those enemies— foreign and domestic—who wrap themselves in a cloak of pseudo-freedom in order to sabotage and destroy a nation that is committed to freedom.

This act of non-violent civil disobedience at this meeting did nothing to advance the cause of civil rights or the cause of freedom. It proved again that there can be no intelligent planning for meetings in the interest of freedom where men do not respect the rights of leaders and delegates who desire to hear and to be heard in an orderly fashion.

7

THE VIOLENCE OF THE NON-VIOLENT CAMPAIGN IN CHICAGO: SUMMER, 1966

CHICAGO, ILLINOIS, the second largest city in the United States of America with a population of more than three and a half million, has an estimated Negro population of 943,000. The city has provided many great economic, scientific, and cultural advantages for all people. Within the metropolis there are outstanding business organizations, strong labor unions, great labor leaders, and many enlightened political and social thinkers. At the same time Chicago is an important educational center with its famous universities and renowned medical complexes. And with its churches and synagogues and world-famous religious thinkers Chicago has taken its place among the cities of the nation. As is true of any great urban community, this one is afflicted by economic, social, moral and political problems. There is far more crime in our streets than we would wish. Suffering and unemployment as well as other negative elements and evils of society exist in Chicago. Racial prejudice, segregation, and discrimination continue to be evident; hence, no patriotic American citizen living in the city of Chicago can overlook the evils of our city or seek to bypass the unsolved problems that confront us in every area of life. Any citizen of Chicago who supports the errors of this community cannot be counted as a loyal American.

There are some signs of encouragement which indicate that the city is not resigned to its plight and has not refused to seek solutions to some of the disturbing problems that confront us.

Before concerning ourselves with the non-violent campaign of the summer of 1966 in Chicago, we should at least recognize what the city possessed and what the visitors who came to the city found, not only negatively, but positively. In 1966 there were Negroes employed and serving in practically every segment of city government. There were seven Negroes in the City Council duly elected from their respective wards and assigned the responsibility of helping to write the laws of the city, to shape its policies, and to help in the affairs of government in general and citizens' welfare in particular. Negroes were also represented in the matter of administration of justice. Eight judges and eight magistrates presided in the courts of the city and had the responsibility of determining and meting out justice in the light of the facts and the evidence presented. In the fire, police, and building departments as well as in other areas of the city's life, top level and prepared Negroes could be found among the other dedicated servants of this city. The Negro community, then, is a vital part of the city's life and has—by vote of the people—been assigned the responsibility of helping to solve the problems confronting our city. We then, as a people, must have some of the credit for the success of our city; we must also accept some of the blame for the unsolved problems that remain.

In Chicago Negroes enjoy membership in one of the strongest, if not the strongest, political organizations in the country. This organization has been led by Congressman William L. Dawson for a number of years. He has been, and still is, one of the most powerful and most influential political leaders in the Congress of the United States of America. He is respected by his colleagues. His decisions are sought on various issues affecting government; and in a quiet but forceful way he has rendered, and still renders, a great service to his district, to the Chicago community, and to the United States of America. As a political leader, he has worked with all groups and sections not only of this country but also of this city. He has done it in such a way that he has served most uniquely the interest of his people as well as the nation itself. He is not without criticism; he is not without opponents and opposition, but the fact is the vast majority of the people of his Congressional District believe in him and trust him as a capable and worthy statesman.

There are many other Negro leaders in politics, business, the professions, religion, and other fields of endeavor. They, too, have made and are still making their respective contributions to the life of the city. While Chicago has gone forward in attacking all problems in general, the city has not overlooked the problem of civil rights. Both Negroes and white leaders have been committed to this cause of justice and freedom for all peoples. This is reflected by the number of civil rights organizations that were operating effectively in the city of Chicago prior to 1966 and which are still carrying forward a program of better human relations. There are in this city forty-three [1] civil rights organizations: twenty-seven of these are private agencies and are carried on by the general public and by special interest groups; sixteen of these are governmental agencies which have been proposed and planned for the purpose of helping to implement the promises of the Federal Constitution and the dreams of all American citizens for full rights and equality of opportunity in every phase of the city's life. These forty-three civil rights agencies were in operation prior to 1966.

The Human Relations Commission is one of the sixteen civil rights organizations sponsored by City Government. It was organized in 1947 and began with an annual budget of $25,000. Today, it has a budget of $400,000. Some of the best trained sociologists and civic workers are listed among the many staff workers that help to carry forward its inclusive program. This Commission is a liaison agency between the city government and the citizens of the community. Any aggrieved person whose

---

[1] Edward A. Marciniak, *Your Civil Rights* (Commission on Human Relations, first printing 1949, the last revision, 1965), p. 43–48.

civil rights have been abridged can make contact with the Commission on Human Relations, and this Commission will direct said parties to the right source for the treatment and solution of their problems. This agency maintains a twenty-four hour service so they may be reached any time of day or night.

In 1963 the City Council of Chicago passed a fair-housing act which outlawed discrimination in housing. A brief quote from this Law will reveal how comprehensive and far-reaching it is. The first two paragraphs read as follows:

It is hereby declared the policy of the City of Chicago to assure full and equal opportunity to all residents of the City to obtain fair and adequate housing for themselves and their families in the City of Chicago without discrimination against them because of their race, color, religion, national origin or ancestry.

It is further declared to be the policy of the City of Chicago that no owner, lessee, sublessee, assignee, managing agent, or other person, firm or corporation having the right to sell, rent or lease any housing accommodation, within the City of Chicago, or any agent of any of these, should refuse to sell, rent, lease, or otherwise deny to or withhold from any person or group of persons such housing accommodations because of the race, color, religion, national origin or ancestry of such person or persons or discriminate against any person because of his race, color, religion, national origin or ancestry in the terms, conditions, or privileges of the sale, rental or lease of any housing accommodation or in the furnishing of facilities or services in connection therewith.

This Law of 1963 represented the thinking, the imagination, and the judgment of some of the best lawmakers in Chicago. At least this is what the voters evidently thought because they elected and sent these men to the City Council. This law does not compromise the rights of individuals to purchase, rent, or own property where their money can buy, nor to live where their financial talents and gifts permit. The Law reflects the City Council's interest in the civil rights of all the people of Chicago. No city council dedicated to discrimination could pass such a law. This Law was passed without intimidation, without threats, and without violence. It grew out of a sense of patriotic responsibility to the City, to its citizens, and to the nation as a whole. This Law still stands. It was tested in the courts by a group of real estate men. These men made no attempt to discredit the City Council or to hinder the operation of the Law but appealed to the courts and awaited the decision of the same. On January 19th, 1967, the Supreme Court of the State of Illinois handed down its decision in favor of the constitutionality of the Fair Housing Ordinance of 1963. No civil rights group or organization of real estate brokers could settle this issue. It was a decision left wholly to the judgment and legal wisdom of the Court.

It is interesting to note that the Chicago Commission on Human Relations was given the responsibility of helping to enforce the Law of 1963. Paragraph 6 of the Law said the following:

Any person aggrieved in any manner by any violation of any provision of the above ordinance may file a written complaint setting forth his grievance with the Chicago Commission on Human Relations. Said complaint shall state the name and address of the complaint and of the persons against whom the complaint is brought and shall also state the alleged facts surrounding the alleged violation of this ordinance.

According to Paragraph 7, the Commission has the right and the power to make a thorough investigation of the complaint. If it finds the complaint to be just, the Commission makes every effort to persuade the violators to change their attitudes and to subscribe to the Law. If this is not successful, then within sixty days after the filing of the complaint, the Commission is empowered to proceed promptly with full hearings of the complaint. This is not only a strong law, but the administrative arrangement for the effective execution of said law reflects the City's concern for the victims and also its determination that violators will not escape the penalty for their infractions.

In 1964, the initial steps were taken by outstanding business-men of the City of Chicago to form what is known as the Chicago Merit Employment Committee. Their motto is: "Merit employment isn't just good citizenship. It's good business, too." They state further, "Merit employment means hiring the best qualified person for each job . . . Without regard to race, color, religion or national origin . . . And providing equal opportunity for all employees to compete for training and advancement." This is a voluntary group that has elected to work for the elimination of discrimination in employment. People are hired on merit and are given a chance to receive on-the-job training if they show ability and willingness to learn. The Committee began with forty-four firms who had voluntarily brought them-selves together for this lofty purpose. The Committee has con-tinued to grow so that by February 6, 1967, 1,191 firms had pledged themselves to follow the principles of merit employ-ment. It is an inspiration to hear these businessmen express their interest and concern in the achievements of merit employment. Their work has been so effective that other cities and commu-nities have followed their pattern of action. Aside from the business aspect, it has engendered goodwill and better human relations within the community. Things are being made better in employment without bitterness. Leaders of industry have made their decisions based on sound economic principles and on the ideals of equality of opportunity and the rights of all men to a fair share in the economic goods of life.

A word must be said about Chicago's system of public edu-cation. The school boycotts in the City of Chicago prior to 1966 grew out of dissatisfaction and complaints against segregation and discrimination in many of the schools. Dr. Benjamin C. Willis served as general superintendent of the Chicago schools succeeding Dr. Harold C. Hunt who resigned in 1953 to join the faculty at Harvard University. The general superintendent had given to the City of Chicago one of the best programs in any large city in the United States of America. The Havighurst Report in evaluating the work both of Dr. Benjamin C. Willis and the previous superintendent, said:

> Under these two men the school system has grown tremendously. The post war increase of births affected the schools first in 1952, but in-migration of low-income people with large families had already pushed up school enrollments to the point that many schools were on double shifts at the beginning of the 1950's. A great building program was carried out, and this eliminated the double shift by 1963.[2]

The members of the Chicago school board were fine citizens of Chicago dedicated to the American ideal of first class citizenship. They along with the General Superintendent recognized many unsolved problems in the field of education. They were working at them and seeking constructive solutions to them. In their wise judgment they did not suspend what they could do until the day of the full realization of all ideals had come. They were carrying forward the program that they had with the facilities and the budget available. But they were also developing and executing plans to remove the limitations and restrictions in order to give to the children of Chicago the best possible quality of education. From 1953 to 1966 Chicago had the services of one of the best trained and most dedicated educators in the United States of America. But many people who did not have a chance to make a thorough study of the plans and programs that the General Superintendent and Board of Education had launched in an effort to solve the remaining problems made sweeping charges against both. The most popular complaint against the school system was that of segregation and discrimination. In order to meet this challenge and to assess and fix the blame the Board of Education invested thousands of dollars to make a study of the system. They called in experienced educators from all over the country. The results of the work of these two committees were given in two reports both

[2] Robert J. Havighurst, *A Survey of the Public Schools of Chicago* (Chicago, 1962), p. 2.

of which were published in 1964. The Hauser Report which included five distinguished educators, one of whom was a Negro, had as their specific objective the study of integration of the public schools of Chicago. In their letter of transmittal the Committee said they were unanimous in submitting their findings and recommendations. They found there was de facto segregation in the schools of Chicago but they also found that the Chicago Board of Education and the leaders, including the General Superintendent, were not responsible for its presence or its design. On this point the Committee stated the following:

This de facto segregation in the public schools is not unique to Chicago. It is a pattern common to many central cities with relatively large Negro populations in the metropolitan United States, even when there is no de jure segregation; that is, legally enacted provision for segregated schools.

In a fundamental sense, de facto segregation is not the results of the intent or design of the Board of Education of Chicago, nor of boards of education in most other metropolitan areas. De facto segregation in the schools, given the wide-spread traditional neighborhood school policy, is a by-product of segregated patterns of settlement and housing in this and other cities. Such concentration of Negro population within central cities are the product of forces built deep into the social, economic, and political fabric of the nation. It is important to understand the demographic, social, and historic background of de facto segregation as a first step toward the solution of the problems which it generates.[3]

This report showed distinctly that the fundamental problem of de facto segregation of the schools in Chicago were due to other causes over which the Board of Education and the General Superintendent had no direct control, but it also showed that they were engaged in seeking solutions to the educational aspect of said problems.

[3] Report by the Advisory Panel on Integration in Public Schools in Chicago, (Chicago, 1964), pp. 3–4.

The Havighurst Report which was concerned about quality education also pointed out that wherever they discovered inferior education in the public school system of Chicago it was not due to any deliberate attempt on the part of officials, staff members, and the school board. The Havighurst Survey says the following:

. . . Pupils in low-income areas generally learn less than pupils in middle- and high-income areas, whether they are white or Negro. However, there is no deliberate attempt to give pupils in low-income areas an inferior education. On the contrary, the school staff worked very hard to find ways to teach effectively in such areas. To date, they have not been as successful as they must be eventually. More money and more creative work must be spent to find out how to teach more effectively children who come from low-income and low-education families, whether white or Negro.[4]

Both of these reports in question condemn racial segregation as being a contributing factor toward reducing the quality of education offered by Chicago or any other city, but the encouraging factors are, there were plans by the General Superintendent and his staff, and there was commitment and dedication on the part of the Board of Education to quality education.

Unfortunately for Chicago so many citizens did not ever know, and many do not know now, what these committed citizens of Chicago were doing to improve the quality of education for all the children of the city. It is unfair to dedicated servants of the people, and to the people themselves, to hold back from them the efforts that are being put forth to solve the problems that can be and should be solved according to the principles of law and order, freedom, justice, and truth.

The Chicago of 1966 was not a perfect city. It had many unsolved problems, but it was a city committed to equality of opportunity and to the defeat of segregation and discrimination. It was a city whose Council had gone on record in the defense of

[4] Op. cit., p. 372–373.

the freedom and rights of all people. It was a city dedicated to solving its problems, to upholding the Federal Constitution, and to the task of making this city a better place in which to live.

While the National Association for the Advancement of Colored People, through its local branch, has carried on full and devoted service in the interest of the civil rights of all people, Chicago has not denied to the civil rights workers of this city freedom of speech, freedom of assembly, and freedom to protest. The records of the city will show that prior to 1966 all civil rights groups were free to picket, to call boycotts, to march, and to demonstrate against any organization, agency, or any public officials. The City Hall, the Mayor himself, the Board of Education and other targets selected by the civil rights workers of Chicago received the words and acts of protest from civil rights leaders. Even the Olivet Baptist Church at 3101 South Parkway was exposed to picket lines by certain civil rights organizations more than once. The City of Chicago has for a number of years carried on a slum clearance program which has resulted in many areas having been cleared, modern structures erected, and improved living conditions for people at all levels.

There is still much that remains to be done, but so much has been accomplished and so much has been done through the organizations of city governments, community organizations, clubs, schools, churches, and other groups that many citizens of Chicago believe that there are not now many problems that cannot be met and solved by the dedicated people of the great city. But, after some months of preparation, a special campaign was launched when the Southern Christian Leadership Conference left its Southern base and came to Chicago on invitation of some civil rights leaders to help save the people of Chicago from ignorance, from slums, from unemployment, and to win for them the unqualified right as citizens on all fronts. *This program in Chicago must be evaluated not in the light of sentiment but in the light of fact* and by the power of truth. The leaders of this Chicago campaign in the summer of 1966 came to enter into the city's life and to try for the first time in a Northern city their program of non-violence and, in some cases, non-violent civil disobedience. They turned to what is called "Operation: Bread Basket," a program of putting pressure on businessmen and employers to hire more Negroes in their firms; yet, before they launched their campaign, there was already in operation a committee called "The Merit Employment Committee" to which we referred above. Of course, there is nothing illegal in seeking to force employment; but, if the employers have organized to do this themselves, it saves time, energy, and money if the employees would allow the employers to fight this battle as long as employers are committed and dedicated.

The Chicago campaign spent much time working with teenage gangs or teenage clubs, organizing the poor of the community, and those who dwell in slums—not for the purpose of harnessing the little money that might be available in order to purchase buildings, give employment, and render unfortunate people more productive with the right of ownership through expanding companies, but the primary purpose was to organize for protest. This is the democratic right of any American citizen, but the time has come when we must decide not only whether we have the right to protest we must also decide where is the most urgent place, what is the most effective method, and when is the appropriate time to employ these methods and to follow these procedures.

The campaign of 1966 is now history. We can observe dispassionately what has been achieved and what has not been achieved. We can observe what was the price and what was purchased by the price. We can ask ourselves the questions: what has been done and what has not been done? Is Chicago better or worse? Is the relationship between citizens purer and better now? Step by step, the organizers and leaders of the campaign gathered data, held community meetings, made speeches, some of which were explosive, some shouted "Peace" but made preparation for war—some uttered essential calls for unity but took steps for divisions and bitterness. They moved from group meetings to community meetings, and finally to the great mass meeting in Soldier Field, at which time they had expected 100,000 citizens to gather. It is said that twenty odd thousand people gathered on this 10th day of July. Songs, speeches, statements, and appeals finally led to deeper feelings of bitterness, anxiety, and frustration. After the mass meeting, the demands [5]—not requests—were taken to city hall and nailed to the door. In a democratic society, citizens make requests of their public officials. In a democratic society, elected officials make requests of their constituents. But, in an autocratic, despotic, and dictatorial government, demands are made, and one is forced to act *according to the demands or be subject to the consequences* thereof. On Monday, after the rally in Soldier Field, a committee called on the mayor of the city to ascertain from him whether or not he was in position to commit himself to the execution of the demands. Some of these demands were of such nature that only the City Council, the lawmaking body of the city, could pass upon them; but the question was thrown in the lap of the mayor of the city. And, when the answers from the office of the Mayor did not satisfy the majority of the leaders in question, they held a long session and, unfortunately, shortly after the close of their session, a dangerous and devastating riot broke out. The so-called non-violent speeches, the non-violent campaigns, as they said, the doctrine of peaceful civil disobedience, as it was expressed, and after all of the talk designed on the surface for the betterment of the City of Chicago, the riot broke out. The leaders could not stop the riot. Buildings were burned, many innocent people hurt, police officers were among the persons wounded; and, during this conflict, twenty-seven people lost their lives. Police Superintendent Orlando Wilson found himself hard pressed to supply enough police officers to maintain the order, to insure the safety of the citizens, and to protect the properties of businessmen from destruction

[6] See Chicago Daily News, July 10, 1966.

by molotov cocktails and by biting flames. Finally, the Governor of the state sent in the National Guard to put down the disturbances. The non-violent leaders did not have the influence or the power to stop the angry people once they were aroused.

To the eternal credit of the citizens of Chicago, it took the leaders of this campaign almost two years to inflame and to sufficiently anger the people and lead them to the state of frustration out of which came mob actions and terror and death. No writer, no observer would speak the truth who would say there were no just causes for dissatisfaction in the city of Chicago—There were persons unemployed; there was sub-standard housing; there were absentee landlords who were interested in collecting the rent while the rats infested their buildings. We do not and will not excuse any shortcomings or any failures in any part of the city's life, but we must admit that stirring people to anger and bitterness has never proved a constructive technique for correcting the ills in which they are involved. Burning down a house that does exist is not an adequate substitute for repairing a house that still stands. Finally, the soldiers had gone and the community marching abated, but it must be remembered that the marchers were not led by people who had no weapons, for the so-called successful marches were led by police officials, armed and prepared to inflict punishment on those who opposed them. Sometimes police officers outnumbered the marchers whom they led. It is almost beyond imagination to expect people committed to non-violence to adopt programs and procedures whose success required uniformed police officers, sometimes two or three to a marcher. According to the report from the police officials, the leaders of the marches at times did not give them the respect of notifying them when and where they were going to march in time for them to get sufficient protection and sufficient leaders. Finally, the marches were stopped because the marchers were enjoined by the City of Chicago [6] and certain stipulations were placed on them.

---

[6] See Appendix, Injunction, pp. 254–255.

That injunction has not been lifted as yet. And among the leaders enjoined was an outstanding white Professor at the University of Chicago who involved himself in these proceedings and in many instances was one of the key advisors and directors. The questions that many Negro citizens living in Chicago have not been able to answer: is this white professor committed to Chicago and to better race relations among the people of the city? Is this professor really interested in first-class citizenship for all peoples? Does he believe in the rights of all the citizens of Chicago and the United States? What has he done to help our people to purchase homes, to buy land, and to build communities? What has he done or said to help protect congregations of Negro churches from being charged enormous amounts for the purchase of old buildings and then high interest rates that sometimes border on extortion? Where is this lover of freedom when innocent Negroes living in Chicago suffer because they do not have the advice that he seems to say he has?

What has the cost been to Chicago? It is said, it cost the City of Chicago upwards of three million dollars in the destruction of property, in overtime pay for police officers, and for the National Guard that came to guard the streets of the city. And, what has been gained? The slum clearance program adopted by the City Council still goes forward with as much emphasis as it did before the campaign of 1966 was launched. The program of building additional houses was not materially helped or advanced. And permanent employment as a result of this campaign must yet be determined. What did this campaign in Chicago achieve?

On the 26th of August there was a summit meeting called by the Conference On Religion and Race for the purpose of stopping the community marches by the Southern Christian Leadership Conference and others. On the same day there had been a discussion in the City Council on the Injunction that had been filed against the marchers by the City of Chicago. After three hours of debate the Council approved and sustained the Injunction by a vote of 45 to 1. The lone dissenter was Alderman Leon M. Despres of the Fifth Ward. In presenting the resolution favoring the Injunction, Alderman Thomas E. Keane of the Thirty-First Ward said: "It was prompted . . . by the tremendous, favorable reaction (to the Injunction) from citizens of all races, religion and ethnic groups. In forty years of public life," said Keane, he "could not recall a greater unanimity of expression in favor of an act taken by a mayor." The Chicago community of all races had sensed the danger and the detriment of these marches. They had discovered that the marchers were using Negroes to incite indignation in white communities for the purpose of forcing city officials to bow to the methods employed by the marchers. The so-called Agreement was reached by a few select people under the guidance of the Conference On Religion and Race. The Conference On Religion and Race does not, and has never, represented the masses of Negro people or the grass roots people in all of the religious denominations in this country. The decisions of the Conference were made by an exceedingly small segment of the three and a half million people who make up the City of Chicago: Among the religious leaders invited to the Conference, practically none of the bishops, presidents of national bodies, presiding elders, moderators, and pastors were included from the Negro community, and few Negroes were invited from Chicago, representing 943,000 Negro citizens. The goals and objectives had been endorsed by the vast majority of Chicago citizens through accepting the Fair Housing Act of 1963, but the City of Chicago did not approve the methods that had been employed through coercion, intimidation, which ended in violence and death. The Negro religious leaders were represented by Rev. Mr. Andrew Young of New Orleans, La., Rev. Jesse Jackson of Greenville, South Carolina, and some other out of town preachers. The Conference on August 26th represented both in its organization and its method of operation one of the greatest demonstrations of segregation and discrimination against any American community. Three and a half million citizens were bypassed while a small minority of Chicago people with visiting civil rights workers attempted to sanction a method of solving problems that the whole city of Chicago would have condemned and disapproved. In the name of acting in the interest of 943,000 Negroes, two or three Negroes were invited to this Conference, but some of the best legal minds, best sociologists, and more experienced business and religious leaders were not included. If Chicago is a city dedicated to the democratic method in solving its problems, then the so-called housing agreement of August 26, 1966 was one of the most tragic events in the history of the City of Chicago, and any city in the United States of America. When Mayor Daley said, "This is a great historic day in the City of Chicago . . . Chicago, as usual, is leading the way for all other cities," he represented the attitude of a tired, perplexed statesman who was doing his best to keep a great city united, and to keep the frustration from occasioning any further violence and death. But as a lawyer and a most successful mayor of a great city he knew that the method employed by the people who had almost forced this negotiation under an atmosphere of threats, of violence and under duress, was not the best for this city or any other city, for he had worked too hard in a series of conferences on civil rights problems trying to negotiate an understanding between all groups including the visiting civil rights leaders.

Bishop James W. Montgomery, co-adjutor of the Episcopal diocese in Chicago, and chairman of the Conference On Religion and Race, said: "I think this represents a great break-through in race relations. It will set a pattern for other cities." The bishop evidently was thinking of the agreement between the people assembled in the room and not about giving encouragement to the non-violent methods that had brought violence as a means of solving the problems of a community. Many Negro religious leaders in Chicago do not believe that Bishop Montgomery thought there were no Negro bishops, presiding elders, pastors,

and presidents of other denominations qualified to sit in such a
conference to discuss the welfare of Chicago. Mr. Ben W. Heineman who was the chairman of the Conference for that day, and
also the successful chairman of the White House Conference On
Civil Rights, June 1965, is a man of broad experience and a
great industrialist. He termed the agreement "a giant step forward in efforts to erase housing discrimination." Mr. Heineman
in this statement seems to restrict his evaluation to the understanding and the agreement of the small group assembled in
the conference room. Evidently he was not thinking of the
Chicago Fair Housing Act of 1963 which was a firm, bold,
courageous, and unqualified pronouncement against housing discrimination in any form.

   This summit conference was hailed as a great achievement
for the city of Chicago, and yet the City Council was not present. People who were present drew up agreements which
amounted to nothing more than intentions that they were going
to work on for the achievements of certain objectives and goals
that had already been set by the enlightened statesmen and
leaders of the City of Chicago. Nothing was done in that meeting to improve upon or to amend the Fair Housing Act passed
by the City Council in 1963. The agreement on the 26th of
August did nothing to transcend or even to match the law
passed. If the law meant nothing, a gentleman's agreement between groups in Chicago means less; and, if those officials who
were a part of the passage of the law of 1963 could not be
trusted to stand behind that law, what assurance have we that
the same officials will back up and stand behind a verbal or
written agreement? The leadership of the City Council cannot
be transferred from City Hall to private hotel rooms with their
powers divided and shared with voluntary community leaders,
some of whom are not voting citizens of the City of Chicago. If
our cities and our states and even our nation are all to remain
intact, they must remain communities of laws with citizens who

are committed to honor and respect these laws. This meeting on the 26th of August did nothing to change the attitude of any of the people in Chicago who have stood against peoples of all groups moving into all sections of the city. Those communities in which people marched for the purpose of granting the rights to others to occupy certain sections have not as yet yielded to the tramp, tramp, tramp of marching feet.

This campaign of non-violence helped to create tensions and, after these tensions, came violence. One newspaper said that the civil rights leaders who had come to Chicago for the summer's campaign had come to bring a revolution. As we look back over the months, we have discovered that no revolution has come to Chicago—increased bitterness, but not a revolution. There has been some divisions, some peoples have lost confidence in some leaders in Chicago, and the campaign of the summer of 1966 has not strengthened confidence on the part of local leaders and peoples in one another. In the city of Chicago, there is more bitterness now than before the campaign of '66. People who believe in race prejudice can be strengthened in their feeling of justification if they could see reasons to believe that the accusations they had heard were correct and that the charges were true. To resort to force of any kind, invites force of a similar kind. To seek to bring a city to its knees by non-violent methods which often turn to violence is an invitation for other peoples to use the means at their disposal to stay up from their knees and to bring their opponents to the same position that their opponents have tried to bring them.

We face a future in Chicago that is not and cannot be dependent upon those devisive forces that create tensions, suspicion, and ill will. People must come to feel more and more that the city belongs to all of the people, and the people have a right to decide who their leaders shall be. When a group of civil rights workers invade a town and seek to dictate to the City Council and to all the elected officials, they, by that act, seek to cut off the democratic process and to control the will of the voters by seeking to control those to whom the voters have entrusted the leadership of their city. It is dangerous in any country to develop a group of leaders who can come to power through threats and intimidations and hold their positions not based on the votes of the people of the community but based on fear and intimidation. Local committees must not be permitted to join hands with visiting diplomats to make policies and programs for city or state that are not submitted to the voters for their approval, for their scrutiny, their investigation, acceptance or rejection. People who march through cities, states, and the nation assuming such authority, working for communities and advancing policies without the approval of the community could become a dangerous fifth column that could usurp the rights of the local democratic community.

The unfinished task of civil rights in Chicago, as well as all other cities, must be faced and faced frankly. The enemies of democracy must be recognized and dealt with through the democratic process, and those who are un-American in their attitudes toward the Federal Constitution and toward the American philosophy of freedom must not be encouraged, condoned, or sanctioned. Those who are not for the American way of life are against it. Those who do not believe in the Federal Constitution are in opposition to it. Those who have elected to live in rebellion to truth prefer error and evil. And those who are too independent to be subject to the just laws of the land are too dangerous to be accepted as members of this body politic and as soldiers of freedom ready to live for the advancement of the country that they love and respect. The campaign in Chicago revealed a great lesson. It revealed that people cannot come into a community so well organized and disorganize it in two or three years. It revealed further that the masses of Negroes, though committed to freedom, civil rights, and first-class citizenship, will not be eternally deceived by those who preach love of race and yet seek to use Negroes to advance their selfish ends and to fill their coffers with coins to satisfy their lust for gain and their love of power. In the injunction [7] drawn against these campaigners in 1966, the city of Chicago did not consider them non-violent but considered them the agents of violence and messengers that had used scathing and inflammatory words to move people to anger and malcontent. But, to the eternal credit of the vast majority of the people, they did not believe these reports and were not misled by them.

One of the dangerous things in a campaign of this kind is the use of half truths and false statements veiled in an intention to win the rights of the people. A committee of us visited the community of Watts, California, in December, 1966. We had heard much of that slum community and were anxious to see it. We had a feeling of horror, dread and fear as the minister took us toward Watts. From what we had read and had heard, we were looking for dilapidated buildings, without paint, without any of the modern conveniences of city life. We expected to find the yards run down, the people living in filth, dejection, and disgrace. But, when we had gone through the community, we discovered it was a community of neat little bungalows, most of which were well painted, the yards well-kept, the streets were clean, the people were clean, orderly, and well-behaved, and then for two hours we observed the Watts parade. This, we thought, would demonstrate bitterness and hatred, but we saw young people—Negroes and whites—carrying the American flag, their bands playing patriotic hymns; they marched with order and dispatch, shoulders back, heads erect, looking like the free people which they were in love with the country of which they were a part. When we left the Watts community, we publicly apologized to the people and to the city for what we had thought of this community. We do not here assume to state why the riot had occurred. We do not here assume that a visit to a city would give one any insights into subtle and hidden prob-

[7] *Ibid.*, pp. 254–255.

lems. Our only statement here is that we had the wrong image and the wrong impression of the people and the community. The truth must be told regarding the growth and the potential and the well-being of our communities as well as the story of their plight and wretchedness. Americans must now become more brave and more courageous in their objection to the over-use of negatives and the under-use of positives. We must proclaim that which is right and through that commit ourselves to the good and destroy the wicked as well as the evil. Campaigns of non-violence that are easily converted into violence cannot be the answer for the vexing problems of human relations in any city in the United States of America.

I consider the flames of bitterness created in Chicago in the summer of 1966 the second great Chicago fire. The first fire, when it was said Mrs. O'Leary's cow kicked over the lantern that set Chicago afire in 1871, was not designed. It was an accident. But much of the city was destroyed. When people, by design and intention, light the fires of hatred and prejudice, as well as move people to throw molotov cocktails, this is an act of destruction by design, a campaign to burn up the values of culture and civilization. For what purpose? Not for the improvement of the city but for its destruction and its defeat. The cities and communities of our nation are too sacred to be used as tools of politics and as playthings of the whims and self-centered ambition of any leaders who love themselves more than their race, their communities, or their nation.

We must not forget those people and groups who have encouraged these campaigns by constantly denying and refusing to take part in building constructive community relationships according to the supreme law of the land. Citizens who insist on denying to other peoples their rights, do create a climate in which campaigns of bitterness can be carried on in the name of freedom, and saboteurs of the nation's life can dignify their cruel efforts of exploitation and destruction by aligning themselves with people who hunger for justice and thirst for freedom and security. People who oppose America's way of life, by that act, invite others to participate in the nation's life who are not committed to the nation as disciples of democracy or friends of truth and understanding. And those political leaders who will cater to groups who seek to defeat America are, themselves, helping to destroy that which they have pledged to save and are helping to tear down that which so many statesmen have suffered, sacrificed, and died to build. We have a great nation and a great opportunity. We have a great culture and a great possibility. We have a great legacy and a great heritage. We must be loyal to these or our present will be jeopardized and the future of our children will be destroyed. We call for unquestioned devotion and loyalty to the nation and to the nation's cause and, by so doing, there will dawn for the cities of America a new day of fellowship and for the nation a new light of freedom and new songs of hope and deliverance.

When one reads the list of demands posted on the door of the City Hall in Chicago one can draw one's own conclusion. These demands were made not only on Chicago and the mayor of the city but on the governor and the state of Illinois, on the banks, labor unions, industry, the Board of Education, the Housing Authority, and all the citizens of Chicago and the federal government also. If these demands had been met we would have had a revolution; for the federal government, local, state government, city government, labor, management, business, free enterprise, education, would have been in the hands of the leaders of the 1966 summer campaign, and they would have been in position to dictate to all groups in America what they should do and when. This is indeed a dictatorial approach to government and such would put an end to government of the people by the people and for the people.

When we compare the purposes, the announced strategy and review the list of demands posted on the door of City Hall on July 10, 1966, we are convinced that this campaign was a failure for several reasons. It did not and has not brought to Chicago the revolution that some of the leaders promised.[8] It was widely publicized in the daily press that they had come to Chicago for the above stated purpose. Furthermore, the campaigns were not non-violent. They were not non-violent in their operation because they were led by armed policemen with weapons which were the signs of possible violence and which carried with them the fear and the possibility of violence. Sometimes there were more policemen than there were marchers. In Section 22 of Chicago's Injunction against the marchers on page 8, the following figures were given to show how many police officers accompanied the marchers in the respective districts:

Gage Park	556	Jefferson Park	258	Belmont-Cregin	1926
Bogan	1732	Marquette Park	2564	Bridgeport	88

Non-violent action should not require that number of armed men if leaders are concerned with the atmosphere and the community relations which would negate violence. The City of Chicago did not consider the leaders of these marches to be non-violent. The leaders were given credit in the injunction against them for much of the disturbances and violence that erupted. Page 4, paragraph 9 of the Injunction says the following:

that one or more or all of the defendants and others were making statements issuing news releases, appearing on other communications media and publicly corresponding with public officials for the furtherance of their announced plan of "creative tension," major civil disturbances erupted in the aforesaid areas of the city resulting in damages in excess of several millions of dollars to private property, the death of 27 persons and injury to 374 persons including 61 police officers.

No one can conclude from these facts given by officials of the City of Chicago that these campaigns were non-violent. Instead

[8] *Chicago Daily News*, February 12, 1966.

of reducing crime these marches occasioned an increase in crime in the City of Chicago according to the Injunction, page 8, paragraph 24 which says the following:

The reduction of police protection in the areas of the city other than those where the demonstrations were taking place resulted in a substantial increase in the crime rate in these areas during the period of the demonstrations. The increase in the crime rate due to incidents directly connected to the demonstration in crimes against persons and property in the areas in which the demonstrations were being conducted is substantial.

The so-called non-violent campaign in Chicago did produce tensions, but these tensions failed to be "creative" of the constructive things for human society. They did not create better human relations, they did not create better race relations, they did not create a deeper sense of responsibility among all citizens for making the city greater and stronger. They did not create more confidence in elected officials of the city. They failed to change the housing pattern of Chicago and added nothing new to the existing intentions and plans of the city for slum clearance and fair housing. They failed to remove from office veteran political leaders, some of whom are Negroes.

It is most fortunate for Chicago and for the United States of America that the campaign of 1966 failed in Chicago. If it had succeeded, Chicago and every other Northern city as well as the nation itself would have been confronted with some serious obstacles and drawbacks. If this campaign had not failed, the leadership of this City would have shifted from the Mayor and the City Council to the hands of visiting diplomats who have not been selected or chosen by the vote of the citizens of this city. If this campaign had not failed, the voters of Chicago would have had, at least temporarily, their right to elect their own officials taken from them. If this campaign had not failed, the rule of law would have ended in this city and the headquarters would have been shifted from City Hall to private offices, hotel rooms, and streets or wherever the visiting diplomats elected to assemble. If this campaign had not failed, Chicago would have become the model by which further confusion and lawlessness would have spread to other cities North, East, and West, in the name of freedom and civil rights. If this campaign had not failed, anarchy would have become the watchword in our American cities, and this whole nation would have fallen prey to vicious and un-godly people who prey on the innocent while they bring shame, disgrace, and destruction upon the nation itself. If this campaign had succeeded, there would have been instituted in the cities of this nation a so-called supra-legal procedure by which individuals could take the property of another without due process and without contract, consent, credit, or cash.[9] When such things are done, any city or nation will be well on the way to a dictatorship under which no citizen is safe, no civil rights respected, and no property rights held intact.

Any citizen of Chicago who loves his community and loves and respects the use of the ballot and who has confidence in the Constitution of the United States of America will have no regrets in knowing that such a campaign had failed in a city of this magnitude and strength. With the failing of the campaign of 1966, civil rights groups must more and more wage the battles for freedom where they should be fought, on the legal soils of the nation and on the terrain of goodwill and the protective guidance of the Constitution of the United States and the courts of the land. It is too expensive in men and materials, in human relations and understanding, to carry forward such campaigns and such battles against the organized life of any American city.

One of the great problems facing America today is that of crime. It is the responsibility of all Americans to so deport them-

[9] Civil rights leaders took over trusteeship of six flat buildings at 1321 S. Homan Avenue, Chicago, without the consent of the building owner Mr. John Bender, 81 years of age. (See Chicago *Tribune*, February 24, 1966, Section 1, p. 3.)

selves that they will not in any wise contribute to crime. Citizens who seek to achieve the highest possible goals in life must do it in such a way that they do not become criminal or occasion crime. Men who advocate and practice segregation and discrimination are committing a form of lawbreaking, and hence a crime against the sacredness of other personalities and against the orderly procedure of a democratic society. It has been said by some, "a skid-row drunk lying in a gutter is crime . . . so is a strong-armed robbery by a fifteen year old boy . . . so is the possession of marihuana cigarettes by a student." [10]

It is the duty of all citizens to work for a more orderly and a more healthy society for the security of all; for if the city, the community, the state, and the nation are criminal in nature, the rights, the property, and the person of all citizens are in danger. The work of making a better society and of removing discrimination and intimidation must not be left to specialists. It is the responsibility of all.

Given enough time and money, specialists can do dramatic things. They can prolong human life. They can make deserts bloom. They can split the atom. They can put men on the moon. However, specialists alone cannot control crime. Crime is a social problem that is interwoven with almost every aspect of American life; controlling it involves changing the way schools are run and classes are taught, the way cities are planned and houses are built, the way business is managed and workers are hired. Crime is a kind of human behavior; controlling it means changing the minds and hearts of men.[11]

In the struggle for first class citizenship and for a free and democratic society in the United States of America, we need more than just laws, we need more than specialists in the many political and sociological fields, we need men and women dedicated to the task of changing the minds and hearts of men.

[10] *The Challenge of Crime In A Free Society* (Washington, 1967), p. 3.
[11] *Ibid.*, p. 288.

8

CONFUSIONISM AND CIVIL RIGHTS

THIS IS A DAY of many *isms.* which are spreading into all sections of the world. I have coined the term *confusionism* not to be in style or to add another word to the chaotic and difficult pattern of modern thought but only because I could not find a term that seemed to define the experiences or the techniques as well as the emphasis of the dogmas and philosophy that are abroad in the world in general and in the United States in particular. The students of the English language will pardon these liberties, but these are liberties that have grown out of a sense of urgency and a sense of necessity to bring into focus some of the problems that confront us in our attempt to arrive at a solution for some of the difficulties that face us in our political and social struggle. These experiences today seem so unique and peculiar that I felt one would be justified in coining a word that would cover the issues and the subjects that we are desirous of discussing. *Confusionism* may be defined as the act of creating tensions, stirring up anger, bitterness and animosities out of which one hopes may come constructive solutions to the evils of present day society. A confusionist believes that lawlessness can be substituted for law and thereby bring to pass an ordered society. *Confusionism* seeks to affirm by denial, to build by tearing down. It teaches that by the disobedience to accepted laws one can build the same type of society that we once believed could come by obeying the tested laws of society. Here one would substitute dis-value for value, error for truth and hatred for love.

In our civil rights struggle many devout workers who say they are committed to the ideals and principles of first-class citizenship are finding themselves adopting the same techniques that have been followed across the years by segregationists who have denied first-class citizenship to others. Historically segregationists have denied the validity of sections of the Federal Constitution that affirm and advocate freedom to all citizens. It is strange that there are persons in the civil rights field today who say they are committed to the task of destroying segregation and yet they are adopting the same attitude and same methods that have been so long followed by those who have sought to defend the cause of segregation. Those who defend freedom are not on safe grounds unless they defend it according to the supreme law of the land and not in the context of lawless society. How confusing it is for the apostles of freedom to adopt the same methods that have been so long used by the enemies of freedom. If this method continues, all of the gains that have been made for freedom through law and through the courts of the land could be easily wiped out. These individuals have believed they could substitute their ideas and their conceptions of life for the laws and the principles of the United States of America. They have no compunction of conscience nor any sense of guilt and would never consider themselves as lawbreakers or as enemies to the American way of life. For more than a hundred years this practice has gone on and has occasioned the chaos that has come in the wake of the thrust for unqualified freedom. No student of law, no leader in the field of religion, can defend this desecration and misuse of the Constitution of the United States of America.

There are those who have resorted to tensions for the purpose of building a democratic society where men live together in a fellowship of understanding. It is impossible to have a government of the people, by the people and for the people based on force and tension. A democratic society is based on choice, understanding, and goodwill. It is impossible to build this kind

of society through tension and yet, tensions have been employed
as the sure method of winning all the rights as members in our
American Society.

The theme of civil rights is freedom. It is the goal and the
object of our striving, but methods have been employed by
which some of the basic freedoms in America have been denied
to others as the quest for fuller freedoms goes on. Some have
been denied the freedom of speech. They must not speak in the
defense of the American Constitution and the American methods of solving the problems that plague a democratic society.
There has been an effort on the part of some to adopt for us in
this country, a monolithic type of thinking and acting. At times
more emphases have been put on direct actions than have been
put on the goals of direct action, which should be freedom,
first-class citizenship and a society of law and order.

One of the other basic freedoms in America is the freedom
of religion. People may worship God according to the dictates of
their conscience. The Constitution of this great republic makes
no attempt to regulate or to define religious worship for any
person or groups; all are left free to make their own decisions
so long as the decisions made do not in any wise take from
another his right to agree or to disagree. Within the last twelve
years there have been civil rights workers who have carried their
campaign of intimidation against leaders of religion and the
church and even church worship. To disagree at any point was
to be put in the category with segregationists and those who
oppose the cause of freedom. Churches at their eleven o'clock
worship hours have been picketed by many persons in the
name of civil rights. Negroes have joined with strange and
bearded white people marching in front of the doors of churches
interfering with the worshipers as they came to worship. This
was done, not because the people assembled inside of these
houses of worship were segregationists or were defending segregation, it was done because some person in that church still
advocated law and order, the courts of the land as the American

method of solving the problem of civil rights. These leaders of picket lines were not interested in the success of the worship service, they were not interested in a better standard of life as proclaimed in the theology and teachings of that church. They were interested in only one thing, compelling the leaders and members of that parish to do and say what the civil rights leaders had ordered and demanded to be done.

Patriotism, or the love of country, frequently is opposed and considered out of step with the times. Often people who preach the gospel of love of country are considered to be "Uncle Toms." The popular speech frequently is the anti-American speech that seeks to discredit, and in some cases, to denounce all of those institutions and organizations that have been counted sacred and dear in American thought and philosophy. Many of our centers of learning have been turned into centers of confusion where the standards of behavior have been lower than the standards of the uninformed, the ignorant, and the uncouth. Any intelligent student knows that scholarship is not produced through the yelling of rowdy mobs and refinement is not the product of uncouth and immoral thinking and acting, and yet scores and scores of our universities have become the scene of brutal and un-Godly behavior requiring the presence and efforts of police officials to bring order and a degree of sanity. Academic refinement, culture and enlightenment are sacrificed in the name of so-called freedom and civil rights, but in reality these are false freedoms and pseudo-civil rights. It is in reality the turning back of the dial of time and a reverting to a primitive type of behavior dominated and inspired by tense emotion, blind passions, and godless prejudices.

In this particular, we do not deny the constitutional right of protest, we have affirmed that right in Chapter II and have, in a way, assumed that right in all of our discussions. We know that the evils of our society must not be condoned or justified. We do know, also, that it is the democratic right of all Americans to throw the weight of their influence and the weight of their thinking against all elements that would negate our freedom and encroach upon the sacred rights offered by the Federal Constitution. But what we point out in these techniques and behavior patterns of *confusionism* is the negation and, in some cases, a direct assault against the very values that we wish to preserve and the very ideals that we seek to enhance and develop.

Confusionism, then, leaves us with no established standard that we must follow, no values that we are duty bound to respect, and no institutions to which we are indebted and to which we owe our unqualified allegiance. Every person is allowed to do that which is right in his own eyesight and to make his conscience the sole guide of what is right, just and true. Here the past is robbed of all of its precious values and the hope of the future rests on the narrow island of our little selves. Human life becomes poorer and is weakened because it is forced to live not on the bread of the present alone but on the husk and chaff of surface things that have no abiding value for the mental and moral life of modern man.

It may be that the most damaging and the most serious aspect of the practice of *confusionism* is the philosophy or the ideology that supports it. Here we come face to face with an eclecticism that breaks the known canons of reason, violates every law of human logic, and sins against the human desire for harmony and understanding. An attempt is made to bring together divergent contrasted and conflicting philosophies of life and weld them into one dominating and compelling philosophy. This is the core of *confusionism,* and it is designed to mis-direct, to mislead, and finally to confuse. Let us note some of the elements of this philosophy. It is made from elements of Hinduism, Henry David Thoreau's view of life without the need of government, a bit of the materialistic philosophy that comes from the brain of Karl Marx. These are combined with the Eighth Century Hebrew prophets and Jesus of Nazareth. When these elements are brought together in an assumed whole, we get the doctrine or the philosophy of non-violent civil disobedience. Here are the personalities of Mahatma Gandhi of India, Henry David Thoreau of New England, Karl Marx with his assumed devotion to the poor, but without the principles and passion of Christian love. Into this group an attempt has been made to bring in the prophets' quest for social justice and the Jesus-idea of the Kingdom of God motivated by love and unselfish devotion to all men.

As we have stated in another chapter, Henry David Thoreau wrote without the experience or the blessings of living in an America with an Emancipation Proclamation that had nullified the institution of chattel slavery that he so much hated; and he finished his work before the evolutionary process in America's legal system put into the Constitution the 13th, 14th and 15th Amendments. And when he spoke against all forms of government, he did not take into consideration the new America without slavery and with an amended Constitution that grants, at least in theory, all men the full right to the ballot and equal share in all of the cultural good of the United States of America. Mahatma Gandhi, the great Hindu saint, is worthy of commendation and praise, but his doctrine of civil disobedience was taken, basically, from Henry David Thoreau of the United States of America, and it was apropos for Gandhi because the supreme law of India was not the Constitution made by Indians of Indians for Indians. It was rather British rule of the British, by the British and for British and finally, Indians. Mahatma Gandhi then needed to do all in his power to break the spell of the imperial power of Great Britain, but he himself admitted that non-violence as a political weapon had failed to unite Hindus and Moslems and had left the soils of India, through riots, stained with the blood of both.[1] Karl Marx gave an economic interpretation of man and his destiny. None of us will deny the importance of economics in human life. Man needs employment, good and fair housing and all the virtues and values that accrue

[1] Chapter IV., p. 87–98.

from a just economic system, but we are not ready to conclude with Karl Marx that any man or any government can live by bread alone and can be comforted by the shelter of houses, be they wood or stone and that if these fail, the whole human spirit will be destroyed. The Eighth Century Hebrew prophets are in strict and stern opposition to the world view of Hinduism and to the godless materialism of Karl Marx and to the anti-government philosophy of Henry David Thoreau. The social justice proclaimed by the prophets referred to above, grew out of and found their basis in faith in an ever-living God. There cannot, therefore, be a working relationship between the religious philosophy of our prophets here under consideration and the world view of any of the other personalities that we have discussed in the system before us now.

Jesus of Nazareth has also been considered as a part of this philosophy that has been made by this eclecticism to which we have referred. He taught a strange doctrine, one that does not allow his followers to fight their own battles, even against known enemies. He did not encourage his followers to use prayer [2] as one of the pressure techniques to compel their enemies to change or subdue those who sought to defeat and to destroy them. His ethical standards were far higher and far richer than the ethical standards that advocate only non-violence. For Him the absence of violence was not a virtue and the refusal to strike with the sword was no indication that in this refusal one demonstrated that one possessed the redemptive power and influence that Jesus proclaimed as the essential equipment for those believers who would help to bring his kingdom to pass. His concept of love was not a love which punished, antagonized, and forced his enemies until they changed their minds and decided to do right. The Jesus concept of love was not the kind that

[2] "And when thou prayest, thou shalt not be as the hypocrites are: for they love to pray standing in the synagogues and in the corners of the streets, that they may be seen of men. Verily I say unto you, They have their reward." (Matthew 6:5).

would block traffic, crowd neighborhoods and sit on the door-steps of oppressors until they willed to end their days of oppression. The love that He demonstrated was the kind that lifted the spirit above and beyond the puny things that enemies would attempt to do. He chose death rather than surrender his right to live sacrificially for the inspiration and the redemption of all mankind. The love that Jesus knows and demonstrates became the theme of Paul's psalm of love in First Corinthians, Chapter 13.

Among the many things that were said in First Corinthians, Chapter 13, "Love suffereth long and is kind," that is, the constructive and creative elements of love can be trusted to purify the soul of the possessor and to have the most creative effect on those who have no merit by conduct or no peculiar value by disposition. The patience of love is clearly known by the disposition of those who embrace it. After suffering long, it is still kind. This does not mean that it ever condones wrong. It means it is never influenced, controlled, or managed by the wrong amidst all the variables that are thrown against any life by those who commit the wrong; love maintains a constant that reflects itself in kindness. "Love seeketh not her own." This is difficult and almost impossible to imagine and unthinkable as a procedural method in a complicated and evil society. This quality of love, being redemptive in nature with a goal which inquest of that which is without merit and lives below the level of dignity and honor, seeks to save whatever lingering spark of life that remains.

I do not advocate or teach that persons who are not followers of Jesus Christ should seek their civil rights. I do not teach here that a non-Christian civil rights movement is illegal or immoral; neither do I sit in judgment on dedicated, patriotic lovers of their race who have embraced the cause of justice and freedom and have not accepted the way of Christ. They are loyal Americans and have their right to choose the way in which they will walk towards the goals of first-class citizenship, but I have made the statement regarding the meaning of the principles of Jesus so that we will clearly understand and know that He cannot be combined in a system of philosophy that is either anti-God, godless or materialistic. The philosophy that supports the views advocated by confusionists is not sound, it is not realistic, and it does not represent in truth all the ideals presented in theory.

Some have asked the question repeatedly: "Are there Communists in those movements that result in race riots, bloodshed and the burning of cities?" We need not ask that question. If confusionism continues, every other destructive *ism* could be put aside for *confusionism* is as deadly or more deadly to the American way of life than all the other *isms* put together and if *confusionism* is allowed to continue, America is headed for a grim and dreadful day that will not only terminate in divisions but in the utter defeat of a way of justice, freedom, and fellowship.

Confusionism has the power to wreck and ruin the American ship of state. How serious and how grim this must be! For the threatening danger comes not from without, but from within. The ship is not threatened by dangerous torpedoes from the depths but by destructive bombs from within. Know we not that the future of every American, the security of every element of American culture, and the destiny of all the people are bound up with the destiny of the Ship of State? If the ship goes down, the passengers and the crew shall be utterly destroyed. *Confusionism* in the name of non-violence has led to a type of brinkmanship that has not only carried the cause of civil rights very close to civil strife and bitterness but has unfortunately linked it to riots and bloodshed. The struggle for civil rights is a noble struggle and such a struggle should never have been associated in any form with race riots and bloodshed. These negatives have come to pass because in the name of non-violence steps have been taken that led to violence; an atmosphere has been created out of which violence logically comes.

The picture is clear before us. Our objectives can now be defined. It is not to discontinue the struggle for civil rights or to delay in any way the journey towards first-class citizenship, but the immediate and urgent task is to seek to untangle the confused pattern involved in method and arrive at a sane and constructive approach to freedom, and all the blessings of American society and culture. We need not discredit any of the elements or independent strains of thought. They must be put in their historic perspective and related to the values and ideas for which they stand. People who believe in the United States of America may cling to American ideals, American principles, and American methods of correcting the evils of society. Those who accept the Christian ideals as the moral and spiritual guides for life need not seek to bind Hinduism to Christian philosophy or to restrict the message of Jesus to the economic and political insight of worldly-minded statesmen. Just let Him stand against the background and the judgment of history, and leave Him to speak His own message and to offer His security to life and society as we struggle to solve the problems that confront us. We must not desecrate the message of Jesus and use His name, His church, or His gospel to deceive innocent believers or to dignify a rough, cruel and sometimes, godless approach to the problems of life. Given the Constitution as the supreme guide in America's struggle for freedom and self-realization and given Jesus Christ as the moral and spiritual influence for lost men, we can overcome the dogma of *confusionism* and go on with the job of building a great democratic state with less bitterness, less confusion and less hatred. It is not too late to lead Americans back to the American way of solving American problems and realizing American dreams in the light of the dynamism of the American philosophy of life and freedom and the Christian concept of love and brotherhood. We must gather up all the fragments of the good so that nothing will be lost and commit ourselves to the task of completing a great democratic state in which all shall be free. Many Negro leaders are still concerned about the victory of the civil rights struggle in the United States of America for they believe it is a definite part of the nation's struggle for fulfillment. Therefore, they are concerned about using those methods that are in harmony with the ideals and principles of the Federal Constitution and about pursuing the goals of first class citizenship according to the directives of the Christian religion.

On November 3, 1966 about three hundred Negro religious leaders from across the nation met in Chicago in a Summit Conference On Civil Rights. They represented bishops, presidents of national bodies, presiding elders, moderators, pastors, and some say leaders from all of the major Negro denominations. They expressed a willingness to cooperate with other groups in the battle for civil rights and the determination to take part in any ecumenical movements that would tend to strengthen and unify their Christian witness, but they were firm in their dedication to law and order as a means of achieving the civil rights goals and commitment to the spirit and principles of Jesus Christ as a means of making the witness of the church more effective. They said if the civil rights struggle is to succeed in the future the following things must be done:

It must be more and more emphasized and conducted as a national cause and not as a Negro cause. For the cause of justice and freedom is the nation's cause. To this end was it created, and to this purpose it is committed.

Only those methods to achieve these rights should be employed that can be sustained and supported by the letter and spirit of the Federal Constitution.

The primary objective of the civil rights struggle is to help make the nation what it ought to be by putting into practice all of its theories of freedom.

Disrespect for law and order, which is sure to lead to lawlessness, confusion, and chaos, must be discouraged by all.

In our determination to improve the lot of all Americans we must at all times guard against those attitudes, tendencies, and overt acts that are sure to destroy our cities and our nation. For it is better to preserve the good things that the nation has accumulated and achieved with patience than in a fit of impatience destroy the good because of the presence of some of the evils that we hate and oppose.

All groups must work together as a unit for the realization of all the high goals of freedom. The North must not be against the South, management against labor, rich against poor, and Negroes against whites. We must discourage every approach in the struggle for freedom that plays one group against another. White Citizens' Councils must become councils of citizens interested in the advancement of their nation and its ideals.

This is a call for correction of the errors of the past and for the concentration on the issues involved. It is also a warning that religious leaders will not be caught in the web of confusionism but will work both as American citizens and as messengers of the gospel of Christ.

Many religious leaders who have gone into the civil rights struggle have deserted the constructive use of the gospel of Jesus Christ. The gospel of Christ in the broadest possible sense is the strongest tool that the Christian leader has for the transformation of society and this transformation is to be brought about not by pressure, not by force, but by persuasion. Are we ready to admit that Christian persuasion must be forsaken and Christian leaders joined with the ranks of those who believe not in persuasion but in force? If the church is to be creatively involved in civil rights or any other struggle it must do so by bringing with it its nature, its message, and its method. It is the right of any Christian citizen to join pressure groups, but it is not the method of the church to pressure people into righteousness, they must be won through persuasion. In confusionism too many ministers are sacrificing the way of the cross to the wish of the crowd. In the language of the historic statement of the Oxford Conference on Christian Life and Work in 1937, "Let the church be the church." Let it be involved in the complete struggle of mankind on all fronts, but let it bring with it its redemptive influence, its commitment, its love, in such a way that it cannot be confused with externalism, with showmanship, and with those methods that will reduce the church to a pressure organization. The church cannot atone for its failure to attract by attacking the leaders in society who are not committed to justice and truth, and it cannot cover up its inability to win people through precept and example by protesting the current sins of the guilty.

9

FROM PROTEST TO PRODUCTION

PROTEST, AS HAS been stated in Chapter II, has its place in our racial struggle. Protest is a vocal and dramatic expression of resentment, and it is a reaction against all forms of segregation and discrimination. Protest is an attempt to impress, to convince, and to persuade the segregationist and all who practice discrimination of the tragic and ill-effects of the sins of exploitation and discrimination against any personality. Protest also reveals how cruel and damnable it is to take from any people their God-given rights and to snatch from them the equality of opportunity to earn a decent living and to make a good life in every area of human existence. Ideally, protest aims at showing to our social order that sins against any segment of human society damages and endangers the whole of it. Protest reveals in practice what is clearly known in theory: that the oppression of the many by the few will soon place upon the spirits of the few the same type of malcontent and will ultimately involve the rich in the same type of insecurities with which the poor have been plagued and doomed. Protest has its place in the economic, political, and social struggle of mankind, and by it much good has been achieved. At its best it has been one of the means of opening the doors of opportunity and granting to peoples once ostracized the right to participate in a larger share of the nation's life. But protest is not enough. We must go from protest to production.

Opening doors of opportunity is very important and redound to the credit of those who had the power and the will to open them. But open doors have little significance unless the individuals in question will go in, seize the opportunities, and make full use of the new ministries and new tasks assigned to them in this new theater of life. In production we harness our gifts and marshall them in an army of creators and seek to produce new commodities. Protest places the blame on others who are guilty of the crimes of exploitation and oppression. Production begins with the act of blaming ourselves for what we have not done and then commanding ourselves to invest what we have in order to help produce the things we need and the things that will enrich our community and our nation. Protest is a reaction against one's environment with a demand for an adjustment in relationships between the individual and his environment, but production is constructive and creative action on one's environment in such a way that the environment will yield some of the goods and values requested. Here is cooperation with and scientific use of the existing forces and laws of the environment. The producer does not approach his environment as a static entity of life, but as a fluid, productive, and life-giving agent. The producer becomes a co-laborer with the laws of life and the evolutionary forces of growth and development. Production is a more difficult task than protest. It involves more risks and more initiative; it entails greater responsibilities and hard work. Production demands of a people a higher and more creative use of their brains and renders them builders and not beggars, sellers as well as buyers, investors as well as consumers. Our strategy in this phase of the struggle must not be based on the assumption that the relationship of manager and laborer, owner and user of capital, will or should always characterize the relationship between white Americans and Negro Americans. Negro leaders who shape their philosophy, theory, and practice as if the end of the economic struggle of the race had been attained when they win the right to be hired in a factory owned by another, disregard the higher powers of their people and can be regarded as traitors to the highest potential of their own race.

While we know employment is an economic necessity, earning and spending do not exhaust the powers of a people to create, produce, and own for themselves. It is a much higher step to own the title to, than to be entitled to use, the available commodities or the goods. The Negro must not shrink from the task of organizing capital, harnessing his earnings, and setting them to work in order to produce more and to develop more economic power and more independence. What has been done in this field, and what is being done, must be greatly strengthened and increased. There are some public relations people who approach white business firms for ads in their publications and they give a strong argument of the importance of the Negro market. One firm pointed out a few months ago that the Negro market in a certain setting amounted to twenty-seven billion dollars. There are some white firms who are kind enough to read or listen to such advertisements and then spend a modest amount in ads with the firms in question. But the joke is not on the white business man. It is on the Negro who has found such great market and such economic potential and has made such little effort to help other Negro businessmen to harness the same. There is no law against Negroes capturing the available markets in any section of the United States of America. We must do more than sell that market to those whose genius can turn it into liquid wealth and organize it into strong and stabilized economic power. We must remember that no people has ever been given its full independence simply on petition, no race has come to its deserved heights of equality by resolutions adopted by powerful assemblies, and no people has ever been fully emancipated by the mere writing of new laws or the amendments of old ones. Neither has any struggling people been moved to the unquestioned heights of freedom by the verdicts of courts or the ruling of judges however lofty and far-reaching the verdicts might be. Free men are not really free until they learn to exercise their newly acquired opportunities to gain for themselves the economic, intellectual, political, moral, and spiritual independence and self-reliance. Hands freed of manacles and limbs liberated from chains will atrophy and grow weaker still unless employed immediately and constantly in the pursuit of larger freedoms. Free men who beg will become beggars. It is the democratic right of any people to demand and to strike for higher wages and better living conditions. It is also their privilege in a free society to organize capital and help to lift the level of production and to increase the output and flow of commodities and thus increase the basis for more employment and the accumulation of more wealth.

This implies increased knowledge both of the tools of production and of the raw materials out of which the ready product is to be made. In this scientific age Negro leaders must more and more advocate and inspire young people to become as efficient as possible in the understanding, the making, and the art of using the tools of production. In this scientific age our manner of life is far from static; the place we win now through protest may not be sufficient in the future unless our talents continue to grow and expand. Any people aspiring for equality of opportunity must commit themselves to those disciplines which will eventually lead to equality in the power to produce and to control not only the tools of production but the raw materials as well. Negro boys and girls must be afflicted with the passion to learn and to know as much as any other student and must be challenged with the task of becoming a producer as well as the users of goods and commodities. From the past history of the Negro in the United States of America, some of those who have made the greatest contributions have been those who have had something to sell and hence have not spent all of their time looking for something to buy. In the field of business we must also accept the call and the demands for equality. We can ill afford two standards in business: one for Negroes and another for white. The community must and will demand equality in the status and soundness of the goods from a Negro businessman as well as from any other man.

There is the need for and the demand for as high a type of

character in one group of leaders as we would expect in another. There is no race that is good by nature, no people who has any exclusive right in the development of character. This field belongs to any group who will pursue it. In spite of the handicaps of the past Negroes have demonstrated that they can produce men and women of character whose moral refinement is above reproach and whose integrity and honesty leaves nothing to be desired. Many of the leaders of the last generation as well as many in the present generation trace their sense of duty, their vision of the right, and their commitment to truth to the training received in some humble home by committed and dedicated parents. The emphasis on character education must not be reduced but increased. It is not enough to know the language of culture and the philosophy and teachings of good men, but young people must be taught to have strong characters, integrated personalities, and be persons committed to ideals and to lofty dreams. As new opportunities are made available and as more and more of our people are elevated to positions of honor and leadership, they must be sound thinkers and men and women of honesty and integrity.

For the last twelve years our voices have been lifted high in the defense of justice, honesty, and fair play. In some cases we have made known the fact that because of the light of our individual consciences we in our moral commitment have been lifted above some of the unjust laws of the land, and large groups have been organized to protest these laws in the name of conscience and of a devotion to a higher law, the moral law. This has put upon Negroes, leaders as well as followers, new demands for displaying within their own person and within their groups the highest possible type of character. The public will demand this of all of us, and we can no longer take refuge in the fact that any drastic judgment that is passed on conduct is a matter of race. If we think or know this, how careful then must we be in our deportment as citizens and as leaders in a great democratic society.

We also have the responsibility of helping to build a better social climate in which it is easier to win not only civil rights, but human rights. There must be a new social order and all American citizens must help to build it. White America and Negro America must be united in the task of building a just society in which free men will not be afraid to practice and to give freedom to others. A morally bankrupt society cannot sufficiently nurture and render secure growing human beings who seek to become the highest and the best within their communities.

A free democratic society is a society of goodwill. It cannot be built on envy or strife, or seasoned and saved by ill will. Goodwill is most essential. In the immediate future Negro leaders must take it upon themselves to help build in the United States of America a greater degree of fellowship, understanding and goodwill among all races and groups. Here the more mature leadership among us must be courageous enough and brave enough to help at this crucial point. It is impossible for white Americans alone to reduce the present tensions in this country. There must be a working together without compromise on the basis of justice and freedom to help clear the air of bitterness and suspicion. Any leaders in any group among Negroes or whites who overlook this need for goodwill will do untold injury to the cause of civil rights and the future growth of the American way of life. Much of the progress made in the struggle for civil rights was due to a reservoir of goodwill. Over a period of years there had been accumulated in the American bank of public opinion an enormous amount of goodwill, and Negroes have done their share in helping to build this accumulated wealth. For a hundred years the voices of the oppressed have been heard, the sorrows of the afflicted have been noted, and the broken bodies of the disadvantaged have been seen and recognized. Many peoples have read the stories of atrocities and racial indignities, have been aroused and have felt they had no weapon with which to fight the ancient tradition of segregation and discrimination. Many white Americans knew how dangerous it would be for them to take an open stand for the equality of opportunity for all peoples, including men and women of color. Many of these statesmen and political leaders knew that the doctrine of "separate but equal" as advanced by the Supreme Court of 1896 was in reality an act that legalized racial segregation and discrimination in certain sections of the United States. They knew that the doctrine of "separate but equal" was a doctrine that was self-nullifying and self-defeating. For if it were equal it need not be separate, and if it were separate, the danger was it would not become equal. There were many Christians North and South who sought a way out and prayed to God to remove the evil from among us that had so bitterly divided the United States into two camps that seemed irreconcilable. There was persistent testimony from both races for the good. The determination and the commitment of thousands of men and women of color to the ideals of the nation in spite of the handicaps inflicted upon them had made a profound and tremendous impression on the hearts of individual citizens and had touched the soul of the nation. And year after year for a hundred years, white America passed through this experience and this searching of heart.

On May 17, 1954, there was a great break-through. The wit and legal wisdom of some of the best lawyers in the United States met, debated, analyzed, and discussed the problem, and nine supreme court judges pondered the issue and weighed with care every bit of evidence and came forth with a decision that made the doctrine of "separate but equal" ancient history and a lifeless tradition of the distant and dead past. Many rejoiced, because at long last, truth had obtained hearing, and America was moving forward towards her desired goal; three years later the United States Congress passed the first piece of civil rights legislation in eighty-three years. These victorious efforts in Congress for civil rights measures continued until 1966, when the first civil rights bill suffered defeat in Congress since 1954.

The reaction against segregation became most intense, most forceful, and more frequent after the decision of 1954. The voice of protest was heard everywhere. Young and old took part in direct actions and in demonstrations. Many of these demonstrations were successful, tolerated; and in some cases, encouraged and led by soldiers of the United States army and by uniformed police officers. Radios had heralded far and wide the militant cries of civil rights advocates. Television cameras had flung to the world the horror scenes of conflicts, and bitterness deepened and increased. In the year of 1966 America witnessed the first organized invasion of a northern city by a southern-based civil rights organization. They came to wage a battle against what they called northern type of segregation and discrimination. They came to a city with a long tradition of assured opportunities for Negroes in many fields. They came to a city where there was Negro and white leadership involved in practically every field of culture and human relations. For the first time since the days of Reconstruction, organized campaigns had been launched in the North with the purpose of condemning the North and putting it on par with the past failures of the South. In this act the Mason and Dixon line faded, and many northern white Americans who sympathized with the civil rights campaign in the South were embittered, and in some cases stunned and horrified. As they moved from community to community, the marchers received more than adequate police protection, and in some cases it seemed that many in the city did their best for the peace and protection of the marchers as they paraded. In this act the sympathies of many white people of the North were withdrawn from Negroes in their struggle and given to white people of the South who had given their interpretation of the Negro problem and of the cause of civil rights, for some of the Negro leaders said that Chicago was worse than the South.

In the Chicago venture a pall of death settled over the type of protest marches that had been hailed before as vital forces by many; and many leaders without knowing it, wrote the last big check on the bank of public opinion and overdrew the accumulated account of goodwill that had been growing by investments, deposits, and by compounding interest. In the elections of November, 1966, much was said about the backlash that defeated some of the distinguished leaders in the civil rights cause. But more than backlash, it was an indication that the account of goodwill had been overdrawn. And when there was an effort to organize a demonstration to protect Representative A. Clayton Powell, to save his chairmanship of the Committee On Education and Labor (January 9-10, 1967) and then to preserve his seat in Congress that he had occupied for more than twenty years, the presence of demonstrators and the voice of protest lifted by them did nothing to save the seat of the Congressman. What the demonstrators did not realize was that the bank account of goodwill had been overdrawn and there was not sufficient funds to honor the voucher. No attempt is made at this point to sit in judgment in the case or to assess blame pro or con but simply to point out the absence of the kind of goodwill that has in the past shown a degree of tolerance in such a crisis.

With this picture before us the task of human relations in America cannot be carried further by threats, and any torn tissues of human relations cannot be mended by any forms of bitterness or repeated acts of intimidations. There must now be a change in strategy, a change in emphasis, and a change in spirit in order to build again the quality of goodwill without which this nation cannot survive as a great free republic and without which any future struggle for improved race relations in the United States will be tedious, to say the least, and maybe fruitless. The voices of more mature Negro leaders in every field in America must be lifted, and there must be launched in every community, town, city, and state, similar campaigns dedicated to the cause of the enrichment of the nation's life and the dramatization of the common brotherhood of all Americans under one flag and one Constitution, and a new drive for the respect for law and order and for a deeper commitment of all peoples to the American way of life. This crusade must be patriotic, for the love of country must be at the heart of it. It must be moral, for justice must regulate it and freedom must inspire it. It must be spiritual, for the divine worth of every human being must again be re-emphasized and men must be re-committed to the kingdom values proclaimed by Jesus of Nazareth, and those who love honor and integrity for themselves as well as their nation, must come to assume a cross that would lead them to suffer within themselves for the victory of principles that they love and have embraced. This type of commitment and living will not only inspire trust and confidence but will become redemptive, in the light of which racial prejudice shall be reduced and animosity of Negroes against whites shall be diminished.

I have long been convinced that protest is not enough; the struggle must move from protest to production. Excerpts from some of the statements and addresses delivered validate this point of view. In Chicago, Illinois, in 1962, addressing an annual session of the National Baptist Convention, U.S.A., Inc., more than 15,000 people heard the following statement:

The American Negro today faces the greatest crisis of his history since the days of reconstruction. And his future as a man and as an American citizen and as a citizen of the world depends on how well he faces the test of this hour and how constructively he uses the opportunities at hand.

With the progressive defeat of segregation in this country, not only are the walls of separation falling from around the Negro community, allowing them the opportunity for larger and unrestricted participation in the nation's life, but the primary force (namely segregation), which has pressed the Negro into a community has been greatly weakened and the Negro community is sure to fall apart or to disintegrate unless some positive force is found as a sure and unfailing bond of racial togetherness.

But because in the past our racial togetherness has been ascribed to segregation, many of us shy away from racial togetherness for fear of being accused of the practice of segregation, and those who would work for racial togetherness in the positive are frequently called uncle toms.

Some of our young people tend to look down upon and to discredit many of those achievements of the race that came (as they could only come in the past), in the pattern and framework of American racial segregation. Hence along with the curse of segregation they tend to discredit and in some cases actually spurn the achievement of their fathers. They would in the language of an old proverb, "throw out the baby with the bath." But if life is to continue and the evolution and progress of the race be maintained, we must learn to draw a line between the soiled waters of the past and the living and growing infant of the present. We must throw out the waters of segregation along with all other social and moral evils, but make sure we keep the baby in our hands, that is we must keep racial appreciation, racial aspirations and a firm patriotic spirit as we move out into a wider circle of participation in the nation's life.

The revolt of the young against their elders and present leaders is wholesome when that revolt is against the shortcomings, the imperfections and the failures of the older generation. But when such a revolt is due to the negative reactions of the young against the values of the past because those values are realized and achieved under the hated system of segregation, then they are associating value with disvalue, and are losing the former because of the latter. In this context the creative days of the past are cursed and the generation labors to destroy the righteous with the wicked, the good with the bad, and the savory with the sordid. While we appreciate all the fine things that this present student generation is doing for civil rights and for racial improvement, but if they be the first to possess a true love of liberty among their people, and must serve as both pioneer and producer, foundation and super structure, then I say the upward journey of racial development is much longer than we once expected, and the task more difficult than we had ever dreamed. For this generation then would be called upon to make brick without straw and to build a durable structure in the present for the present and the future without an adequate supply of material from the generation of the past.

We also face the further danger of mistaking means for ends, acquired opportunities for achieved objective realities. Any defeat of segregation by the forces of integration is at most the creation of another opportunity for further growth and development. If the opportunity is not used and the values at hand not invested then the potential fruits of the privileged will fade and die in the bud of promise, and the second state will be worse than the first.

The next forward step in racial development and progress will not be made by our white friends for their Negro neighbors, but will be made by Negroes for themselves. And this step depends not on what Negroes can force others to give or do for them, but what Negroes in the light of new opportunities will do for themselves and for the social order in which they live. We then must possess a new courage to face frankly the failures and shortcomings in our local community, and address ourselves with boldness to the correction of the same; for it takes far more courage to face the personal problems in our lives and those in our immediate families and communities, than it does to analyze the shortcomings of those who oppose our growth and development. We must go from protest to production.

My economic philosophy as it relates to our racial struggle has been stated more than once, so by this time many of you should be able to state it as clearly as I can. But because of the nature of our struggle, and because of different views regarding it, I think it wise to state again my economic philosophy with some further amplification.

Protest has its place in our racial struggle. It is a vocal and dramatic expression of our resentment and reaction against all forms of segregation and discrimination. Protest is an attempt to impress, convince and persuade the segregationist and all who practice discrimination with him of the tragic and ill-effects of the sins of exploitation and discrimination against any personality; and it also reveals how cruel and damnable it is to steal from any people their God-given rights and to snatch from them the equal opportunities to earn a decent living and to make a good life in every area of human existence. Protest ideally aims at showing to our social order that sin against any segment of human society damages and endangers the whole of it. Protest reveals in practice what it is clearly known in theory; that the oppression of the many by the few will soon place upon the spirits of the few the same type of mal-content, and will ultimately involve the rich in the same type of insecurity with which the poor have been damned and doomed.

Protest has its place in the economic, political and social struggle of mankind, and by it much good has been achieved. But I repeat, protest is not enough. We must go from protest to production. That is, we must seize every opportunity new and old in order to become creators as well as consumers of goods, we must become inventors as well as the users of the tools of production and also the investors of capital as well as the spenders of it. Our strategy in this struggle must not be based on an assumption that the relationship of manager and laborer, owner and user of capital, will or should always characterize the relationship between our white opponents and the Negro race. Any Negro leader who shapes his philosophy, his theory and his practice as if the end of our economic struggle has been attained when we win the right to be hired in a factory owned by another, is a traitor to the highest potentials of his race and a dangerous enemy to social progress, and a stumbling block to mankind. While we know employment is an economic necessity, earning and spending is not enough for a progressive people. After we have earned our money there is no economic necessity laid upon us to spend it all within twenty-four hours for things that are not economically essential or morally sound. It is not wise to talk big and to spend big and then to save and invest little. We must learn how to organize our capital, harness our earnings and set them to work for us so that we may produce more and finally develop independent factories and companies of our own. Remember my friends, that no people have ever been given their independence simply on petition, and no race has come to its deserved heights of equality by resolutions adopted by powerful assemblies, and no people have ever been fully emancipated by the mere writing of new laws or the amendments of old ones. Neither have any struggling people been moved to the unquestioned heights of freedom by the verdicts of courts or the rulings of judges however lofty and far-reaching the verdicts might be. Freed men are not really free until they learn to exercise their new acquired opportunities to gain for themselves the economic, intellectual, political, moral and spiritual independence and self-reliance. For hands freed of manacles, and feet liberated from chains will atrophy and will grow weaker still unless employed immediately and constantly in the pursuit of freedom and in the task of human betterment, moral and spiritual uplift. Freed men who beg will become beggars, and the liberated who seek to ride another's train without paying the just fare will become hobos and tramps. For hobos and tramps seek more for themselves than they are willing to pay for, and ask for more than they hope to give in return. They would gather where they have not strewn, reap where they have not sown, and borrow with no intention of ever paying it back. Some persons fitting this description may have college and university degrees. They may dress in Hickey-Freeman suits, wear fifty dollar hats and drive cadillac cars too big for the land they own, and too long for their short pocketbooks, and occupy high offices in school, church and state. But they are as truly hobos and tramps as are the ragged, unkempt and hungry beggar who has just arrived in the city on the last freight train.

Direct action has been the theme and the technique of many modern civil rights organizations. Under this caption many and varied methods have been employed, including boycotts, pickets, sit-ins and many other forms of demonstrations. I have also repeatedly advocated direct action, but with a different emphasis; the emphasis should be positive as well as negative and should, by all means, be productive and not destructive, creative and not only consuming. On this matter the following statement was made in Cobo Hall Arena (September, 1964) in Detroit, Michigan, at an annual meeting of the Convention before fifteen thousand people:

We have heard much in recent months about direct action in terms of boycotts, pickets, sit-ins, and demonstrations of various kinds. In each case the purpose as stated is a lofty one; namely, the winning of civil rights and the achievement of the equality of opportunity. I repeat, these are worthy ends and desirable goals, but this kind of direct action is orientated against others, and for the most part, must be classified in the negative since they have been designed to stop, arrest, or hinder certain orderly procedures in the interest of civil rights. In some cases however, these actions have been against practices and laws considered to be both evil and unjust.

Today, I call for another type of direct action; that is, direct action in the positive which is orientated towards the Negro's ability, talent, genius, and capacity. Let us take our economic resources however insignificant and small, and organize and harness them, not to stop the economic growth of others, but to develop our own and to help our own community. If our patronage, withdrawn from any store or business enterprise will weaken said enterprise, why not organize these resources and channel them into producing enterprises that we ourselves can direct and control. In the act of boycotting, our best economic talents are not called into play, and we ourselves are less productive and seek to render others the same. Why not build for ourselves instead of boycotting what others have produced? We must not be guilty of possessing the minds and actions of a blind Sampson who pulled a massive building down upon himself as well as his enemies and died with them in a final act of revenge. No act of revenge will lift a race from thralldom, and any direct actions that reduce the economic strength and life of the community is sure to punish the poor as well as the rich. Direct actions that encourage and create more tensions, ill will, hostility, and hate, will tend to make more difficult the mental, moral, and spiritual changes essential to new growth and creativity in human relations. Remember that when we seek to change certain acquired notions and habits of men we are seeking to change that which is very vital in human nature. When we labor to change segregationists and racists who believe they are right, we are facing the task of re-conditioning human emotions and building within new patterns of thought, and changing human nature itself. In addition to that type of direct action which is negative and aimed at the correction of others, we need the type of direct action also that starts with ourselves which tends to produce a higher type of life within us as well as within others, and which aims to build a better community in which the available moral forces may be used to create new attitudes and new dispositions where human beings will regard others as they regard themselves. Why should we expect direct actions against others to bear immediate fruit, and then procrastinate and postpone the direct actions that will make us better business men, better statesmen, better thinkers, and better men and women with better homes and better fellowship NOW? Now must not only be applied to the needs for changes and attitudes of segregationists, it must also be applied to us as a people and as a race when we aspire for the best and seek the more constructive and creative methods of life. We can be better now. We can acquire a better education now, we can organize our capital now and receive our share in this economy of free enterprise now. In spite of all that we have attained as a people we have not exhausted our possibilities, and the past does not define the limits of our potential. Are we not as well equipped to respond to the call of the right, the just, the good, the highest, and the best as are the white segregationists against whom we fight? Has not the great God put in our souls the thirst for truth and righteousness? Are we not endowed as co-workers with the great creative spirit of the universe? Then we need not wait until all is well before we harness our resources and venture upon new ways of life and creativity.

We must not play ourselves too cheap or postpone the day of greater things when the hour of fulfillment is already at hand. To the leaders of school boycotts who have called children to remain out of school in order to help correct the evils and errors of an imperfect system of education, are you willing now to use your influence to lead young people to desert the ranks of drop-outs and struggle now to make the best out of the education that is now available? The call to stay out of school does not appeal to the highest in students, but to the ordinary and the easy. It requires less initiative to stay out of school than it does to attend school. It requires less mental alertness to refuse to study than it does to study. Is not some education better than no education? Of course, we should get all the education possible and go as far up the ladder of intellectual attainments as our powers will allow us. We must strive for the very best opportunities, the best possible schools, and the best possible teachers, but if these are not available to us then let us make the best use of what we do have. Remember that the future is with the person who knows, thinks, understands, and who has character and soul, and who can produce, invest, create and live in harmony with the highest and the best. Of course, we adults must continue to correct all the evils which make education more difficult. We must strive for quality education and seek to make available all the resources possible for the education of the young, but our young people must keep their feet in the upward path of learning and their minds stayed on the quest for truth.

THE PROGRESS OF THE RACE LIES NOT IN CONTINUED STREET DEMONSTRATIONS, AND THE LIBERATION OF AN OPPRESSED PEOPLE SHALL NOT COME BY ACTS OF REVENGE AND RETALIATION BUT BY THE CONSTRUCTIVE USE OF ALL AVAILABLE OPPORTUNITIES AND A CREATIVE EXPANSION OF THE CIRCUMSTANCES OF THE PAST INTO STEPPING STONES TO HIGHER THINGS.

A call to production does not mean that the day and time of protest can be eternally abandoned. Life is not lived in tight compartments but as a whole. Here we do not call for a surrender of the right of free speech or of the right of democratic expression. Here the call is to a new emphasis, that is, an effort to concentrate and to make production the primary objective and purpose. This is not a statement of utter condemnation, but it is in fact an appreciation of elements of the past and a challenge for the present and the future. History attests to the fact that the greatest and most enduring gains of any people are registered at the level of production. We remember with keen delight John B. Russwurm who graduated from Bowdoin College in 1847. A year later he, with Samuel Cornish, founded *Freedom's Journal*, the first Negro newspaper in the United States of America. While Russwurm was fighting a battle for freedom, he did not overlook the importance of producing a weapon or agency by which to carry on the struggle. His actions have been a source of inspiration to many journalists and to many founders and publishers of weekly and daily newspapers until this time. Possibly the greatest and best known of these champions of freedom was the golden-voiced, gifted thinker and great American orator, Frederick Douglass. He, by his intellectual ability, entered the mainstream of American life and took his place along side of and above many of his peers and compatriots. He traveled over the nation and in parts of Europe and was recognized wherever he went as a man of talent and rare ability. He stated his cause with clarity. His arguments were logical, and he was creative as a statesman and many of the gems of truth uttered by him are still available to inspire and to guide young Americans of all races and nationalities.

A visit to many of the best colleges and universities of this country would reveal the existence of the host of Negro scholars who have accepted the challenge in the field of research and thought and who have taken their places by the side of other American scholars regardless of race and nationality. Some have produced textbooks, others like George Washington Carver have used their insights and scientific gifts to extract from mother nature precious commodities unheard of before in scientific research. There have been heroic souls who have occupied classrooms and as teachers have captured the imagination of young minds and have led growing young people to new levels of intellectual speculation and discovery. In these days of stress and strain many of these gifted servants of the people have gone forward in the pursuit of their duties in many cases, underpaid, without honor or even words of commendation from those whom they served. They may be found not only in large metropolitan centers, universities and colleges but also in the humble school houses in the rural areas of this country. They have been in many instances the unsung heroes in the struggle during the past twelve years. They have guided the minds and the attitudes of thousands of young people towards the constructive way of wholesome living and creative thinking.

In spite of the scarcity of money, the curse of poverty and humble circumstances, we must recognize among us business leaders, organizers of insurance companies, bankers and others who have learned something of the technique of employing money and commanding dollars to be the servants of mankind. In practically every area of life Negroes may point with pride to some who have made distinct contributions in their respective fields through the art of production. Time and space will not allow the extension of the list of these worthy servants of humanity. But we must include in this section the productive work of the Christian Church. In Chapter Two we dealt with Negro slave songs as, in part, expressions of protest, sign language and means of directing fellow slaves in plans for their secret meetings as well as dealing with problems of their contemporary history but the author of *Negro Slave Songs of the United States* admitted that religion, in some form, was in both the life and the music of these slaves. Dr. Fisher says, ". . . African life was not partitioned. All of it was religious, and thus the music was also." [1] The songs then could deal with an immediate contemporary situation and still be religious. The words and message of the songs might point to a desire to return to their native Africa or to be exempt from the lash of the master's whip and still be religious. A people whose life is interpreted in terms of invisible or spiritual forces could use the same expressions in dealing with their desires whether said desires pointed to things material or immaterial and things physical or extraphysical. The African slaves believed in a world of spirits and hence their physical environment and their geographical surroundings did not wholly exhaust their concept of home and friends. Death was as real to them as was the auction block and hence could be interpreted, not only as a separation, but as a long journey to a different world. The song "Swing Low Sweet Chariot, Coming For to Carry Me Home" could be the longing for some little ocean vessel that would take them back to their native Africa and the words, "I looked over Jordan, and what did I see, A band of Angels coming after me," could also be interpreted in terms of their return to the shores of Africa. The Atlantic Ocean could be Jordan and those manning the ships could be considered as angels if they were the agents returning a lonely people to their home. But in the setting of religion, the imagination could also leap across a dark and unknown stream of death and envision a life that continues after the physical frame was cold and motionless. These slaves were tolerating and enduring

[1] *Negro Slave Songs of the United States*, p. 6.

but not accepting their cruel lot as just and final. These sorrow songs represented, according to many, the religious aspirations of an oppressed people. They were songs of hope in times that could have been surrendered to the night of despair. They represented the soul's attempt to love while being confronted with an opportunity to hate and to seek to destroy. These were lonely people in a strange land. They had come from a climate of sunshine where nature smiled upon them, where only little effort produced the needed food and shelter, but now they lived in a country of some rain, snow and ice as well as a few days of bright sunshine. When you add to this their afflictions and their chains, it is clear that they could not explain their troubles and yet they sought to see a glory that would defy the gloom. Says one spiritual, "Nobody Knows the Trouble I've Seen, Glory Halleluja!" Through their music the slaves escape the logic and the loathesomeness of their chains as they looked, longed for and waited for brighter days. It was their way of saying, "No" to their masters without violating the laws that punished and compelled them. When every visible sign had failed and there was no strength within the slave camp to match the might and power of the masters, the slaves looked through their childlike faith for a deliverer that no powers of earth could turn back or conquer. This was not wishful thinking. This was rejection of the present plight through the hopes and dreams of a more desirable future.

The slave songs had a message for the problems that confronted the slaves, and they believed that spirits were not conquered by time and space or wholly subdued by death. In this deeper meaning of life the slave songs moved from their protest to a form of moral and spiritual production which gave them victory and hope in the present set of circumstances that were most grim and most tragic. In an attempt to explain these songs one must admit that they represent the slaves' reaction to trouble and sorrow. They brought with them a mind and spirit that responded with deep tones and melodies of grief instead of shrieks of anger and testimony of bitterness of mind and soul. They were indeed different from those bound men who admitted they could not sing the songs of Zion as strangers in a strange land.

When we visited Africa many years ago, we did not find the type of melody and sweetness in their music as we had expected. At their funeral dances there was ritual, but little music. In their churches their music was cold and almost lifeless. They sang without feeling and depth as are reflected in the slave songs. It seems that the affliction and the troubles that played upon their spirits created the notes and their expressions that came forth from their souls. What is this that these people brought with them? According to some thinkers they had kinship with some ancient culture and deep in the recesses of their being there lived a creative greatness that came forth as they met new experiences in the new world and the new circumstances. A British historian tells this story;

In the age of Western history a distinguished Negro American singer felt the thrill of making a surprising discovery when he came to realize that the primitive culture of his African ancestors, of which a musical echo had survived the shock of enslavement and transplantation to a new world, was spiritually akin to all the non-Western high cultures, and to the pristine higher culture of the Western world itself, in virtue of its having preserved a spiritual integrity which a little modern Western secularized culture had deliberately abandoned. '. . . I have made many discoveries. They began when I was still a student. I came in contact with Russians at college. I heard them sing their native songs and was struck by their likeness to Negro music. I began to make experiments. I found that I—a Negro—could sing Russian songs like a native. I, who had to make the greatest effort to master French and German, spoke Russian in six months with a perfect accent, and now, finding it almost as easy to master Chinese. I discovered that this was because the African languages—thought to be primitive because monosyllabic—had exactly the same basic structure as Chinese . . . I found the African way of thinking in symbols was also the way of great Chinese thinkers.[2]

There is something mysterious and mystical about the music of these slave songs. They speak to the deeper regions of the human spirit and they stir the most profound emotions and leaves one thinking in terms of the highest and the best; wherever these songs have been sung, there has been a similar reaction and response. The response is not light-hearted or frivolous, but serious and moving. This is true on farms, in fields and factories where humble people labor under conditions that are hard, difficult, and sometimes oppressive. The same spirit is recognized on college campuses, among scholars and thinkers in practically every field. The message of slave songs have captured the imagination of kings and queens and heads of state, and they have appeared possessed with the spirit of reverence and deep appreciation for the higher values of life. These slave songs carried not the message of slavery alone, but they carried aspects of trust, confidence, hope, and an expectation of deliverance. In them the human spirit seems to find a new lease on life and moves out, above, and beyond the ordinary and the commonplace things of life and history. The Negro spirituals have come down through history flooding the minds and souls of men with rare gems of inspiration and impressing upon the puny and the weak a sense of belonging to a vast dominion of eternal values that chains, dungeons, and prison houses can never crush or destroy. In the mysticism of this strange music it seems that a prophetic spirit has visited the humble and touched the lips and hearts of slaves and lifted them to a grandeur that can only be possible through the bounties of divine grace. They sang not to the victory of the master and his cruelty. They cringe not before the cursed afflictions of heartless masters. They have seen an order above the curse of chains, they have heard a voice that speaks in more tender and redemptive tones than those

[2] Arnold Toynbee, *A Study of History*, VIII (London, 1955), 500.

expressed by the lips of a demoniac master. It is difficult, yea impossible, to chain these songs to the material and to the logic of things physical and things perishable. Whether by accident or design, the slaves in their protest or inspite of it, produced not only America's original music, but gave to Negro America one of the tools for creative endurance when they had not the light of learning to guide them, or economic wealth and power to protect them. Of these songs a learned scholar gave this testimony:

Little of beauty has America given the world save the rude grandeur God himself stamped on her bosom; the human spirit in this new world has expressed itself in vigor and ingenuity rather than in beauty. And so by faithful chance the Negro folk song—the rhythmic cry of the slave—stands today not simply as the sole American music, but as the most powerful expression of human experience born this side of the sea. It has been neglected, it has been, and is, half despised, and above all it has been persistently mistaken and misunderstood; but notwithstanding, it still remains as the singular spiritual heritage of the nation and the greatest gift of the Negro people.[3]

It seems that the same spirit that inspired the slaves to sing gave birth to the Negro church and sent it forth as a messiah to humble people in the United States of America and as the messenger of the great Messiah of truth, Jesus Christ, the Son of God. It is true that the Negro church began in protest—in protest against a double standard in the gospel of universal redemption, and against man-made restrictions to "the whosoever will of Jesus Christ." The origin of the Negro church basically sprang from the Negro's rejection of a segregated gospel and a segregating church. Time would fail us to recount the tragic and heroic stories of how disappointed men and women of color early discovered that the gospel of discrimination was not the true gospel of Jesus Christ. Then the words of the white preacher became as dust in the mouths of those who hungered

[3] W. E. B. Dubois, *The Soul of Black Folk*, (Greenwich, Conn., 1961), pp. 181–182.

for living bread, and segregated pews became too hard and repulsive to sit upon, and these humble people lost all confidence in a church that would sing about the redemptive blood of Jesus Christ and yet close its doors against weary souls whose faces were black. The segregated Christians made no efforts to disturb or to interfere with the segregating church. They had been disappointed, they saw no hope, and they elected to depart. They had approached the fig tree of professed Christianity but found only withered leaves. They had approached what they thought was a refreshing stream in the desert for their thirsty souls, only to discover that for black men and women there was no water to drink. If they had lingered and had elected to spend the rest of their lives villifying and cursing the leaders and members of the segregating church these pioneers would have lost their souls, lost their vision, and lost their opportunity to become servants of the most high God, and flaming evangels of the Cross of Christ. They moved from protest to production.

Today the Negro race is better because the Negro church has created a climate of hope and appreciation for those values and gifts that God in His providence has bestowed upon us. The Negro church though humble has been powerful enough to inspire millions of Negroes to turn from the shadows of ignorance and go in quest of the light of learning. Out of their humble and meager incomes they have founded little schools and have helped spread the gift and the light of learning. Out of these churches have come directly or indirectly many of the Negro men of professions; lawyers, doctors, teachers, and those in many other areas of life. When there was no Negro press, the Negro preacher helped to spread the news of life and of hope. Out of these churches have come some of the truly great preachers of the United States of America and of the world. They have in their humble way used their talents for the advancement of the gospel of the Son of God. They have through prayer and meditation opened their minds and their souls for the direction and the use of the eternal spirit, and they have been a source of hope and a tower of strength to a people when the nights of suffering were long and hard and the days of ostracism were dark and dreary. The Negro church is a concrete illustration of what happens when we move from protest to production.

Arnold Toynbee, the great British historian, sees in the Negro church a potential and the promise that could well be the fertile soil in which a vital, contagious, and a redemptive Christianity of the future could sprout and grow and thus save the church of Jesus Christ from stagnation and death. Toynbee says the following:

The Negro appears to be answering our tremendous challenge with a religious response which may prove in the event, when it can be seen in retrospect, to bear comparison with the ancient Orientals' response to the challenge from his Roman masters . . . The Negro has been adapting himself to the rigors of his new social environment by discovering, in Christianity, certain original meanings and values which western Christendom has long ignored. Opening a simple and impressionable mind to the Gospels, he had divined the nature of Jesus' mission. He has understood that this was a prophet who came into the world not to confirm the mighty in their seat but to exalt the meek and humble . . . It is possible that the Negro slave-imigrants who have found Christianity in America may perform the greater miracle of raising the dead to life. With their childlike spiritual intuition and their genius for giving spontaneous aesthetic expression to emotional religious experience, they may perhaps be capable of re-kindling the cold, grey ashes of Christianity which have been transmitted to them by us, until in their hearts the divine fire glows again. It is thus, perhaps, if at all, that Christianity may conceivably become the living faith of a dying civilization for the second time. If this miracle were indeed to be performed by an American Negro church, that would be the most dynamic response to the challenge of social penalization that had yet been made by man.[4]

[4] *A Study of History,* (II) 219–220.

What a challenge! What an opportunity! Arnold Toynbee has summoned the Negro church to a great and worthy task. If said church never reaches the goal as stated the pursuit of it would be most rewarding. It would inspire the most noble thinking and the most lofty living. The end results for both the Negro church, the Negro race, and the nation itself would mean a new moral and spiritual upsurge of life on every front. To such a quality of life men of all races and nationalities would be drawn, asking, "Sirs, what must we do to receive the vision, the insights, and the grace and glory of the Christian religion?" It is exciting to know that Negroes live in a nation that owes to them a debt in the form of full equality of opportunity and their rights as first class citizens. But it is most disturbing to think that the Negro church has been blessed with some values and insights that renders it a debtor to their fellow-men and to the nation as a whole. Such thoughts should occasion great humility, repentance, and confession of sins and limitations. If such a noble challenge is to be met it must be done creatively by seeking the constructive power that comes from loyalty and devotion to the way of Christ. The quest for civil rights is a worthy one but it is far more lofty to seek a kingdom of values that would inspire in all men a sense of brotherhood and will bring to the hearts and minds of the peoples and nations of the world the way of justice, righteousness, and peace. Here is an opportunity that no human hands can snatch away, and here is a rare privilege where there can be victory without victims. In reality, this is a cause, and a cause involves a cross and this cross can be born only through the power and strength of the living Christ. This is not a call to protest, it is a challenge to produce.

10

THE TEST OF A PEOPLE'S GREATNESS

THE LONG AND TEDIOUS journey was over. The errors, mistakes, and blunders were now parts of the history of the struggle. In the far-off wilderness the bleached bones of the dead testified to the long delay that had accompanied the effort of these tired pilgrims to reach the land of Canaan. They had arrived now. They saw the land, they beheld its promise, but they knew the labors were not over. When Joshua assigned to the children of Joseph their territory, they were not satisfied for they believed that the land offered did not match their greatness and that they had merited more than this. And then the question was asked of Joshua: "Why hast thou given me but one lot and one portion to inherit, seeing I am a great people." [1] Joshua did not try to stop this protest, he did not attempt to dismiss it as the empty and meaningless words of misguided and misinformed people, he accepted the statement as being real and true. The children of Joseph said further, "The hill is not enough for us." [2] The children of Joseph not only had seen a hill but they had a vision of a mountain vast. The hill is never enough if a mountain is possible. The children of Joseph refused to be satisfied with what they had because they were moved and disciplined and conditioned by the vision of an available mountain.

Traditions are great and history should always be respected and revered, but the man who buries himself in a grave of a past and disregards the call of the future, sins against the most noble

[1] Joshua, 17:14.
[2] *Ibid.*, 17:16.

principles of his own being and forfeits his right to new powers in a new day and age. One of the best ways to preserve the glory of the past is to go on to even larger and higher goals of life. How often have men been heard to make the figurative expression, "don't forget the bridge that brought you over the stream." This is accepted as a statement of wisdom, that is if we can remember the bridge without parking on it or camping there. For if we did the latter we would not only negate the purpose of our crossing but would block traffic so that other travelers would not have the chance to pass over without hindrance and hazards.

The history of ancient China reveals that they were a great people. They can boast of some of the wisest sages and philosophers of recorded history and have made some lasting contributions to human progress. They went further than most ancient nations in the practical application of the ideals of peace, and some of the wise sayings of Confucius are still valuable in this modern age. But one of the primary reasons why China was for a long time a retarded nation was the fact that she loved her ancestors too well and was too much committed to and enslaved by the old tradition of the country. She worshiped the past at the expense of the forward call of a great vision. China had the land, the wide open spaces, the manpower, and the genius but in the distant past she did not have the vision necessary for the higher response to the future. Hence China was at ease, complacent and satisfied because she saw no threat to her security and no danger to her future. But she was looking in the wrong direction. She had turned her back on the budding tomorrows and sought security in the spirit of her ancestors. But dead ancestors cannot guide well the feet of posterity on highways that the forefathers never knew. History has recorded, science has proved, and philosophy has validated the fact, that where there is no vision the people perish. Where there is no vision people become self-centered and satisfied with their past and present attainments. They build altars and erect shrines at the tomb of the dead past and worship the created goods of life instead of facing a future of creativity. Men without vision spend a life time building fences around their little possessions and fighting bloody wars to have and to hold that which has been bequeathed to them as a legacy from the past. A great people is a people with a great vision,—a vision that brings into their reach lofty values that the past has not fully yielded and all the wonderful gifts of life that are yet to be achieved. A vision for a people is a light of faith breaking in the darkness of the present and pointing toward the unexplored regions of the future. Vision is the people's torch, a brilliant light that sparkles and burns and guides the footsteps in quest of new worlds, new possessions, other lands, and other experiences. When the children of Joseph saw the great mountains standing in the distance with all their potentialities and great possibilities, they cried aloud to Joshua, "the hill is not enough for us." The valleys of life are enough if there be no hills. The hills will satisfy the basic needs if there are no mountains in sight. A little education will suffice if there is not the age of scientific knowledge with all the modern inventions and a new technology that summon men to new heights of living both in theory and practice. For this the masses sometimes need leaders with genius who would teach them to look beyond the valleys to the hills, and beyond the hills to the mountains. The majority may never see or sense immediately the vision for the future. Majority rule is a rule for conserving value, but not for discovering them. In a democracy we must depend on the leaders; the few inspired people of the community, to see the vision first and then try to win others to their conviction and to their discovers and bring the majority to accept the new light that points the way to a new future. Hence a great people is a people who produce, encourage, and then follow their leaders.

A nation or a race that demands of its leaders to follow them is a people who will surely perish in the wilderness of a dead past. The leader must be brave enough and love his people enough to share with them the verdict of his vision though it causes him suffering and even death. The leader must rise up early and endure the solitude of the night and maybe walk alone until his fellow-sufferers catch the vision and come to the brightness of its rising. For fear that they will not see the vision in his day, the leader must write it and leave it to history to preserve until men grow to see it and appreciate it. A great people will somehow produce great leaders. A great people will grow great men in whom the idealism of the race or nation will come to life in concrete forms as personal desires and as social concern. There will be incarnated in the soul of a few the basic hopes and the most lofty dreams of the people. The philosophical thought of ancient Greece rose to new heights and power in the soul and mind of Socrates, and behold a new system of ethics was born. In the walk of Abraham the ancient Hebrews came to a new venture of faith and new standing with Jehovah, and hence a great religion leaped forth into the stream of history. A people must keep always on hand some star gazers who will watch for the signs of a higher revelation of truth and find and follow the sacred star of hope until it stands in all of its blazing brightness over the place where revealed truth is born. People are sensitive to the light of vision and somehow they follow almost instinctively. In a democratic society the tendency is to pick the men of larger vision for the larger responsibilities of state.

From 1789 to 1829, the first forty years of American history, there were seven presidents to preside over the nation; two of whom came from Massachusetts. The other five came from Southern states. They were George Washington of Virginia; Thomas Jefferson, Virginia; James Madison, Virginia; James Monroe, Virginia; Andrew Jackson, Tennessee. These were the formative days for the United States of America. In the first forty years the thirteen original colonies were merged into a young and promising nation. This small group under the Federal Constitution in 1789 became a nation more united and more powerful as a republic. It was in this first forty years that the American economic life took on a more fixed and enduring pattern. It was in these first formative years that the American experiment stood the test and gave promise of a long and eventful history. Many of the leaders then were Southern statesmen who were consumed by a world-embracing vision of freedom and an unqualified longing for justice, and a desire to build a republic that would survive the ravages of time and stand the test of ages.

But later an awful pall fell over the nation's life and a shameful blot marred the records of its existence. The country was divided on the issue of slavery. So deep was the wound, and so wide the chasm that both sides took up arms each against the other. The South struggled in the defense of the institution of slavery; the North fought against it. While the cause of freedom triumphs, the nation paid a great penalty. That penalty was not only the sacrifice of some of the most promising sons of the republic on the field of battle, but it caused many of the great American statesmen of the South to turn their attention to the defense of themselves and to the defense of their future, and to the defense of the former institution of slavery. Many of our fine Southern statesmen have been busy defending the hills; the hills of limited human relations, the hills of a segregated society, and have not had the time or the vision to behold the mountain of all inclusive freedom and equality, and the brighter world of unrestricted democracy. Hence during the past one hundred years, with the exception of Missouri, Tennessee, and Texas, no Southern state had sent a single son to occupy the White House. It is not a matter of geography or climate, for the South has many great and worthy statesmen and has had for the past one hundred years. But the South has demanded from her statesmen to give a larger portion of their time to the defense of the cruel institution of a segregated society; but as the South now turns her mind more and more towards unlimited freedom of opportunity for all, there shall be more voices heard from the Southland and more statesmen recognized as the leaders and spokesmen not only for the South but for the nation as a whole. It is not too much to expect that with the expanding vision among many of the leaders of the South, that the next progressive step that America will take in building a greater democracy will be determined largely by the attitude and disposition of leaders and statesmen of the South. The South may yet determine whether America shall remain the moral leader of the free world or whether she shall by her own action become to the rest of the world mockers of democracy and a hindrance to the growth of freedom. A great people is a people with a great vision who will not be satisfied with less when their abilities and their capacities warrant.

The final and all important element in the test of a people's greatness is their ability to produce. Joshua's reply to the children of Joseph reflected his belief in what was and is the greatest test for any people's greatness. Joshua answered them, "If thou be a great people then get thee up to the wood country and cut down for thyself." Joshua was telling the children of Joseph that there is land, there is wooded country; but there is no prepared place for you. If you are great, no place has been arranged to house your greatness. You must build out of the raw materials and by the power of your own vision and strength. This reflects what Katherine Anne Porter makes one of her characters to say in her novel, *Ship of Fools*. "The place to which you are going does not exist yet. You must build it when you come to the right spot." [3]

What is vision must be turned into reality and what is theory must become practice and what one is entitled to get must be gotten by labor, sweat and sacrifice. There is no neat, cozy place ready made for members of any society. There is no reserve station in life to be given to any people for the asking or for the marching. They must build when they come to the right spot. In our social struggles there is no one single problem that we

---

[3] Katherine Ann Porter, *Ship of Fools* (Boston, 1945), p. 146.

can solve and end the struggle once and for all, for the solution of one problem is often the beginning of a new and different problem. Success demands and requires hard and difficult work. I agree with the great scholar who says:

> Growth is not an automatic process, but is the hard-won reward of effort that makes a continual and exacting demand on the growing individual's or growing society's will power, since it has to be perpetually renewed in a series of responses to challenges in which a successful response to one challenge always evokes a fresh challenge, with the consequence that every solution to one problem brings with it the presentation of another.[4]

In a social struggle we must build when we get to the right spot. We are now at the right spot to build a strong, healthy and democratic society. We have the records of some economic, cultural, and scientific achievements to encourage us. We have some of the most far-reaching legal supports in the field of civil rights, supported and passed by the Supreme Court and the Congress of the United States of America. More progress has been made in this field in the past twelve years than was made in the previous one hundred years. The ballot has been extended to more citizens than ever before in the history of the country and the ballot is the strongest and most powerful weapon that any citizen can receive. The standard of living in this country puts at the disposal of all groups greater advantages than are enjoyed by any other people in any other section of the world. Already there is enough capital passing through the hands of Negroes to make a great and powerful economic force if organized and properly directed. We are at the right spot to become productive. We are at the right spot to become creative. This is our task and our responsibility. Any further delay in this noble venture must be laid at our own doors. This is the time to move from the emphasis on protest to the commitment of production.

[4] Arnold Toynbee, *A Study of History*, (VIII,) 497.

When the pilgrim fathers set sail to this country in quest of the land of freedom and opportunity they found a vast wilderness and not a cultivated, well-developed, and ready land. They had to build when they reached the right spot. When they set foot on Plymouth Rock, they had reached the right spot to begin. Plymouth Rock to them well could have been called the rock of the pilgrim's potential and promise, for from there they went on to turn the wilderness into a fertile land and make the desert bloom like a rose as they built a great nation and a glorious people. If every opportunity sought in the struggle for civil rights were granted today, there still would be a need for building and producing, for there is no soft ready-made place where men can fit in without effort and without labor. They must be creative, they must be productive, they must seize and hold the opportunities and turn raw materials into finished products. It is glorious to seek the spot; it is most urgent to build on it. Whether in politics, in education, business, or religion, we must build if we be great enough to build. In a college or university all that the committee on admissions can do is to admit a student based on his record, credentials, and recommendations. But the status of that student must be determined by himself, by his dedication to study, and by his commitment to his task. He decides his rank, what his average shall be, and his scholastic standing in general. Shall he remain in school or not? Shall he be at the foot or the head of his class? There is no law for or against; he must build for himself.

Joshua called his people up to the wood country. Go up where the raw materials are. Seize every opportunity and build. Do not only contest what others say but also construct what your vision gives. Do not continue to beg, but build. Do not argue the point of your greatness, but demonstrate it in constructive and creative actions. If the present borders are too limited then break over them by effort and expand the area with dispatch. It is difficult to enslave true greatness. Visions will not be blinded by the fog of hate, the wings of hope will not be hindered by the dangerous clouds of despair, genius cannot be bound with cords of ignorance and superstition, and the glory of the human spirit will never be eternally damned in the gloom and corruption of material things. If we be great, we build.

11

WORKING, WINNING, WAITING

FOR THE SAKE OF clarity, a discussion must be divided into topics, but life itself is not so divided. It is rather a whole that brings all the parts together in a vital working and inter-related organism. While the title of this chapter will be dis-cussed under three headings, but in reality these headings are so related that in practical life they frequently take place al-most simultaneously.

Working is man's efforts applied to some object or to some problem for the solution of the same. By our labors we seek to remove obstacles and then go on to attain the goals that are set before us. As has been reflected in the previous chapters of this treatise, much work has been done for the cause of freedom and for the equality of opportunity to all citizens. It has been noted in forms of protest as well as in the challenge and labors of production. In this struggle many have been more than con-sumers of goods, they have addressed themselves to the task of producing goods. The federal government as the agent has done much work in this field, and the laws on the statute books and the verdicts of our courts reveal the same. Freedom, justice, and the security of all citizens is the purpose and the objective of the United States government. Although it has not done all within its power to achieve these goals it has at no time denied its intention or changed its lofty course. It is still striving to bring to full fruition all of the ideals and dreams of the founding fathers. Though an imperfect machinery it is nevertheless an existing machinery functioning theoretically at least, for the well-being of its citizens and it has not failed in all of its attempts. Much remains to be done still, but much has been done already. It has brought together and held together, in a modest way, many different races and nationalities and has merged them into one nation, under one flag, and guided by one supreme law of the land. America has not won the battle for complete freedom and equality for all as yet. But neither has it lost this battle. It is winning. There are many who are convinced that it is not winning fast enough and has delayed too long in working seriously and courageously for all of her promised values. But the victories of the past inspire faith in the present and hope for the future.

Individuals and groups as we have observed, have also been at work for the achievement of civil rights and for the strengthening of the fibre and soul of the nation. These have been at work since the very birth of the nation. This has not been a racial struggle alone. It has been both interracial and bi-racial. The champions and apostles of equality and freedom have been found on both sides of this struggle and the cause of justice and freedom has drawn support from the various fields and levels of life and experience. Both the learned and the unlearned, the rich and poor, saints and sinners, have done their bit in this noble and lofty struggle. The people are still working because they believe in the object of the struggle and have been inspired in the belief that they are in process of winning the desired victory. Many people can recount in their own lifetime, victory after victory that they have seen for the betterment of the lot of all and for the expansion of freedom and for the spreading power of justice. It takes the most blatant sceptic to say that in the United States of America we are not winning the war against ignorance, diseases, crime, segregation, and oppression. All the Americans who have helped in this struggle should share in the promised reward. There is not a single organization in the United States whether it be civil rights or not, that has not and cannot count some definite achievements as the results of the efforts, sacrifices and labors in the past for the cause of freedom. Our reference to the above things is by way of summary of some of the previous discussions in this document. We have brought together the three ideas in this chapter for several reasons: First, because we wanted to point out that they are not as separate as they may seem, and in the second place, because we felt that something needed to be said as an antidote to impatience that can lead to frustration. There are those among us who have said repeatedly that we cannot wait, that all the great values of freedom must be given now, and then they hasten to conclude that we have already waited long enough and maybe too long. And they say any reference to patience is a counsel to postpone actions and to yield to the power and the forces of those who oppose the progressive efforts for freedom. We have brought these three ideas together so that the first two will be a source of strength for the third, and the third idea (that is waiting), would not be construed as a negation of the first two, namely; (working and winning). It should be clear to all of us that unless we know the logic and the wisdom of waiting we might unwittingly and unknowingly penalize the work that has already been done and negate some of the lofty gains that rightfully belong to ourselves, to our nation, and to the cause of freedom. Notre Dame and Michigan State football teams were matched in the fall of 1966. Both were considered the top teams of the season and many called it the game of the year. They played to a tie, but it was the conviction of many who saw the game that the scores would have been different had the linemen of Michigan State been patient enough to remain on the line and in place until the ball was snapped. But on several occasions there was an off-side penalty which cost important yardage and position because these players became too anxious to await the time to move logically and accordingly to the rules.

Let us come now to address ourselves to the meaning of the term waiting as used here. In this context the term waiting may mean several things. But it never means the postponement of what one can do now. It is never procrastination or putting off until tomorrow what one can do today. It is not laziness and the finding of alibis to justify indifference to duty and apathy in the face of responsibility. It is not the passive acceptance of the old, the traditional, and the consumer way of life because it may seem convenient and easy. Waiting, or the exercise of patience is a constructive attitude towards those situations that we cannot control after we have done all we can to master them. It assumes the application of one's self to a particular task and the harnessing of all the resources at one's command to find a solution to a problem that still remains unsolved. There can be no real waiting then, unless there has been some serious effort put forth out of which one has a right to expect certain constructive results. In waiting one keeps the torch of expectancy burning brightly though the shadows seem deep and impenetrable. Timely and constructive efforts must always precede a season of expectation or the time of hopeful waiting. In waiting one refuses to accept the present as the finished, sealed, and final work of destiny. And inspite of all the discouraging reports from the past and the counsels of despair proclaimed in and by the present, one refuses to break off negotiations with the future.

Patience is not willful delay in order to avoid the pain and price of progress. Rather, patience is the constructive acceptance of an enforced delay. It is the endurance of a hinderance accompanied by a sustained hope of inevitable victory. Patience is the acceptance of a temporary delay as one of the short steps on the long journey of human progress. It is a means to renewing strength and the act of rising higher so that we can go further. Patience is running without becoming weary at the task, and walking constantly and persistently toward our desired goal without fainting in the heat of oppression or tiring under the hot sun of human affliction. Patience does not mean "go slow," it means to go as fast as you can whenever you can, wherever you can. It means that when we have come to our wits end we must know that the journey is not at an end. For if the only struggle for justice is man's struggle, then the cruel chains of slavery will be the common lot of all. And if the only defense of truth is human, then the day of doom is near. But we are co-laborers with creativity and are workers together with the God of truth, justice, and eternal goodness. And be well aware that patience and persistence are twin brothers in the struggle for civil rights, human fulfillment and the spiritual battle for the full realization of the Kingdom of God.

Henry M. Wristun said, "In the discipline of imagination, persistence comes next to patience. As patience realizes that great results will not be easy, persistence appreciates that even slow progress will grind to a halt unless effort is vigorous and continuous." [1] A person who waits gathers gleams of promise from the past and embraces reasons for hope while he struggles in the present, and by faith tarries for the fulfillment that the future would bring to the present visions that gladden the mind and feeds the human spirit.

A skilled and experienced prize fighter would like to get rid of his opponent as quickly as possible but knows he must defend himself and wait for the opening that allows him to reach his target with the greatest force with as little damage as possible to himself. He who fights a trained opponent must spend well his season of training, getting the proper rest, and observing all the rules of health and the strategy of battle. Then when he is in the ring he must abide his time and deliver the desired punch at the right spot. He may win by a knock-out or he may be forced to go the distance be it ten or fifteen rounds. Then when the last bell rings tolling the end of the contest, the victorious fighter must still await the verdict of the judges and the decision of the referee.

In this vast universe there are laws of growth that no person can ignore, disregard or break and arrive at the normal goals of maturity. In every sphere of life fulfillment depends on and must await the operation of the prescribed laws of growth. In

---

[1] *The Age of Revolution*, July 1961 Issue of Foreign Affairs, p. 535.

the attempt to build an orderly society we must not leave anything to luck or chance, we must do our full share. We must in every way cultivate the soils of human relations and fertilize the same with goodwill and understanding, and then plant the seeds of justice, freedom, love, and await the work and the reward of the same. When we deal with human plants or thinking, self-conscious, and emotional beings, we cannot predict the length of the season or measure and determine with accuracy the span of time.

.The freedom of choice is the right of all men to help or hinder the onward march of truth, push or postpone the advancement of personal and social righteousness in the present world. Freedom means this kind of risk. A free person with the power of choice is not wholly subject to the determinism of nature or wholly controlled by the forces of human nature and the principles of cause and effect that play upon him. He can break the cycle of nature by his will and arrest external pressures by personal desire and inner compulsion; so when one group of persons have made known their desire and their determination to secure their full rights, and when they have been committed to all the ideals and principles and rules of life that would achieve well the goals in question, unfortunately they must still face the emotions, wills, resentments, and the opposition of others who differ with them. There are some who will see the logic of the law and understand the moral ground of the cry of others for all the fruits of freedom, and they will still struggle to hinder them because of some ancient tradition which blinds them to the logic of reason. Human beings who oppose the truth cannot be killed enmasse or removed from the state by death individually or collectively as the means of building a just, free, and democratic society. They must somehow be won. In clearing new ground a farmer may cut down the trees, pull up the stumps and burn them, but in an attempt to build a just and free society social engineers cannot be so drastic with human beings that stand in the path of truth and righteousness. You

cannot always even threaten or intimidate them and influence
them to stand for the right. You cannot stampede human beings into a way of fellowship by threats, or pressure them into
a life of purity. The whole philosophy of our democratic society
rests on the notion that people can be won to obedience and
loyalty to the laws of justice and to the righteous government
of a free state. But the genius, the enlightened statesmen and
chosen leaders of the people must teach and lead a recalcitrant
multitude into the way of understanding and dedication. This
means education, and in some cases, social redemption. For
knowing does not always mean doing. There is indeed a wide
gulf between the two. This Shakespeare must have had in mind
when he said:

> If to do were as easy as to know what were good to do, Chapels
> had been churches and poor men's cottages prince's palaces.[2]

Knowing this plight of mankind, leaders should not mislead
people or withhold from them the knowledge of the truth, for a
delay in giving them the right knowledge will delay even longer
their accepting the duty that the knowledge imposes. Many
leaders of the United States of America have admitted their
errors in condoning for more than a hundred years the evils of
racial segregation and discrimination, and all too many young
people have been reared in a tradition that taught them that
these evils were right and that the vice of hate was a virtue
that they would do well to practice. Within the last twelve
years, thanks to the Supreme Court's decision of May 17, 1954,
and the many programs of education and other forces and influences, many Americans have re-thought the old concept of
racial segregation and have committed themselves to the enlightened vision of the highest court of the land and have set
their feet in the path of justice and freedom, and now are on
their way to new heights and new experiences that are destined

[2] *Merchant of Venice,* Act I, Scene III, Line 13.

to lead them to become better and stronger Americans dedicated to the building of a just and great society.

I repeat, for the complete blessings of full first-class citizenship, no one should have to wait for the full deliverance of all the blessings of these rights; America should not wait for she has the resources even now. But these things cannot be achieved until Americans will with all their mind and spirits that they will be achieved now. Ancient Israel had all the assets essential and yet they were detained for forty years in the wilderness because they had not willed to go into the land of promise. They had been motivated by the hatred of the cruel pharoahs and by the burden of making brick without straw, and by the pain and lash of the master's whip. They were running from Egypt but had not been sufficiently inspired by the love of the land of Canaan.

We face a danger today of being too concerned with an escape from something. Some are motivated with a desire to escape the burdens and the unkind past of segregation and discrimination, and like some of the ancient Hebrews we hate the Egypt of past bondage more than we love the Canaan of available but unfulfilled promises. The evil of the past might repel a people and encourage them to flee, but only a love for the promised values will strengthen their power of choice and push them forward armed with a determination to pay the price whatever it might be. Being out of Egypt and beyond the Red Sea for the ancient Hebrews was not the land of Canaan by a long shot. For when the early stages of their journey brought them from the curse of Egypt and they could no longer hear the cruel voices of their unkind masters demanding their cruel task, they embraced a complacency that was not helpful, and some turned their minds back towards the fleshpots of Egypt and longed to be back to labor where they could be without personal and productive responsibility. A generation perished in the wilderness because they had not willed to enter the land of Canaan. No people can reach full maturity as a free people who would avoid the risk, the responsibilities, and the voluntary sacrifices that freedom involves. Exploring and exploiting the new privileges outside of the land of one's former captivity on the road that would lead to, but is not the promised land, can cause a people to postpone the day of their full deliverance and maybe doom them to disintegrate and perish before the richer things are seen and achieved. No people have willed to be free until they have willed to pay the full price for this precious prize. For the price comes before the pleasure of possession, and he who seeks the pleasure by avoiding the price will never see the full day of the pleasure, for it will never come. A pause to shout "black power," as a separatist move against the white community and then adopt the other slogan, "whitey must go," is just as prejudicial as the cruel voices lifted against Negroes in the past. If we are desirous of conquering prejudice and putting an end to segregation and discrimination we must not only oppose it in the minds and hearts of others, we must by clear thinking and noble living drive it from the sacred chambers of our own minds and give it no place in our hearts. If a part of our social order still makes choice of a manner of life less than that which freedom demands and proclaims, then the whole nation will be plagued and penalized thereby. Negroes by force or intimidation cannot compel white America to will and work for a great free republic. The freedom that we seek can only come to the race when America is free. One tenth of a population of almost two hundred million people cannot render the other ninety per cent free. Part of the Negro population, however committed, cannot force all Negroes to will to pay the full price for a day of freedom for the whole race. The whole is always burdened by and responsible for the parts, and the parts have the power to slow down, handicap, and penalize the whole. In any social order the good is penalized by the bad. The present virtues are hemmed in by current vices. Saints are tied to sinners, hope is taunted by despair, and the wisdom of the wise is reduced in power and strength by the ignorance of the unwise, and the heighth of a few is always modified, and in fact, imperiled by the degradation of the many.

The destiny of the people of America is tied to the destiny of this nation and it matters not how anxious we are and how determined to receive the full gift of freedom, we cannot be blessed with so precious a gift until the commitment has been made by all Americans of all classes and kinds. For leaders cannot arrive without the people, and the whole cannot reach maturity without the growth and the fulfillment of the parts. All Americans must make their choice and be and do those things that would lead to the promised land. The writer was more than a poet, he was a philosopher when he wrote these words:

> Where there is a will there is a way my lad.
> If the will has the strength to serve.
> The goal isn't reached in a day my lad,
> But winning takes patience and nerve.
> It's a long long way and a hard hard road,
> And a life time is hardly enough.
> But you'll win if you stick to the roadway you pick,
> And your heart is the right kind of stuff.

From another point of view the whole struggle for civil and human rights is a process and a movement towards desired goals that can be realized in a democratic society comprised of free citizens and free people. The true drive for civil rights in the United States of America need not be revolutionary in character but evolutionary, for it is not against, but in harmony with the Federal Constitution and supported by the American promise and philosophy of democracy. It need not be as much of a revolt against past evils as it is a joint venture and joint action in pursuit of a fellowship of free people who take the supreme law of the land seriously and seek to regulate their plans and programs thereby. It is not expected that the task will be fully completed at a particular time in history when all persons can and will retire from the great struggle of improved and just human relations. Society and life are not so static as that. This whole enterprise becomes a way of life in which all groups shall live and participate, and not a fixed goal that they shall reach and then retreat from the struggle. This is a progressive plan and an endless cycle of efforts on the part of all the people in the name of justice and for the cause of freedom. The quest then is for more than particular laws to correct the errors of the past (as important as this may be.) The quest is for a way of thinking, feeling, and living towards the social order and toward one another. This becomes an experiment, an investigation, and a practice in living together that will finally establish new habits, new patterns, new constructive and creative character products. In this process the American principles of justice, goodwill, and respect for human personality will become incarnated in the lives of more and more people so that individuals and groups will gain and reflect new ideals, new emotions, and new thoughts that will tend to dispel old prejudices and old fears. Citizens will be working on the side of freedom in order to win the victory not for themselves alone, but for all Americans and ultimately for all mankind. The highest purpose of citizenship will not be the getting of rewards and benefits for the individual and his group, but the creation of a political, social, cultural, and moral atmosphere in which all of the highest faculties of human beings will be harnessed and released for the good of all. With such a commitment to this process of democratic thinking and living, working for the good will become an aspect of winning the good, and winning the good, a vital phase of waiting for a fuller fruition of the good. For not one of these three aspects of life can be wholly completed without the other. This implies a new and vital interpretation of citizenship in the United States of America. It shall no longer be the defense of the individual rights of individual citizens against the encroachment of organized society. Neither shall it be the state's attempt to overtax or misuse its citizens; but a joint venture on the part of all for the realization of the values of all including both the individuals and the state.

In the next place, there will be tolerance on the part of the advantaged for the disadvantaged, and the granting to the latter the latitude and time for growth. In this the advantaged recognizes the potential of their less fortunate brothers and sets themselves to the task of working for and on the side of those forces of freedom that shall go on winning victories in both the segregated and the segregators. Not all Americans have had the same opportunities in the past, and all may not be as fruitful in the present as their potentialities warrant. While all must be given equality of opportunity there must be a season of tolerance for those who may be a little delayed or tardy in developing their talents more fully. Here we do not plead for extra privilege in the present and future for those against whom the tides of misfortune have surged; but would suggest that there may be the need for more tolerance and more time for the fullest unfolding of the latent powers of the unfortunate ones.

White backlash against those who have tried to help in the growth and progress of democracy is an act of intolerance that will not and cannot help to build a stronger nation in the interest of freedom. A punishment of any American citizen directly or indirectly because of what he has done or tried to do to help develop this great republic is an attempt to hinder the work for freedom and to arrest the progressive thrust for a greater victory for America. We must not be too hasty in turning against those who have done their best as they saw and understood it in the past. It sometimes requires time to understand motives and purposes and also time should be granted to heal the hurts of life and to help the weak and unfortunate.

Wholesale condemnation of a people based on traditions of the past is a hasty judgment that tends to hinder the growth of freedom both in the judges and in the judged. We must at some time rely upon and wait for the creative march of eternal truth and trust to the order of eternal providence those aspects of our case that we ourselves cannot wisely handle or master intelligently. Believing that there are such forces at work in the world, our Christian faith demands that we seek to be in tune with, and in harmony with the plans of the great Determiner of Destiny for the salvation of men and nations. The tide of years must come to help carry into the main stream of human existence and effort our ships of life. And no man can push himself safely and successfully against the waves of evil on the great ocean of human existence if there be on his side no power that makes for good and works for righteousness. To surrender to all of the grim and inadequate things of the present means to deny the rightful place of the creative and redemptive forces of the universe.

Impatient and frustrated church leaders and churches must be on guard against the doctrine of godless materialism. Godless materialism is too much for us. It goes beyond the call to work for better housing, slum clearance, and all of the other political and economic goods that rightfully belong to all American citizens. Our energies and our talents must be harnessed to attain all of these lofty goals in America for Americans. But to say that poor housing, slums, and economic disadvantages will damn the souls of its victims eternally is godless materialism. To say that people must postpone a serious quest for character at its best until all of the social evils of city, county, state, and nation have been corrected, is godless materialism of the worse kind. Godless materialism sees nothing in a situation to sustain and lift human life aside from bread and meat, shelter, and all the other human securities that are designed for the comforts of human life. While human beings must work to improve their lot, to harness the economic and political forces for the blessings of life and health, they must not surrender their right to embrace the higher powers available to them as they learn to live on that which is not bread and to have contact and communion with the Determiner of Destiny that is not at any time the victim of fate or the helpless slave of destiny. We shall go on working for the right in harmony with the will of the Lord of life. We shall work on, winning the battle for love, justice, and goodwill while we await the coming of the complete victory of all of these constructive forces over corruption and evil. It is expected that people will grow weary with toil if there be no forces or power on which and on whom they can rely. Faith in the victory of the good dictates that we must at some times seek the will and the way of the God of goodness. If there were no visible sign of victory for past effort, by faith we would still be sustained by the presence of the power that is not of ourselves but is still at work for righteousness in the world.

This was the reason that the writer of this treatise suggested that Negro Americans would make some use of the power of religion in civil rights shortly after the death of Medgar Evers the Executive Secretary of the National Association For The Advancement Of Colored People in the state of Mississippi. The writer arrived in Washington the same morning that the flag-draped casket of Medgar Evers with the funeral party arrived for burial in Arlington Cemetery. The writer was enroute to a White House Conference on Civil Rights called by the late President John F. Kennedy. At the close of this conference many of us left Washington in the late afternoon and early evening for our respective destinations. We were scheduled to go to Birmingham, Alabama where the Board of Directors of the National Baptist Convention, U.S.A., Incorporated was in session. Enroute to the railroad station that evening in Washington I asked the minister who was taking me, to allow me a chance to stop at the church in which the body of the slain hero for civil rights lay in state. As I approached the church and the huge crowd, I saw young Negro boys passing out hate literature and some were cursing the very soul of the nation. The intense bitterness thus expressed was blaming a whole nation for the brutal murder of Medgar Evers. While we too wanted the guilty one apprehended and brought to a speedy trial, we knew that this was not our task. We felt we needed a point of view to save us from despair and to arm us with courage to go on. When we left this grim and pathetic scene the thought kept recurring that those who believe in religion should seek to make use of this grim hour to turn the souls of the people away from bitterness, frustration, and despair. It seemed to us that the drive for civil rights could continue as we drew closer to the divine forces and petitioned the God of all history to give us strength to endure through such a sad hour. At our special board meeting in Birmingham, Alabama, the matter was presented to the Board of Directors and adopted by unanimous vote. A brief quotation from that message reveals the spirit and religious intent encouched therein.

5. We suggest that all public demonstrations in the form of pickets and marches be prayerfully suspended in favor of the silent and prayerful mourning for Medgar W. Evers. That we allow the eloquent testimony of his sacrificial death to be heard, and that we will seek to release new spiritual influence and power that will help to change the minds and hearts of those Americans who have not as yet willed the full freedom for all men.

6. We further recommend that during this sixty days of mourning we will do the following:

a. Do all within our power to support the President's Civil Rights Legislation and to cooperate with him in his constructive efforts to relieve tensions in this country, and pray for his continued strength and vision as he leads forward this great nation.

b. That we will send telegrams and letters to our respective Congressmen and Senators urging their support of the President's Civil Rights Program and in helping to make America a greater and more complete democratic country for free men.

c. That we will send letters of congratulations to those groups and organizations who have voluntarily set up a program of desegregation and who have committed themselves unreservedly to the American way of life.

d. That we will pray for all the governors of states and local leaders who are committed to the cause of justice and freedom without qualification.

e. That we will pray and work for goodwill and better relations among all the peoples of the nation.

There were many civil rights leaders and workers who raised their voices in hot protest against the sentiment expressed, but time has proved that the civil rights leaders and the civil rights movement needed that type of divine reliance to renew their strength, to save them from weariness, and to preserve the soul of the movement from frustration and almost despair.

One of the serious problems of this age is that of intolerance and impatience. Men are committed to, and in quest for the place, rank, and reward of society but are not wholly committed to the pain, labors, and price to be paid. Some human beings tend to judge most harshly the failures in their fellow-men and their social order, but would overlook the same failures in themselves. All of us would do well to remember that it may take as long to change the mind of others for good as it does to change our own. In a society of imperfect men working, winning, and waiting must be a part of the pattern of life for all who desire a better, more just, and a greater society.

At the White House Conference on Civil Rights called by President Lyndon B. Johnson June 1-2, 1966, he warned the delegation that they must not and could not expect anyone to correct or set right in a day what it has taken generations to set wrong. Said he: "Do not expect from me or from any man, a miracle. Do not expect us even together to put right in one year or four all that took centuries to make wrong." The president had called together civil rights leaders, religious leaders, business men, school teachers, labor, management, and people from all walks of life in an attempt to bring some degree of unity to the legitimate struggle for civil rights. But while the delegation worked, on the inside of the hotel on the problems and programs set before us, there were some civil rights people who were picketing the entire hotel on the outside. They were not willing even to wait to see what the outcome of the meeting would be and what would be the plans for achieving the proposed goals. Some civil rights groups refused an invitation to come and be a part of the meeting. Such actions make the following questions very logical and significant: Are such workers for civil rights concerned about the solution to the problem or about keeping the problem alive? Do they wish to find an answer to the old questions of civil and human rights, or do they seek to prove that the question cannot be answered by the United States of America?

In medical science there must be the patience for a thorough diagnosis and scientific prognosis for the treatment of patients. All of these require time and a patient must endure them all. But there must not be any encouragement of any unnecessary delay between diagnosis and prognosis. But when there has been delay, the skilled and dedicated physician will work as fast and as hard as he can, but the patient still must wait the application of the remedy; then both the physician and the patient must further await the response and the reaction of the latter's system and allow the prescribed time for the healing forces of the patient's body to act and to react. There are many reasons why we should not have waited this long for our full civil rights. The application of the laws of justice and freedom for the defeat and the destruction of segregation should have been in operation long ago. There are legal and moral reasons why the United States of America should not have procrastinated until now in the enforcement of the rules for first class citizenship for all. We see now that the nation is reaping a grim harvest of its misdeeds at this point in the form of unrest, division, strife, and bitterness. And the sons of America of both races are dying now on foreign battlefields to prove the nation's commitment to freedom when the mere report of how democracy works in the United States of America should have been enough to influence the rest of the world by precept and example. No, we do not wish to wait any longer. But having said this, there are reasons that we must wait if we are to build to health again the body politic of this nation that has been seriously afflicted with the disease of hate and the malignant growth of social ostracism and segregation. There is a body politic however, though diseased; it has enough health and soundness to merit the care, the protection, and the salvation that the best scientists of human relations can give. Any quest for civil rights is also a practical quest that must be judicious in an attempt to preserve the good in the nation's life while fighting against what is bad. The good in this nation must not be destroyed in the attempt to eliminate the evil. The righteous must not be destroyed with the wicked. The barn full of corn must not be burned down to catch the corn-eating rats. The right traps must be set to catch the rat while the barn and the corn are left intact. No liberal is an asset to this nation who is not also conservative enough to work for the preservation of the values of the past. No radical is trustworthy who is not also reasonable enough to draw the distinction in this nation between the wheat of liberty and the chaff of license, and no militant in this social struggle is a true soldier of freedom who is not mindful of the material to preserve as well as he is of the mess and the misery that ought to be and must be destroyed.

Dedicated statesmen know of this two-fold responsibility and work to include both in their plans and programs. Religious leaders also are aware of this and combine the drive for social and cultural growth with plans for the redemption of the individual and the social order. Many Americans who are concerned about the growth of their country know this and they take both a short time and a long-term view of the struggle and even the most militant civil rights leaders who are also dedicated to the life of their nation know and recognize the two-fold aspects of the problem and they address themselves to both. In their speeches and direct actions and in all forms of protest they say what all Americans say who love the cause of freedom, and that is we want these promised values NOW. This is the same insistence that this writer proclaimed in his plea for the ballot in the annual address before the National Baptist Convention, U.S.A., Incorporated in Denver, Colorado, in 1956. But the militant civil rights leaders as well as the rest of us know there may be some time before all the dreams of victory can be realized and all the promises of freedom fulfilled. They pledged to work; if the work in the present day does not bring the desired reward, they have consented to wait for another day. And they have taken the words of one of the sorrow songs of the Negro church which testifies that victory will come if we do not fail within ourselves. Note the words:

> I'll overcome some day,
> If in my heart I do not fail,
> I'll overcome some day.

This is not only a commitment to the struggle, it is a confession that the struggle will not be a failure and the victory may not come today. They admit the time cannot be specified nor the day catalogued or named, but what the struggling spirit knows, is that "I'll overcome some day." Here the faith of the radical, the hope of the conservative, and the expectation of the dedicated leaders of protest and the activism of the militants are joined in a common testimony that some day the victory for justice and the right will come. This long-range faith has kept all devotees of freedom working, winning, and waiting. What is it that gives any person or group the right to sing "I'll overcome some day?" It is not the burden of the many years of oppression and discrimination stretching from the dark night of chattel slavery to this new day of postponed deliverance and hopes deferred. It is not the majority vote of those who still believe that racial prejudice and discrimination are legitimate means of protecting the virtues of the majority from the vices and evils of the minority. It is not the hard and difficult road that remains ahead to be traveled and endured. It is not the absence of the stress and strain of the human struggle. Rather, it is a vision of an eternal constant for good that will not be downed by the variables of evil and corruption. It is the vision of a victory that is too great to be matched by human defeat or death. It sees a vital truth in every tragedy; a beauty of life in every ugly scene of human existence and relationships. It beholds some gems of eternity in every matrix of time and breathes a clean fresh breath of life in every throb of death and beholds a Christ that calls, claims, redeems, and delivers in every cruel and crushing crisis. It is not our strength but the producer of that strength which springs from the creative forces of the universe. This song is not the toast to human perfection and greatness. Rather, it is a cry of hope and certainty as human beings find solace in the shadow of the Great Rock of security that is the hiding place from the winds of adversity and a covert from the tempest of despair. We will overcome some day.

Freedom is a vital part of the moral structure of the universe. It is not only written in the heart and soul of human creatues it is written in the decrees and promises of the universe. Freedom has been and still is the invaluable prize toward which men in every age have aspired and for which they have paid the greatest price.

Also in every age of human history there have been hindrances to freedom. The dark clouds have been seen in the form of chattel slavery, imperialism, oppression, and every form of human life and organization which tend to enslave the spirits of man. But in spite of these unholy shadows of all kinds, freedom's holy light still shines for there has been no darkness strong enough to put it out. We will overcome some day because truth will overcome error, justice will overcome injustice, freedom will conquer servitude and America will overcome all those forces that have hindered and are now hindering the upward thrust of a more perfect democracy. We wish this victory had already come. We wish it were today or tomorrow or the next day, but if not then, we will continue to work because we are assured by freedom's holy light and all of the other constructive forces of life that we shall overcome some day.

APPENDICES

APPENDICES

APPENDIX A. Letter From Senator John F. Kennedy who was elected president of the United States November, 1960.

APPENDIX B. The Call To National Unity

APPENDIX C. Some Endorsements Of The Call To National Unity.

       1. Editorial, Nashville Banner,
       2. Letter From Robert E. Lillard, Councilman, Nashville, Tennessee.
       3. City Council of Kansas City, Kansas
       4. Mayor Travis H. Tomlinson, Raleigh, No. Carolina
       5. Governor John H. Chaffee, Rhode Island
       6. Governor Carl E. Sanders, Georgia
       7. Governor Otto Kerner, Illinois

APPENDIX D. Chicago Fair Housing Act of 1963

APPENDIX E. Injunction of the City of Chicago Against the Chicago Marchers the summer of 1966.

U. S. SENATOR...

JOHN F. KENNEDY
FOR PRESIDENT
★　　★　　★　　★

HEADQUARTERS · 261 CONSTITUTION AVE., N. W. · WASHINGTON, D. C. · NAtional 8-8206

August 3, 1960

Dr. Joseph H. Jackson
Mt. Olivet Baptist Church
3101 South Parkway
Chicago, Illinois

Dear Dr. Jackson:

Through many of our mutual friends, I have learned of your long interest in the cause of human freedom, and but for our full schedules of the past year, I am certain these friends would have arranged for an earlier meeting and discussion between us.

Especially have I been impressed with your ideas regarding the strength and growth of our nation and with the statesmanship you have demonstrated in your world travels, representing your organization and America as one of its most distinguished citizens.

I join you in your faith in a strong America for all of the people and, with you, I believe that every American citizen has a contribution to make if we are to solve the many challenges of the new frontier in human affairs. For these reasons, I am inviting you to help me by joining my group of consultants on the various issues of the campaign. In particular, I would welcome your assistance in the formation of an active group of representative clergymen and lay religious leaders to carry the message of the Democratic Party's Platform to all parts of the country. Your acceptance of such an assignment would be a source of real encouragement to me and I would hope for an opportunity for an early meeting with you.

In the meantime, I have asked Mrs. Belford Lawson to be in communication with you.

With every good wish, I am .

Sincerely yours,

John Kennedy

John F. Kennedy

JFK:pd

A CALL FOR NATIONAL UNITY

By

DR. J. H. JACKSON, *President*

NATIONAL BAPTIST CONVENTION, U.S.A., INC.

The United States of America is a great democratic republic dedicated to human dignity, justice, freedom, and equality of opportunity for all. Her supreme law, the Federal Constitution, is so constructed and so structured that it allows for political, social, and economic evolution and basic changes by amendments. Therefore, all Americans—both conservatives and liberals—can support and be loyal to the Federal Constitution and to the nation itself. All citizens can obey its fundamental principles and take part in its evolutionary changes through amendments when time, experience, and change demand it.

In this hour of crisis we call upon all American citizens and all groups to support the fundamental principles of the nation's life. We would call upon all to support the following ideas:

1. Unqualified loyalty to and support of the nation as a whole.

2. Risk all that we have and possess for the life, soul, and salvation of the nation, and trust a just nation to protect and save us as citizens and all that we hold dear, so long as it does not include the values of religion which are above the dominion of the state.

3. Let us recognize that our common enemies are those persons and groups who by ideology and purpose are committed to the destruction of this nation and that these enemies make use of all of our divisions to weaken and to destroy this republic.

4. We must recognize the fact that it is better to live in an imperfect America with the freedom to work for its improvement and fulfillment than to be a helpless slave in a perfect totalitarian state without the freedom even to question its policies or to change its evil practices.

5. Let us always recognize the right of freedom of thought, freedom of expression, and freedom of action as well as the right to differ with and to be different from others. But let us never seek to defend and protect these differences by denying to others their constitutional, just, and God-given rights as free men in a free society.

6. Let us be as wise as the enemies of this nation who—when it is to their advantage—will join with any groups in the United States and work through them for their evil purposes. If being a segregationist furthers their cause, these enemies will join the ranks of segregationists. If and when they find being an integrationist serves their purpose to negate the nation's life, they will become integrationists and work through integration to achieve their negative ends. They will also play one group against another to divide and to weaken the nation.

We are in a national crisis and at this moment are engaged in a bloody conflict with international communism in Vietnam and are potentially in conflict with the same forces throughout the world as well as at home. Americans can no longer afford the luxury and the negative weight of past prejudices, hatred, envy, discrimination, disrespect for law and order, disrespect for one another, race riots, and blood-shed. All of us must unite and work together as one for the nation's life and cause, or we will eventually perish.

7. All groups are called upon to rise above the differences of creed, color, caste and to join together as Americans in order to work for, live for, and—if need be—die for the ideals, values, and principles of justice, freedom, and equality as proclaimed by this great nation.

8. We are called upon not only to obey federal law, but also to rise above it and make a good-neighbor policy of our own by which we will build a community spirit and erect community organizations based on goodwill for the education of our children, for the security and development of our family, for the advancement of culture, and for the moral and spiritual growth of all who dwell therein. This can be done only by cooperation and not by contest and conflict. Such community spirit will not only enrich our several communities but also will greatly strengthen our national government both at home and abroad.

9. This call is for positive thinking and for positive action. It is not enough to be anti-communist, anti-poverty, anti-segregationist, anti-integrationist; we must be pro-America, pro-freedom, pro-justice, and pro-goodwill. A commitment to build a great democratic society for the enrichment of human personality is far more elevating and for more lofty than setting ourselves to the task of destroying the enemies that disturb us.

10. A cooperative venture among the citizens of the United States for the advancement of the ideals of justice and freedom does not in any way jeopardize the legitimate privileges and the moral goods of free enterprise nor does it imperil the personal rights of individuals and groups. To paraphrase the historic statement of the great educator Booker T. Washington, in all things strictly personal and in all matters purely private we can be as separate as the fingers, but one as the hand in all things tending toward the mutual progress of the individual, of groups, as well as the fulfillment of the nation's life itself.

Page 16—Wednesday Afternoon, Dec. 1, 1965

Nashville Banner.

Nashville's Oldest Newspaper—Founded April 10, 1876

E. B. Stahlman, *Publisher, 1885-1930*

James G. Stahlman, *President and Publisher*

E. B. Stahlman Jr., *Exec. Vice-President and Co-Publisher*

Charles Moss, *Vice-President and Executive Editor*

Fred Russell, *Vice-President*

Alvand C. Dunkleberger, *Editor*

Robert E. Finley, *Secretary and Treasurer*

F. C. Stahlman II, *Assistant Secretary*

"Were it left to me to decide whether we should have a government without newspapers, or newspapers without a government, I should not hesitate to prefer the latter."
—THOMAS JEFFERSON.

A BIBLE THOUGHT

Truth shall spring out of the earth; and righteousness shall look down from heaven.—Psalms 85:11.

Call For National Unity:

To The Heart Of America, A Ringing Message

FOR NATIONAL UNITY in its full, meaningful sense, no declaration could be of greater timeliness—or more perceptive of ideal and the method of achieving it—than the 10-point formula advanced by the National Baptist Convention U.S.A., Inc.

That body, representing a 5,500,000-member Negro religious organization, has fashioned a document of American purpose as sound as the respect for law on which it rests. And the Metropolitan Government of Nashville, solicited yesterday to join this movement of internal national solidarity, can well lead out in what should be an affirmative nation-wide response.

The depth of this message was recognized when it was presented at the 85th annual convention of the NBC in Jacksonville. Written by Dr. J. H. Jackson of Chicago, president of that body, the import of it is shared by colleagues locally. Dr. J. Lewis Powell and Dr. D. C. Washington presented it for Nashville consideration as a premise for community action. It is the call of men concerned for their country's future and well aware of its danger in an era of divisive movements. The answer to that is UNITY on the principles of America and Americanism.

All groups, it notes, "are called upon to rise above the differences of creed, color, caste, and to join together as Americans in order to work for, live for, and—if need be—die for the ideals, values, principles of justice, freedom, and equality as proclaimed by this great nation."

"We are called upon not only to obey federal law, but also to rise above it and make a good-neighbor policy of our own by which we will build a community spirit and erect community organizations based on goodwill for the education of our children, for the security and development of our family, for the advancement of culture, and for the moral and spiritual growth of all who dwell therein."

★ ★ ★

THAT IS ENLIGHTENED statesmanship, of responsible appeal at the grassroots level—with the worthy objective of relating rights to responsibility. It accents law as the instrument of government, protective of society; but no less does it underscore the obligation of society—in all its parts—to deport itself with intelligence, dignity and conscience, within that framework.

In the final analysis, the moral standards that will preserve the nation—or by neglect and dissolution destroy it —rest on faith. As confirmed by the spiritual precept, faith without works is dead. In the knowledge of that, these men propose a WORKING faith, addressed to national survival in the environment of freedom in which— and for which—it was born.

They propose no arbitrary amalgamation, the pressure cooker approach appalling in its consequences, disrupting and antagonizing. They stand obviously opposed to the extremisms visited—by either side—on a controversy playing into the hands of the nation's enemies; and seized upon for exploitation as an issue to divide.

★ ★ ★

CLEARLY DEFINITIVE is Point 10, as a summary of righteous and patriotic intent: It is:

"A cooperative venture among the citizens of the United States for the advancement of the ideals of justice and freedom (that) does not in any way jeopardize the legitimate privileges and the moral goods of free enterprise; nor does it imperil the personal rights of individuals and groups. To paraphrase the historic statement of the great educator Booker T. Washington, in all things strictly personal and in all matters purely private, we can be as separate as the fingers, but one as the hand in all things tending toward the mutual progress of the individual, of groups, as well as the fulfillment of the nation's life itself."

Heed it, America: A call to unity as elementary as the vision of need, and sense of duty, on which it rests.

BEVERLY BRILEY, MAYOR

Metropolitan Government of Nashville and Davidson County

MEMBER OF COUNCIL
XXXXXXXXXXXX
NASHVILLE, TENNESSEE 37201
333½ 4th Ave. N.
December 9, 1965

Dr. J. H. Jackson, President
National Baptist Convention, U.S.A., Incorporated
3101 South Parkway
Chicago, Illinois

Dear Dr. Jackson:

I congratulate and commend the National Baptist Convention,
U.S.A., Incorporated, under your able and capable leadership, upon the adoption of one of the greatest documents
compiled in the twentieth century. "A CALL FOR NATIONAL
UNITY" should be read and digested by not only every American
citizen, but by mankind universally.

When the Call was first publicized in this city, I procured
copies from Dr. Washington and forwarded them to every member
of the Metropolitan Council, as well as the local press. I
am enclosing a photostatic copy of the accompanying letter.

Nashville has a forty member council, composed of liberals,
conservatives and extremists of various political affiliations.
The Resolution, sponsored by me, received the unanimous en-
dorsement of the total membership. The City Clerk, by provision of the Resolution, was directed to send you a copy.
I am sure you will receive it in the very near future.

Again, congratulations, and best wishes for your continued
success.

Very truly yours,

Robert E. Lillard

REL/ld

RESOLUTION NO *19566*

WHEREAS, the National Baptist Convention, U.S.A., Inc.,
in its eighty-fifth session in Jacksonville, Florida, September,
1965, unanimously adopted "A Call for National Unity," a document
consisting of ten fundamental principles aimed at preserving the
ideals of justice, freedom and equality; and

WHEREAS, "A Call for National Unity" asks all American
citizens to rise above differences of creed, color, caste, and to
unite and work together as one for the nation's life and cause;
and

WHEREAS, at a meeting of the Board of City Commissioners,
The Reverend E. A. Freeman, pastor of the First Baptist Church of
this City, together with a group of Baptist ministers, urged the
City Commissioners' loyal support of this call to develop community
spirit, goodwill, and security in our nation.

NOW, THEREFORE, BE IT RESOLVED BY THE BOARD OF COMMISSIONERS OF THE
CITY OF KANSAS CITY, KANSAS:

That the Board of City Commissioners unanimously adopts the
principles contained in "A Call for National Unity," as adopted by
the National Baptist Convention, U.S.A., Inc., and strongly urges
the citizens of this community, particularly in this time of national
crisis, to lend their wholehearted support to the preservation of
these principles and to cherish the ideals and obey the rules embodied
therein.

ADOPTED BY THE BOARD OF COMMISSIONERS OF THE CITY OF KANSAS CITY,
KANSAS, THIS _2_ DAY OF _December_, 1965.

George D. Groneman
_____
City Clerk

City Of Raleigh
North Carolina

OFFICE OF THE
MAYOR

January 5, 1966

Dr. J. H. Jackson, President
National Baptist Convention, U. S. A., Inc.
3101 South Parkway
Chicago, Illinois

Dear Dr. Jackson:

Mr. O. L. Sherrill, Executive Secretary, General Baptist State
Convention of North Carolina, Inc., was kind enough to deliver
one of the brochures entitled, "A Call For National Unity" to me
during December.

I wish to express appreciation to Mr. Sherrill for delivering this
brochure and to you for your work in connection with the adoption
of the Resolution by the National Baptist Convention, U. S. A., Inc.,
in session in Jacksonville, Florida, September, 1965.

Dr. Jackson, I just want to say that I think this is a very excellent
document. The goals expressed are worthy of consideration of all
of our citizens and if properly followed would result in a better
life for all of our citizens. I sincerely hope for you and your
organization much success in promoting the ideas contained in
this brochure.

I would like to have fifteen or twenty additional copies of this
brochure for distribution to some of our positions of leadership
in this community if they are available.

Thank you again for your interest and your efforts.

Sincerely yours,

Travis H. Tomlinson
Mayor

THT:phw
CC: O. L. Sherrill

STATE OF RHODE ISLAND & PROVIDENCE PLANTATIONS
EXECUTIVE CHAMBER
PROVIDENCE

JOHN H. CHAFEE
GOVERNOR

December 17, 1965

Mr.J.H. Jackson
3101 South Parkway
Chicago, Illinois 60616

Dear Mr.Jackson:

Thank you for your letter. I read your pamphlet
A Call For National Unity. It seems to me to express
clearly and well the ideals of this country, and I think
it is an important statement. For that reason I will
certainly support it.

If the members of your convention will support
it and publicize its message, it can have an important
effect on this country.

With very best wishes.

Sincerely,

John H.Chafee
Governor

JHC:fm

Executive Department
Atlanta

Carl E. Sanders
GOVERNOR

John C. Harper
PRESS SECRETARY

December 13, 1965

Dr. J. H. Jackson, President
The National Baptist Convention, U.S.A., Inc.
3101 South Parkway
Chicago, Illinois 60616

Dear Dr. Jackson:

Thank you for your letter of recent date and the accompanying pamphlet, <u>A Call for National Unity</u>.

Your plea for national unity in face of growing tensions in South Viet Nam and other areas of the world today is indeed valid. Citizens of the United States must be aware of the dangers of disorder from within, and, although we champion freedom of speech as one of the four basic freedoms guaranteed to us in the Constitution, we must also recognize the truth in Abraham Lincoln's words, "A house divided against itself cannot stand."

I heartedly endorse your call for national unity and wish you success in your endeavors to bring about a greater understanding and fellowship among the citizens of the United States.

With best wishes, I am

Sincerely yours,

Governor

CES/egv

OFFICE OF THE GOVERNOR

SPRINGFIELD

OTTO KERNER
GOVERNOR

January 10, 1966

Dr. J. H. Jackson
3101 South Parkway
Chicago, Illinois 60616

Dear Doctor Jackson:

    I regret very much that we were unable to visit personally, since the affairs of State have kept me in the Springfield area for a longer period than I had expected after our return from the Far East Trade Mission.

    However, I wish to add my unqualified support of "A Call for National Unity". The precepts and philosophies are greatly needed in the United States and I compliment The National Baptist Convention for their foresight. A call to return to the philosophies stated by the founders of the United States is a need of our day.

    I will be pleased to join with you in the promotion of your program.

Sincerely,

Governor

APPENDIX D

Chicago Fair Housing Act of 1963

CHAPTER 198.7-B.
CHICAGO FAIR HOUSING ORDINANCE
DECLARATION OF POLICY

1. IT IS HEREBY declared the policy of the City of Chicago to assure full and equal opportunity to all residents of the City to obtain fair and adequate housing for themselves and their families in the City of Chicago without discrimination against them because of their race, color, religion, national origin or ancestry.

2. It is further declared to be the policy of the City of Chicago that no owner, lessee, sublessee, assignee, managing agent, or other person, firm or corporation having the right to sell, rent or lease any housing accommodation, within the City of Chicago, or any agent of any of these, should refuse to sell, rent, lease, or otherwise deny to or withhold from any person or group of persons such housing accommodations because of the race, color, religion, national origin or ancestry of such person or persons or discriminate against any person because of his race, color, religion, national origin or ancestry in the terms, conditions, or privileges of the sale, rental or lease of any housing accommodation or in the furnishing of facilities or services in connection therewith.

3. In order to effectuate this policy and to eliminate as far as legislatively permissible, all forms of discrimination and segregation in the field of housing,

BE IT ORDAINED BY THE CITY COUNCIL OF THE CITY OF CHICAGO:

That it shall be an unfair housing practice and unlawful for any real estate broker licensed as such by the City of Chicago:

A. To make any distinction, discrimination or restriction against any person in the price, terms, conditions or privileges of any kind relating to the sale, rental, lease or occupancy of any real estate used for residential purposes in the City of Chicago or in the furnishing of any facilities or services in connection therewith, predicated upon the race, color, religion, national origin or ancestry of the prospective or actual buyer or tenant thereof.

B. To publish, circulate, issue or display, or cause to be published, circulated, issued or displayed, any communication, notice, advertisement, sign or other writing of any kind relating to the sale, rental or leasing of any residential real property within the City of Chicago which will indicate or express any limitation or discrimination in the sale, rental or leasing of such residential real estate, predicated upon the race, color, religion or the national origin or ancestry of any prospective buyer, lessee or renter of such property.

C. To refuse to sell, lease or rent, any real estate for residential purposes within the City of Chicago because of the race, color, religion, national origin or ancestry of the proposed buyer or renter.

D. To discriminate or to participate in discrimination in connection with borrowing or lending money, guaranteeing loans, accepting mortgages or otherwise obtaining or making available funds for the purchase, acquisition, construction, rehabilitation, repair or maintenance of any residential housing unit or housing accommodation in the City of Chicago because of race, color, religion or national origin or ancestry.

E. To cheat, exploit or overcharge any person for residential housing accommodations in the City of Chicago because of race, color, religion, or national origin or ancestry.

F. To solicit for sale, lease or listing for sale or lease, residential real estate within the City of Chicago on the ground of loss of value due to the present or prospective entry into any neighborhood of any person or persons of any particular race, color, religion or national origin or ancestry.

G. To distribute or cause to be distributed, written material or statements designed to induce any owner of residential real estate in the City of Chicago to sell or lease his property because of any present or prospective change in the race, color, religion or national origin or ancestry of persons in the neighborhood.

H. To deliberately and knowingly refuse examination of any listing of residential real estate within the City of Chicago to any person because of race, color, religion or national origin or ancestry.

4. Any person who shall exercise within the City of Chicago any function of a real estate broker, shall be deemed a broker for all

purposes hereunder and shall be subject to all applicable provisions hereof.

5. It shall be the duty of the Commission on Human Relations to:

A. Initiate or receive and investigate complaints charging unlawful housing practices;

B. Seek conciliation of such complaints, hold hearings, make findings of fact, issue orders and publish its findings of fact and orders in accordance with the provisions of this ordinance and with the ordinance establishing the Commission;

C. Render from time to time, but not less than once a year, a written report of its activities and recommendations with respect to fair housing practices to the Mayor and to the City Council; and

D. Adopt such rules and regulations as may be necessary to carry out the purposes and provisions of this ordinance.

6. Any person aggrieved in any manner by any violation of any provision of the above ordinance may file a written complaint setting forth his grievance with the Chicago Commission on Human Relations. Said complaint shall state the name and address of the complainant and of the persons against whom the complaint is brought and shall also state the alleged facts surrounding the alleged violation of this ordinance.

7. Said Commission is hereby fully authorized immediately to investigate every such complaint thus filed. If the Commission determines that the respondent has not engaged in any unlawful practice, it shall state its findings of fact in writing and dismiss the complaint. If the Commission determines after such investigation that probable cause exists for the allegations made in the complaint, the Commission shall set a date for a conciliation hearing. At such hearing, the Commission or any member thereof shall interview the complainant and the person or persons against whom the complaint has been directed and shall attempt to resolve the complaint by all proper methods of conciliation and persuasion. If such attempts at conciliation are not successful within sixty days after the date of filing of the complaint, the Commission shall then proceed promptly with full hearing of the complaint.

8. Such hearing shall be conducted by the Commission, or any member thereof, upon due and reasonable notice to all parties. The Commission shall have full power to subpoena witnesses and perti-

nent documents, which power may be enforced by the Commission by proper petition to any court of competent jurisdiction. The Commission shall have power to administer oaths and to take sworn testimony. At the conclusion of the hearings, the Commission shall render a written report and recommendations, which shall be served by mail upon the complainant and the respondent. No report shall be delayed more than sixty days after the date of the issuance of notice for commencement of the first hearing.

9. The Commission shall be empowered at the conclusion of such proceedings and as part of its report, to recommend to the Mayor of the City of Chicago the suspension or revocation of the broker's license of any broker licensed by the City of Chicago who shall have been a respondent to any proceedings thus filed and found guilty of violation of any applicable provision of the within ordinance. Any broker whose license has been suspended or revoked by the Mayor, or any complainant aggrieved by the decision of the Mayor, shall have full right to appeal from such order of suspension or revocation in accordance with procedure specified in the Administrative Review Act of Illinois. The order of the Mayor shall be final and transmitted to the Commission as part of its record and it shall serve a copy thereof upon the respondent, and any appeal may be taken thereafter.

10. In addition thereto, the Mayor may direct the Corporation Counsel to file with the Department of Registration and Education of the State of Illinois a complaint against any real estate broker found guilty of violating any provision of this ordinance, seeking suspension or revocation of the license issued to such broker by the State of Illinois.

11. If any section, subdivision, paragraph, sentence or clause of this ordinance is for any reason held to be invalid or unconstitutional, such decision shall not affect any remaining portion, section or part thereof.

12. This ordinance shall take effect upon its passage and due publication.

APPENDIX E

Injunction of the City of Chicago Against the Chicago Marchers the Summer of 1966

STATE OF ILLINOIS)
      SS
COUNTY OF C O O K)

IN THE CIRCUIT COURT OF COOK COUNTY

CITY OF CHICAGO, a municipal
corporation; ORLANDO W. WILSON,
Superintendent of Police of the
City of Chicago,

       Complainants,
     vs.

REV. DR. MARTIN LUTHER KING;
REV. JAMES BEVEL; REV. JESSE
JACKSON; REV. ANDREW J. YOUNG;
ALBERT RABY; FRANK DITTO; ELBERT
RANSOM, also known as BERT RANSOM; REV.
WILLIAM ALVIN PITCHER; individually and
as members of THE SOUTHERN CHRISTIAN
LEADERSHIP CONFERENCE, THE CO-
ORDINATING COUNCIL OF COMMUNITY
ORGANIZATIONS, and OAKLAND COM-
MITTEE FOR COMMUNITY IMPROVE-
MENT; and all other persons acting by,
through or in their behalf,
       Defendants.

NO.

IN CHANCERY

C O M P L A I N T

Now comes the CITY OF CHICAGO, a municipal corporation,
and ORLANDO W. WILSON, Superintendent of Police of the City
of Chicago, and complain against the defendants:

1. That the CITY OF CHICAGO is a municipal corporation, both a body corporate and politic, exercising public and essential governmental functions and has all powers necessary and convenient to carry out and effectuate the purposes and provisions of an Act of the General Assembly of the State of Illinois creating said municipality.

2. That ORLANDO W. WILSON is Superintendent of Police of the City of Chicago and that as such he is the Chief Executive Officer of the Police Department; that he has the power and duty to administer the affairs of the Department as Chief Administrative Officer; that it is his duty and the duty of the Police Department of the City of Chicago and its members to devote their time and attention to discharge the duties of their stations according to the laws and ordinances of the State and City and the rules and regulations of the Department to preserve order, peace and quiet and enforce the laws and ordinances throughout the City.

3. The defendants are persons who purport to be the leaders of groups of citizens of the United States who act in concert under the name and style of unincorporated associations of individuals, such as, THE SOUTHERN CHRISTIAN LEADERSHIP CONFERENCE, THE CO-ORDINATING COUNCIL OF COMMUNITY ORGANIZATIONS, and OAKLAND COMMITTEE FOR COMMUNITY IMPROVEMENT, for the purpose of petitioning for redress of their alleged grievances under rights guaranteed to all citizens by the Constitution of the United States and this State.

4. That one or more or all of the defendants and others have from time to time chosen as the method of their petition for redress an action in concert by a number of persons which has come to be described in recent years by various names, such as "civil rights marches" or "civil rights demonstrations."

5. More specifically, during the years 1965 and 1966, in the City of Chicago, County of Cook and State of Illinois, one or more or all of the defendants and others organized and participated in several civil rights demonstrations involving parades of several thousand people from the general area of Grant Park to City Hall. These parades were conducted under permit and in an orderly manner along various streets in the downtown area of Chicago.

During the same period there were a number of "civil rights

marches" and "civil rights demonstrations" organized by one or more or all of the defendants and others which were conducted without parade permit. During the course of these latter marches and demonstrations there were many civil disturbances resulting in the arrest of 1,327 persons.

6. During the months of June, July and August, 1965 one or more or all of the defendants and others organized and participated almost daily in a "vigil" before the City Hall and other public buildings in the City of Chicago in numbers varying from ten to several hundred. During the latter part of 1965 and during the winter and spring of 1966 one or more or all of the defendants and others organized and participated in a number of other demonstrations in various areas of the City of Chicago in numbers varying from several to several hundred persons.

7. During the years 1965 and 1966 on the occasion of each of the marches or demonstrations referred to in paragraphs 5 and 6 above, the Police Department of the City of Chicago in no way interfered with but rather affirmatively *assisted* and *protected* all who were engaged in said marches and demonstrations who conducted themselves in a peaceful and orderly manner.

8. In January of 1966 one or more or all of the defendants and others advised officials of the City of Chicago, and the news media particularly, that they intended to embark on a program of developing "creative tension" in the City of Chicago during the summer of 1966 in order to clearly articulate to the people of the metropolitan area of Chicago and of the nation as a whole the objects of their petition for redress.

9. During the months of June and July, 1966 in several areas of the City of Chicago, where one or more or all of the defendants and others were actively engaged in organizing the people of specific communities, namely, the Near West Side, Wabash, Lawndale, Englewood and Woodlawn, to protect against alleged violation of their civil rights, and during a period of time when one or more or all of the defendants and others were making statements, issuing news releases, appearing on other communications media and publicly corresponding with public officials for the furtherance of their announced plan of "creative tension," major civil disturbances erupted in the aforesaid areas of the City resulting in damages in excess of

several million dollars to private property, the death of 27 persons and injury to 374 persons, including 61 police officers.

10. In order to contain the several disturbances on the West Side of Chicago, it became necessary for the Illinois National Guard to assist the police in containing the disturbances. In the course of these disturbances over 536 persons were arrested.

11. During the months of July and August, 1966 (the specific dates of concern are set forth more specifically hereafter in this Complaint) one or more or all of the defendants and others embarked upon a procedure of organizing and leading demonstrations in individual neighborhoods of the City of Chicago.

12. The pattern of the demonstrations is as follows: A substantial number of persons, usually several hundred in number, being led by one or more or all of the defendants and others, assemble in some public area of a specific neighborhood. Carrying signs, singing and chanting slogans, they proceed from the public area on foot on the sidewalks of the involved community to real estate offices or churches in the neighborhood, where they kneel on the sidewalks and recite prayers in furtherance of their objectives.

13. This procedure has been followed in Gage Park, located in the general area of 55th Street and Kedzie Avenue, in the City of Chicago, on the 23rd and 24th day of July, 1966, and on the 14th day of August, 1966; in the Bogan area, located in the general area of 79th Street from Western Avenue to Pulaski Road, in the City of Chicago, on the 12th day of August, 1966, and on the 14th day of August, 1966; in Jefferson Park, located in the general area of Foster Avenue and Milwaukee in the City of Chicago, on the 14th day of August, 1966; in Bridgeport, located in the general area of 35th Street and Lowe Avenue, in the City of Chicago, on the 20th, 21st and 22nd days of July, and on the 3rd, 4th, 8th, 9th and 10th days of August, 1966; in Marquette Park, in the general area of 67th Street and Kedzie Avenue, in the City of Chicago, on the 16th, 29th, 30th and 31st days of July, 1966, and on the 1st, 5th, 6th days of August, 1966; in Cragin area, located in the general area of Central Avenue and Fullerton Avenue, in the City of Chicago, on the 2nd, 3rd and 7th days of August, 1966; all in the corporate limits of the City of Chicago.

14. On the 14th day of August, 1966, three groups of demonstra-

tors, each led by one or more or all of the defendants, went into three separate neighborhoods, Gage Park, Bogan and Jefferson Park. The neighborhoods are separated from each other by substantial distance and the times of the demonstrations were either simultaneous or overlapped.

15. On that date, while the several demonstrations were going on in the three separated neighborhoods, in still another neighborhood adjoining the Bogan neighborhood a severe civil disturbance involving the same subject matter arose in Marquette Park involving several hundred participants.

16. On the 16th day of August, 1966, six groups of demonstrators, each led, convened or organized by one or more or all of the defendants, went to six separate locations in the downtown area of Chicago, demonstrated and held prayer vigils at these locations. On the same date six groups of demonstrators, each led, convened or organized by one or more or all of the defendants, proceeded to the Jefferson Park neighborhood, arriving as darkness fell and proceeded to demonstrate until after midnight.

17. In each of the demonstrations set forth above in Paragraphs 13, 14, and 16 above except with respect to those marches and demonstrations held in the downtown area on August 16, 1966, large crowds of persons other than the participants in the march, varying in size from several hundred to several thousand people, gathered along the line of the march carrying signs, hooting, throwing rocks, firecrackers and other missiles at the marchers endangering the persons and property of the marchers and other citizens. Several dozen automobiles owned by the marchers and other citizens were burned or in other ways substantially damaged. Access to the sidewalks was denied to non-participating citizens, the normal flow of traffic both pedestrian and vehicular was obstructed, substantial damage was done to private property along the routes of the march and 177 persons were arrested.

18. During each of the marches and demonstrations referred to in Paragraphs 13, 14 and 16 above, the Police Department of the City of Chicago in no way interfered with but rather affirmatively assisted and protected all who were engaged in said marches and demonstrations who conducted themselves in a peaceful and orderly manner.

19. During the period of all of the over 200 demonstrations set

forth above in Paragraphs 5, 6, 13, 14, 15 and 16, the Police Department of the City of Chicago was notified of the locations, character and extent of the demonstration planned on only two occasions in writing. On no other occasion was notice given which was accurate, timely and verifiable.

20. This failure to give adequate notice to the Police Department has occurred despite assurances made by the Rev. Dr. Martin Luther King and others that it would be given.

21. Requests that adequate notice be given the Police Department have been made repeatedly by Superintendent Wilson and as recently as August 4th, 1966, Rev. Dr. King agreed to do so. No such notice has been received. The failure to give such notice to the Police Department of the City of Chicago has resulted in an unreasonable waste of manpower which could and would have been used for preventive police work as well as crime detection in other areas of the City.

22. In the various demonstrations occurring in the past month, referred to above in Paragraphs 13, 14, 15 and 16, it was necessary, in order to protect the marchers from injury, and in order to protect the persons and property of the citizens of the City of Chicago who were neither participating in the marches or in the attacks on the marchers, for the Police Department to assign the following numbers of men to special duty for the specific purpose of protecting the marchers:

Gage Park	556
Bogan	1732
Jefferson Park	258
Marquette Park	2564
Belmont-Cragin	1926
Bridgeport	88

23. The assignment of officers to this special duty removed them from their normal duty posts and reduced police protection in the areas where they would, under normal conditions be assigned by a substantial degree.

24. The reduction of police protection in the areas of the City other than those where the demonstrations were taking place resulted in a substantial increase in the crime rate in these areas during the periods of the demonstrations. The increase in the crime rate due to incidents directly connected to the demonstrations in crimes against

persons and property in the areas in which the demonstrations were being conducted is substantial.

25. The effective police patrol force during a normal period of a patrol watch is approximately 1,020 men, exclusive of detectives, traffic officers, and juvenile officers.

26. The burden placed upon the personnel of the Police Department to protect marches conducted at simultaneous times in widely separated areas of the City, as on the 14th day of August, 1966, in Gage Park, Bogan, and Jefferson Park is demonstrated by the fact that 1,279 policemen were assigned for special duty protecting the marchers on that date.

27. Although it has been requested of defendants that they cease and desist from placing this unreasonable burden on the Police Department of the City of Chicago and the rights of other citizens of the City to have their persons and property protected by the City, the defendants have continually refused and failed to do so and threatened, not only to continue their demonstrations in said unwarranted and injurious manner, but to expand the demonstrations into many other neighborhoods at simultaneous times.

28. The City of Chicago and the Police Department have been informed that the defendants intend to proceed with this course of action forthwith.

29. If defendants are permitted to proceed with simultaneous marches, it will be impossible for the Police Department of the City of Chicago to protect the defendants, the marchers, public and private property and the life and property of the more than 3½ million citizens of the City of Chicago, who are not participating as marchers or as protestors to the marches, from the clear and present danger of riot, civil disturbance, and the deleterious effects of unreasonably overburdened police duties.

30. The defendants' actions during the past month and particularly their actions on the 14th and 16th days of August, 1966, and their announced intention to expand the demonstrations into many neighborhoods at simultaneous times, constitute a clear and present danger to the order, peace and quiet, health, safety, morals and welfare of the City of Chicago.

31. The action proposed by the defendants as outlined above is an unreasonable, unwarranted and unlawful means of citizens' petition for redress of alleged grievances.

32. Plaintiffs state that none of the defendants or others have been in the past or are now or will be in the future deprived of any of their rights as citizens of the United States, the State of Illinois, or the City of Chicago by any action of the City of Chicago, or by any of its agents, officers or servants without due process of law.

33. Plaintiffs recognize that the defendants and all citizens of the United States have the right to petition for redress of grievances and in furtherance of that right have the additional right to conduct reasonable demonstrations to call attention to their claims.

34. Plaintiffs state that the pattern of action set forth above in this complaint does not constitute reasonable demonstration in support of any petition for redress of alleged grievances under the Constitution of the United States or of this State.

35. If defendants continue unreasonable marches and demonstrations in many and widely separated neighborhoods in the City of Chicago at simultaneous times, without adequate notice to the Police Department, during peak traffic periods and after darkness had fallen; the public sidewalks will be blocked, the normal flow of traffic, both pedestrian and vehicular, will be obstructed and substantial and irreparable damage will be done to the persons and property of the public in general.

WHEREFORE, plaintiffs ask judgment that a temporary injunction issue immediately without notice and without bond upon the filing of this complaint; that upon the final hearing said temporary injunction be made permanent restraining REV. DR. MARTIN LUTHER KING; REV. JAMES BEVEL; REV. JESSE JACKSON; REV. ANDREW J. YOUNG; ALBERT RABY; FRANK DITTO; ELBERT RANSOM, also known as BERT RANSOM; REV. WILLIAM ALVIN PITCHER; individually and as members of THE SOUTHERN CHRISTIAN LEADERSHIP CONFERENCE; THE CO-ORDINATING COUNCIL OF COMMUNITY ORGANIZATIONS; and THE OAKLAND COMMITTEE FOR COMMUNITY IMPROVEMENT; and all other persons acting by, through or in their behalf, their agents, employees, representatives, and all other persons who have, may now or may hereafter combine, conspire or act with them, or as individuals, from conducting, organizing, or participating in unreasonable demonstrations in support of a petition for the redress of alleged grievances; to-wit:

(A) From organizing, conducting or participating in any march, assembly, gathering or meeting on public property in more than one specific area of, or location in the City of Chicago on any given date.

(B) From conducting, organizing or participating in any such march, assembly, gathering or meeting on public property unless such march, assembly, gathering or meeting is limited to such numbers as will not obstruct traffic, either vehicular or pedestrian, in an unreasonable manner, and, in any event, such march, assembly, gathering or meeting shall be limited in size to 500 persons or less.

(C) From conducting, organizing or participating in any such march, assembly, gathering or meeting on public property unless the Police Department of the City of Chicago has been given notice in writing of the location, number of people participating, and the names of the organizers of any such march, meeting, gathering or assembly, its route, and time of inception, at least twenty-four (24) hours prior to its inception.

(D) From conducting, organizing or participating in any march, meeting, assembly or gathering on public property in the City of Chicago except during daylight hours and at times other than peak traffic periods (7:30 A.M. to 9:00 A.M. and 4:30 P.M. to 6:00 P.M.)

Plaintiffs, CITY OF CHICAGO, a municipal corporation, and ORLANDO W. WILSON, Superintendent of the Police Department of the City of Chicago, further pray for such other and further relief as the court in its discretion deems meet and equitable in the premises.

CITY OF CHICAGO, a municipal corporation,

By————————————————————————
RAYMOND F. SIMON, Corporation Counsel

————————————————————————
ORLANDO W. WILSON
As Plaintiff and as agent for the City of Chicago in this behalf.

RAYMOND F. SIMON
Corporation Counsel of
  the City of Chicago
SYDNEY R. DREBIN
Assistant Corporation Counsel
Room 511 City Hall
Chicago, Illinois 744-6900
THOMAS A. FORAN
Special Assistant Corporation Counsel
Room 610 City Hall
Chicago, Illinois
744-6972

STATE OF ILLINOIS)
                       SS
COUNTY OF C O O K)
  ORLANDO W. WILSON, being first duly sworn on oath, deposes
and says that he is the Superintendent of the Police Department of
the CITY OF CHICAGO. That as such Superintendent, as one of
the plaintiffs in this cause, and as agent for the CITY OF CHICAGO
in this behalf, he has read the above Complaint by him subscribed,
knows the contents thereof, and the same is true in substance and
in fact.

                                    ORLANDO W. WILSON

SUBSCRIBED AND SWORN to
before me, this ————
day of August A.D. 1966.
———————————————
Notary Public

BIBLIOGRAPHY

Allport, Gordon W., The Nature of Prejudice, Cambridge, Massachusetts: Addison-Wesley Publishing Company, Inc., 1954.

Fischer, Lewis, *The Life of Mahatma Gandhi,* New York: Harper & Brothers, 1950.

Fisher, Miles Mark, Negro Slave Songs in The United States, New York: The Citadel Press, 1963.

Franklin, John Hope, *From Slavery To Freedom,* New York; Alfred A. Knopf, 1947.

Montgomery, D. H., *The Leading Facts Of American History,* Boston; Ginn And Company, 1910.

Plato, *The Republic,* Benjamin Jowett, Trans., Cleveland, Fine Edition Press, 1946.

Porter, Katherine Anne, *Ship Of Fools,* Boston, Little, Brown and Company, 1962.

Smith, Lillian, *Killers of The Dream,* New York: W. W. Norton & Company, 1949.

Thoreau, Henry David, *Walden and Civil Disobedience,* New York: W. W. Norton & Company, Inc., 1966.

Toynbee, Arnold J., *A Study of History,* Volumes II & VII. London: Oxford University Press, 1955.

REPORTS

A Plea To The 1964 Congress For A Strong Civil Rights Bill, National Baptist Convention, U.S.A., Incorporated. Congressional Record-Senate, p. 2348, 1964.

Affirmation of Faith in The Nation, National Baptist Convention, *U.S.A., Inc., Dallas, Texas, 1966.*
1960.

Hauser, Philip M., et al., eds., *Report to the Board of Education,*

City of Chicago, by the Advisory Panel on Integration of the Public Schools, 1964.

Havighurst, Robert J., *The Public Schools of Chicago.* Chicago, 1964.

Plan For Racial Self-Help, National Baptist Convention, U.S.A., Incorporated. Congressional Record. Appendix, p. A2079, 1961.

The Challenge of Crime In A Free Society, A Report by the President's Commission on Law Enforcement and Administration of Justice, Washington, D. C., 1967.

Jackson, J. H., *Annual Address to the National Baptist Convention, U.S.A., Inc.,* St. Louis, Missouri, 1954.

——————, *Annual Address to the National Baptist Convention, U.S.A., Inc., Memphis, Tennessee,* 1955.

——————, *Annual Address to the National Baptist Convention, U.S.A., Inc., Denver, Colorado,* 1956.

——————, *Annual Address to the National Baptist Convention, U.S.A., Inc., Chicago, Illinois,* 1962.

——————, *Annual Address to the National Baptist Convention, U.S.A., Inc., Detroit, Michigan,* 1964.

——————, *Annual Address to the National Baptist Convention, U.S.A., Inc., Jacksonville, Florida,* 1965.

——————, *Annual Address to the National Baptist Convention, U.S.A., Inc., Dallas, Texas,* 1966.

Manifesto From Negro Religious Leaders, (Unpublished Report), 1966.

PAMPHLETS

Jackson, J. H., *A Call To National Unity,* Sponsored by the National Baptist Convention, U.S.A., Inc., 1965.

——————, *Cooling The Long Hot Summer of Mal-Content With Justice, Understanding, and Goodwill,* 1965.

LEGAL DOCUMENTS

Chicago Fair Housing Ordinance, September, 1963.

Complaint and Petition For Injunction, The City of Chicago Against the Southern Christian Leadership Conference, other organizations and Individuals, August 19, 1966.

The Order Granting The Temporary Injunction Subsequently Issued In the Circuit Court of Cook County.

NEWSPAPERS

Chicago *Sun Times, Injunction Against Southern Christian Leadership Conference* and Others Endorsed by City Council by vote of 45 to 1, p. 3, August 26, 1966.

Chicago Sun Times, August 30, 1966.

Chicago *Tribune, City Council Lauds Injunction Against Marchers,* August 26, 1966.

Chicago *Daily News, Text of Demands by the 1966 Marchers in Chicago,* July 10, 1966.

The Morning Advocate, Baton Rouge, Louisiana, June 20, 21, 22, 26, 30, 1953.

The *State Times,* Baton Rouge, Louisiana, June 24, 26, 1953.

New Reader, Baton Rouge, Louisiana, June 27, July 4, 1953.

INDEX